DICK LANDY'S DODGE

Landy's Dodges

GEOFF STUNKARD

The Mighty Mopars of "Dandy" Dick Landy

CarTech®

CarTech®, Inc.
838 Lake Street South
Forest Lake, MN 55025
Phone: 651-277-1200 or 800-551-4754
Fax: 651-277-1203
www.cartechbooks.com

Edit by Wes Eisenschenk
Layout by Monica Seiberlich

ISBN 978-1-61325-248-2
Item No. CT561

Library of Congress Cataloging-in-Publication Data

Names: Stunkard, Geoff (Geoffrey F.), author.
Title: Landy's Dodges : the mighty Mopars of "Dandy Dick" Landy / Geoff Stunkard.
Description: Forest Lake, MN : CarTech, [2016] | Includes index.
Identifiers: LCCN 2015041396 | ISBN 9781613252482
Subjects: LCSH: Dodge automobile–History. | Chrysler automobile–History. | Automobile racing drivers–Biography. | Landy, Dick, 1937-
Classification: LCC TL215.D6 S78 2016 | DDC 629.222–dc23
LC record available at https://lccn.loc.gov/2015041396

Written, edited, and designed in the U.S.A.
Printed in China
10 9 8 7 6 5 4 3 2

Front Cover: *In late 1967, Dick Landy introduced one of his most famous cars, the 1968 Hemi Charger R/T. He is seen here during a professional photo session at Orange County International Raceway. (Photo Courtesy Landy Family Archive)*

Frontispiece: *Dick Landy is interviewed during his first clinic trip to Fresno, California. (Photo Courtesy Landy Family Archive)*

Title Page: *Dick Landy and his Dodges were always entertaining. Here, at the 1971 AHRA Winter Nationals at Beeline Raceway in Phoenix, Arizona, the Challenger gets going onward and upward on another hard run. (©TEN: The Enthusiast Network. All rights reserved.)*

Contents Page: *Bob Lambeck in the SS/EA Coronet, 1969. (©TEN: The Enthusiast Network. All rights reserved.)*

Back Cover Photos

Top: *The 1967 Coronets during the first year of the legendary clinic program. Dick had a full plate with wrenching, racing, and the Performance Clinics. (Photo Courtesy Landy Family Archive)*

Bottom Left: *Dick talks with Plymouth team member Buddy Martin at York in 1969. At this point in their careers both Landy and Sox & Martin were conducting Performance Clinics at every stop on the schedule. (Photo Courtesy Landy Family Archive)*

Bottom Right: *A hard launch behind the starting line shows the bite was there at Bakersfield; Landy took home the win in the abbreviated field at the 1970 March Meet to get his first personal Pro Stock crown and Dodge's first title for the Challenger in Pro Stock. Bob Lambeck can be seen in the background. (Photo Courtesy Landy Family Archive)*

Publisher's note: Some of the vintage photos in this book are of lower quality. They have been included because of their importance to telling the story.

DISTRIBUTION BY:

Europe
PGUK
63 Hatton Garden
London EC1N 8LE, England
Phone: 020 7061 1980 • Fax: 020 7242 3725
www.pguk.co.uk

Australia
Renniks Publications Ltd.
3/37-39 Green Street
Banksmeadow, NSW 2109, Australia
Phone: 2 9695 7055 • Fax: 2 9695 7355
www.renniks.com

TABLE OF CONTENTS

ACKNOWLEDGMENTS

To document a person or race team can be daunting. This project was in the works for almost a year, but it actually began the first time I met Dick Landy, in 1992. Who could have guessed then that our paths would cross on multiple occasions, as I wrote features on drag racing history and on restored race cars, and even worked with Landy during my tenure as editor of *Mopar Muscle* magazine? As can be imagined, I was saddened by his passing in early 2007, after seeing him in challenged health the previous summer. When asked to put this book together for CarTech, I agreed to do so only under the condition that his family would be involved.

As a result, I can offer nothing but humble and gracious words for Gean Landy, who was married to Dick most of her life, loved him, and documented his long career in a priceless collection of scrapbooks and mementos. This organized material formed the research basis for this book. During the week I visited California, Gean allowed unconditional access to this very personal material. To her I dedicate this finished effort: Gean, you gave your love and affection to your high school sweetheart but also gave those of us who loved Chrysler racing a hero. To become that, your husband and our friend was away from home much more than either of you would have liked. Thank you.

Meanwhile, the three adult Landy children, Richard, Danette (Satenstein), and Robert, proved to be indispensable during this project. Richard and his wife, Peggy, hosted me during a stay in Southern California, and Richard's personal collection of memorabilia was available to examine and copy as needed. Danette agreed to do the huge job of copying materials from the scrapbooks after I left, and both of them managed the flow of the content in Gean's possession to allow its use. Robert, who worked with Dick at the Dick Landy Industries (DLI) shop the longest, gave me his reflections and read the manuscript; his insight provided some of the most colorful statements you will read here. Richard also gets credit for making contacts for me, including with Dick's brother Mike Landy. Mike was an integral part of Dick's career for the entire Dodge and DLI era.

For research beyond my personal archive of interviews with Dick over the course of two decades, I made use of numerous period feature stories and interviews by the likes of Bob McClurg, Dave Wallace Jr., and the late "Diamond Jim" Kelly. The many friends and fans of Dick Landy on Facebook also helped me access rare resources, with more than 1,000 of them supporting the page created for this volume, and with more supporting associated pages on Landy and on drag racing.

Illustrations came from a number of sources but can primarily be attributed to the Landy family archives. A very special thanks goes to researcher Thomas Voehringer at the Petersen Publishing archives of TEN: The Enthusiast Network, who worked hard with me to secure hard-to-locate images in those vast holdings, and to assets manager Sidney Hidalgo, who then steered the legal process to allow me to use them. Other photos herein can been attributed to Dan Williams, Charles Milikin Jr., Tommy Erwin, Jeff Husk, David Hakim, Erik Lindberg, Ed Strzelecki, and my own quartermilestones.com archive. David Carl Peters, a talented and recognized commercial motorsports artist, gave me access to a number of his wonderful Dick Landy paintings. Additional video interview footage came courtesy of Jim Amos of Bee-On Video.

Vehicles that have survived to the present were available for documentation thanks to past and present owners, including Todd Werner, Mike Guffey/Nick Smith, Dean Klein/Marco DeCesaris, Pete and Renee Haldiman, Erik Lindberg/Greg and Kathy Mosley, Ed Vandersnick, Bernie Mangnitz, Elana Scherr/Tom Yeager, and Ron and Roseann Sites. A very special thanks goes to David Hakim, who knew Dick Landy well from his own career at Mopar Performance. Dave secured a pilot 392-ci Scat Pack Challenger from acquaintances at Chrysler for media use and then accompanied me on a 17-day coast-to-coast cross-country journey to get *Landy's Dodges* started. Thanks, pal!

To my wife, Linda, thanks once again for putting up with my mindlessness and the endless piles of research paperwork stacked inconveniently all around the house, and for believing in me. I love you. The Bible says, "Trust the Lord with all your heart, and lean not on your understanding; acknowledge Him in all your ways and He will make your path straight" (Prov. 3:5–6). I did, and He did.

FOREWORD *by Butch "The California Flash" Leal*

I grew up in the San Joaquin Valley, and I started racing in 1960 with my 348-ci El Camino. I had won locally with it and so I went down south, over "the hill" to San Fernando Raceway, a track I had heard about and the one closest to me. That day, there was a yellow Ford with "Andy Andrews" on the side, one of the first stockers that had lettering on it; that was the first time I met Dick Landy. After I got my 409 Impala, I raced him again at the Pomona drags, and we also raced each other when he had gone to Dodge and I drove a Thunderbolt for Mickey Thompson in 1964. That year, Dick let me use the Automotive Research shop to do a cam swap in the Ford, and I even drove the Max Wedge version of the car for him once, since I weighed less than he did.

Anyhow, we would go to Lions in Long Beach and stop at this little driving range off the 405 freeway because I liked to play golf. We would hit balls and Dick later told everybody he had taught me how to play golf! He took me to a local bar and taught me how to drink a little, too, and we matched-raced each other a bit. I remember one match race where we were running on this airstrip up north. We were lined up and we looked up and this Cessna was coming in. We pulled off to the side and it landed right on the track where we had just been!

When Ford had no deal for me even after I won Super Stock class at Indy in 1964, Bob Cahill hired me on at Chrysler in 1965 to drive an altered-wheelbase car for them. Dick and I were goods friends by then, and we flew out together to Detroit to see the new car that winter. I'll tell you, our mouths hit the ground when they rolled that thing out; we couldn't believe they had altered the wheelbase that much. The plan was Dick and I would both be 4-speed drivers, and we both had to go back to Detroit to pick up the cars. I remember that was in a big snow storm and it was a miserable trip for myself and H. L. Shahan, my crew chief. Dick, who was a good 4-speed driver, ended up going back to the automatics because he had some parts problems. I spent three or four days doing nothing but setting up the clutch in my car and H. L. did the engine work, so we got it figured out. That car was *fast.*

When the clinic deal came around, Dick told me that he was thinking about doing it, and later Mr. Cahill asked me if I was interested. I told him "No"; at that time, I was still a pretty young guy and did not want to tie that much time up in it. Dick was a little older than I was, and he did a great job with those; the one they offered to me ended up going to Don Grotheer and instead I built the Logghe Barracuda Funny Car I raced.

Then Pro Stock started, and Dick and I battled each other again. Ron Butler built me a new car, a 1971 Duster, and we raced every Saturday night it seemed like. Back and forth; it was him, myself, and Bill Bagshaw battling at Orange County, Irwindale, everywhere around the West. His son Robert always came over and hung out with me; a lot of fun, and I teased Dick about it. "Hey, are you sending that kid over to see what we are doing here again!?" Those were good times.

When the boycott stuff happened around 1974, we were both back in Super Stock again. Butler built me a 1965 Plymouth that worked almost like my 1973 Duster, but it was Super Stock legal, and Dick had a Challenger. I became "Mr. Direct Connection" after that and ran Chrysler Hemi Pro Stocks until 1981 or so. I drove a Pontiac for Gil Kirk and the Rod Shop in the 1980s.

Dick Landy was a good friend during my career. The shop did a lot of machine work for me. Dick worked hard on that small-block thing because he had the shop and wanted to stay out there, but I had to change; they (the rulesmakers) made it impossible. He was loyal to Chrysler like that, and they were loyal to him. I had always been of the idea that "You see the green, you start the machine." I talked with NHRA people such as Bernie Partridge and told them how crazy things were, as they kept redoing the rules like the weight on the Chryslers. I told them they should set it up just like Funny Car and Top Fuel: do a flat 500-ci engine at 2,350 pounds. When they finally changed the rules for the last time, they did just that.

Dick was done driving by then. A few years later, he came out to Pomona for the Winternationals, and we were hanging out in the staging lanes; I was getting ready to make a run in the Pontiac and it was *flying*. He grinned and told me "Go kick their asses!" and when we got through talking, he looked at me and just said, "I love you, man." That was crazy. You know, I about lost it; he just wasn't that kind of person. "I love you, too, buddy," was all I could say back to that.

I'm sorry that he is gone. We enjoyed making the history of drag racing in its best era, and I even drove Super Stockers for him a couple of times. You know, I wouldn't trade my career and those memories for anything.

INTRODUCTION

It is often said that timing is everything. For young men maturing in America in the late 1950s and 1960s, a newfound emphasis was placed on the ownership of a personal, and personalized, automobile. Certainly there had been hot rodders before, but the popular culture now started portraying this activity as a regular facet of being part of the "in crowd." Movies, music, and media all helped stimulate interest in this idea, and nowhere was this pressure more evident than in Southern California.

Not every teenager was a hot rodder, but for those who chose this as a passion, it was a wide-open world of opportunity. In Southern California, despite a host of activities that could occupy your time due to the pleasant climate and good economic conditions, it was possible to find both avocation and vocation in the field of automotive performance and modification. Customizing paint and hot rod parts helped execute a mechanical vision. With V-8 engine designs becoming commonplace, the growing speed equipment industry offered a solid selection of components for most makes, including the latest cars from Detroit. From that perspective, even the manufacturers had begun to grasp the profitability of this market, and began offering cars directly from the factory in performance trim.

It was here that young Richard Landy realized his calling. After a short stint in the world of custom speedboats, he returned to the performance automobile world that had been part of his high school years. Working with a promotionally minded performance car dealership, Landy began drag racing first in the latest Fords, and that in turn caught the attention of a major player in Chrysler's racing efforts, Ronney Householder. Householder was looking for a good representative for Chrysler's expanding racing program. Landy admitted years later he was not impressed at all with the styling of the 1962 Plymouth that Householder suggested for him. But the potential of the 413 Maximum Performance engine and the direct factory assistance that Householder was willing to provide sealed the deal.

Dick Landy was not an engineer or a grad student beyond his two years of junior college. But he did have three very important things that helped make "timing everything." First and foremost was an intrinsic mechanical ability that set him apart from his peers. Dick Landy was never afraid to experiment, and he was constantly looking over possibilities for bettering performance. As part of his efforts with Chrysler, he opened a dynamometer

A look of confidence and an understanding of the value of promotion helped Dick Landy attain superstardom in drag racing. This photo is from his publicity campaign in 1967. (Photo Courtesy Landy Family Archives)

This 1969 clinic poster showed Landy as a sponsored professional who thrilled crowds with extreme performance in Detroit's latest cars. This Dart ran in A/Modified Production.

shop he called Automotive Research. Although it made its "bread-and-butter" doing tune-up work on all makes, it became the headquarters for the Dodges that Landy began to race starting in 1964. His race work eventually forced its closure as a commercial enterprise, but it was succeeded in 1971 by Dick Landy Industries, which he operated until his death in 2007.

The second thing he possessed was an understanding of the media. Landy received what some might consider an inordinate amount of publicity on many of his cars. Although some of this is certainly attributable to his commendable performances, it also was in making himself and his race cars available for promotions. With many nationally recognized automotive magazine titles in the Los Angeles area, Landy readily opened his doors to give the media people the latest, greatest tips (although I would be remiss to say he always "told them everything") as well as test car tune-ups. He was also available as a spokesperson for drag racing in general, and even hired publicity agents to handle this aspect of his career. All of this played a major role in the value he gave his sponsors as well.

The final thing that cannot be overlooked is that Landy took a good deal of care to represent himself and whoever was supporting his racing effort properly. Eric Dahlquist of Petersen Publishing is the one who tagged him "Dandy Dick." The rhythm of the nickname worked, and although that moniker might not be considered a manly phrase in the 21st Century, the former high school sports star stuck with it.

Landy and his crew wore clean clothes, sometimes with spotless white tennis shoes, and looked the part of at-ease professionals. The ever-present unlit cigar was a source of interest that gave him a unique calling card. That Landy eventually piloted some of the most dangerous stock-bodied creations to ever hit the dragstrip only added to the dichotomy of all this.

It was also mentioned in the news reports of that era that Dick always took time to talk with amateur racers and potential Dodge customers, even very young ones. This fact perhaps played a pivotal role in Dick Landy becoming Dodge's best representative at its dealerships, and one of the most important in its racing program.

In the following pages, I tell the story of Landy's Dodges, the cars that Dick raced and won with. It was a unique time in automotive history, an era of opportunity that has long since passed. Dick Landy was a man of his time, and he participated in that moment to the utmost, creating a legacy of performance still remembered today.

Robert, Danette, Gean, and Richard Landy in 2015.

CHAPTER 1

HOT RODS, CIGARS AND ROOSTER TALES

The Landy Legacy and Dick's Racing Efforts before 1964

Southern California was a land of dreams and promise for many. Some came for the climate; others arrived for a chance at fame in the growing Hollywood movie business; still others came because "going West" simply landed many wanderers in the growing Los Angeles area and surrounding hills. For Henry and Genevieve Landy, son Richard was the fifth addition to an eight-child farm family in what was then a still-rural Granada Hills. Located just north of Hollywood in the San Fernando Basin, the area that came to be referred to simply as the Valley, was filled with nicely irrigated homesteads. Indeed, the house that Dick grew up in still stands on Tulsa Avenue, a long residential block, but at the time of his birth, in March 1937, it was part of a recently built small farmstead called Sunshine Ranch, which featured a house, barn, garden area, and grove of orange trees.

The Landowski family had first immigrated to Wisconsin, and four of the five family patriarchs shortened that name to Landy when they opened a family auto repair business in the early 1930s. Henry had moved to the Golden State after contracting tuberculosis. The climatic change from Milwaukee was medically required, and the new California home was purchased sight unseen during the same year that Dick was born. Once healed, Henry opened a collision shop called Landy Auto Body Works in San Fernando. A machinist who had plied his trade at International Harvester, Henry had also worked for the growing Chrysler Corporation as a vehicle repossession agent before the move; he jokingly told Gean Landy years later that he had been shot at only once! In the late 1930s, Henry even owned a prewar hot rod built around a 1917 Model T Ford, complete with a Fordson-valved flat head, high-lift cam, DD4 magneto, and custom crankshaft.

Growing up, young Richard Landy found ample time to develop the type of mechanical prowess that marked his later engine-building career by working on family cars. Of course, those formative years included World War II and the soon-to-boom postwar economy; both helped fuel another pastime that became known as hot rodding. By then, Henry had closed the body shop and was working in the aerospace industry as a fabricator, using a small home-based machine shop for doing odd jobs on the side.

Chrysler hired the model for the photo shoot for the new 1962 Plymouth, but wife Gean's support of Dick's tireless racing efforts was a huge part of his success. They were married for more than 50 years, until Dick's passing in 2007. (Photo Courtesy Landy Family Archives)

The 1917 Ford that Henry Landy hot rodded around in during the 1930s. Note the flow-through pipes. (Photo Courtesy Landy Family Archives)

Dick and Gean's 1947 Cadillac was both a powerful tow vehicle for the Drag 'n' Ski boat business and a nice ride for the young family. (Photo Courtesy Landy Family Archives)

Dick's first car was this 1941 Chevy convertible. (Photo Courtesy Landy Family Archives)

Southern California was the hotbed of hot rodding activity. Equipped with prewar dry lakes experience and the economic optimism that marked the era, a ready group of young men who had come from the armed services with skills and fearless determination led the movement. That in turn meshed with the newly developing youth culture, so it is not surprising that Dick Landy as an older teenager became interested in this pursuit in the early to mid-1950s.

Among other activities at Notre Dame High School in Sherman Oaks, Dick played football through his junior year, at the tackle position, and he laid bricks during the summer. This job financed his first car, a 1941 Chevy convertible. Dick's fourth year was at San Fernando High School, where he joined the Ignitors car club. He also met the good-looking Gean Beahrs; she jokes that she was the "spoiled brat only child" of a doctor and nurse and that Dick had brothers and sisters. The chemistry was there; they were married just two weeks after his graduation in 1955. Although he and friend Vali Goelz had played around with a 1953 Ford, this is when drag racing first became part of his life. The apartment he and Gean rented was only about a mile from the San Fernando Raceway, and they could hear the cars running on Saturday evenings and Sundays.

The Landy Auto Body Works in San Fernando operated from 1938 until the advent of World War II. Owner Henry Landy, Dick's father, is standing second from the left. (Photo Courtesy Landy Family Archives)

Ford Days: 1956–1962

"In 1956, a friend of mine bought a new Ford truck and we decided to go out to the San Fernando dragstrip,"

Dick and Vince Hart with Hart's 1956 Ford truck, already showing some signs of modification. (Photo Courtesy Landy Family Archives)

Dick summarily noted in a later interview. "I was doing both the driving and wrenching."

Landy did not state what condition this truck was in when it was purchased, except to note it was new, soon was stripped down, and had a V-8 under the hood. He and his construction business friend Vince Hart became serious enough about racing that it won. A lot. He later told writer Bob McClurg that he guessed it took home 40 trophies that year. Hart was happy being able to ride shotgun, which was part of racing at the time. Dick recalled that the truck eventually ran 92 mph. The team raced on the track and made the occasional dry lakes run.

Dick did chassis changes, and it is likely that he rebuilt the engine in addition to adding speed parts. The two young men campaigned it with success at the legendary Pond (the nickname of the Harry Hibler–managed San Fernando track), which had a class specifically for pickups, as well as at Lions Associated Drag Strip in Long Beach and at the Saugus Drags. In part because the rules for pickups were much looser than those for stock, it was the first of the Landy-associated machines to make a name for itself by performance. However, when the navy called Vince to go to sea; before he left, he sold the truck. Dick was now in college, studying mechanical engineering, plus working at masonry jobs to support his young family.

By this date he was also involved in a new performance business, but not on pavement. With Pyramid Lake and other recreational waters close by, weekend boating and water-skiing became Dick's second vocation. He started a small business called Drag 'n' Ski. Soon afterward, in a verbal partnership with Irv Brendell, the duo opened Brendella Boats. Dick proved to be very adept at the custom fabrication of fiberglass, engine support framing, and hot rod engines for their new high-performance SK-class watercraft. Drag racing was no longer a priority, until the day in 1960 when Dick's older brother Les bought a new 352-inch Ford.

While completing his junior college studies, Dick raced Hart's truck and worked at Brendella Boats, building custom boats and boat engines for water-skiers. (Photo Courtesy Landy Family Archives)

Big-Block Starliner

This car, a Starliner, was powered by what many consider to be one of the first big-block muscle car engines, the 360-hp version of the Ford Y-block FE series. Free-flow exhaust manifolds, an aluminum intake supporting a Holley 4-barrel carb, an open-element air cleaner, a hotter cam, solid lifters beneath heads featuring adjustable rocker arms, and a dual-point/mechanical advance distributor all made it go. Once again, Dick was responsible for tuning it up and getting the suspension ready, and soon he had the car running at local tracks. However, he recounted later that the biggest change was receiving some attention from Fran Hernandez.

With tuning becoming his specialty, Dick campaigned Andy Andrews's big Ford cars with success around tracks in Southern California. (Photo Courtesy Landy Family Archives)

Andy Andrews's multicar team en route to the races. Andrews raced multiple brands to promote his used-car business. Dick drove the Ford he supplied. (Photo Courtesy Landy Family Archives)

At the time, Hernandez was a noted veteran hot rodder associated with fabricator Bill Stroppe's shop in Long Beach; he also represented Autolite's racing interests. According to Dick, Hernandez was willing to set up an account for parts and racing pieces from the company. Because of Stroppe's close relationship with Ford, when Autolite was purchased by Ford in 1961, Hernandez was suddenly elevated to a much more important role in racing at Ford Motor Company. By this time, Dick was driving a new 4.05-inch-bore 390-ci Galaxie that came courtesy of dealer Andy Andrews.

Andrews was a dynamic young car dealer who specialized in high-performance vehicles only, both new and used. He recognized that Dick Landy was a clean-cut, responsible young father who had the looks and ability to sell cars but also the additional talent to keep them in tune. He first asked Dick to tune his dealer-backed 1961 Ford and then asked him to drive the car. Whether Andrews had any prior association with Hernandez is unknown, but he did sell all makes and models, and this car came into Dick's use because of Andy's business. Some pictures show the Galaxie that Dick drove for Andrews being flat-towed along with a 1961 Chevy that Andrews may have also been campaigning. Well versed in shifting and suspension tricks, Dick rented a small shop on Ventura Canyon Avenue and soon had the Andrews Ford making waves at local tracks in the stocker ranks. It was Andrews who gave Dick a visual trademark that lasted his entire career.

Andrews ran this yearbook ad in Dick's alma mater Notre Dame High School in Sherman Oaks. (Photo Courtesy Landy Family Archives)

A Cigar and a Nickname

"I'll always remember Dick Landy as the mysterious guy who never fired up his cigars," mused writer Dave Wallace Jr. in a 1976 *Drag News* story about Dick Landy Industries. Andy Andrews seems to have liked smoking them, and he gave Dick a victory stogie at the races. Andy soon had Dick keeping a supply on hand to use in his publicity efforts, but Dick personally found that unlit cigars simply put his mind at ease. He noted in multiple interviews that he did not like to smoke, but he got a fresh one ready before each run. That big unlit cigar,

The Fords were hot race cars in the pre-1962 era. Dick races one of his Automotive Research customers in this snapshot. (Photo Courtesy Landy Family Archives)

clenched between his teeth as the car launched, fascinated then-12-year-old Wallace and other media types. It also became a point of humor in race reports, which might end with something like, "Chomper Landy won enough money tonight to buy himself cigars for two whole months!"

Then there was the "Dandy Dick" nickname, although it was applied a little later. It came from a noted media friend whom Landy had met during his early racing efforts, Eric Dahlquist of *Hot Rod* magazine. Dahlquist, looking for a hook on a story he was writing about Landy in 1964, put the tag on Landy as a rhyme. Dick took it in stride, but he did note in an interview years later that it was somewhat scandalous to his staunch Catholic family; to them, he was always Richard.

However, he was already using the nickname Dick on business cards and sponsor references. Besides, the Dandy part did fit; he understood from those early efforts at business and racing that looking professional made a big difference. He did not look like the greasers that many people associated with hot rodders, wryly noting in one interview that some of them looked as if they had been working in sewers. This good grooming effort came even before his Andy Andrews "charm school" era. With his clean shoes, button-down shirts, and flat-top haircut, the big former football star was exactly what the promotionally minded auto representatives wanted, especially because he was adept enough at shifting to win races.

Hernandez was in. After his move to Detroit, Fran pulled strings and got Dick and Andy the latest car for their drag racing program. It was a yellow tri-power 405-hp 406-inch 1962 Galaxie without undercoating; Dick prepped it for the track, rebuilt the engine, and continued to find the winner's circle. By then, Andrews had asked him to stop doing outside tune-up work. Instead he focused mainly on cars at the dealership; he had already put his boat-building days behind him.

However, Chevrolet had arrived with the hot 409s, and the big Ford was not as competitive as it once had been. Even with Hernandez's association, Landy did not enjoy the same rapport that local older racers Les Ritchey and Gas Rhonda enjoyed with Ford.

Enter the B-Body

That same spring (1962), Chrysler's recently redesigned midsize unibody was released with a new engine, the 413 Maximum Performance Wedge. At this point Dick, who did not like losing, began to consider a switch. He recalled in a *National Dragster* interview that it was Bob McDaniel and Ronney Householder (both with deep California roots) who had first recognized his racing efforts. Bob was a young regional Chrysler executive who actually did some drag racing, and Ronney was a former Indy car driver who was now spearheading Chrysler's factory racing efforts. Householder reported directly to executive Bob Rodger, inventor of the Chrysler 300, in Chrysler's executive offices. There can be little doubt that the no-BS Householder held a good deal of respect, whether standing in the legendary pagoda during the Indy 500 or in meetings at the corporate offices back in Detroit. He liked Dick Landy; plus he smoked his own cigars constantly.

At this time, recently positioned Chrysler president Lynn Townsend became serious about marketing vehicle performance. The 413 package had come about as a direct result of multiple factors, one of the biggest being Townsend's teenage sons noting to "Pop" that the kids in high school had no respect for Chrysler's street manners. Soon afterward, in October 1961, Townsend authorized an in-house performance-engineering group,

This early business card shows that Dick primarily focused his business on late-model Detroit package cars, the Super Stocks that arrived in the early 1960s. (Photo Courtesy Landy Family Archives)

The 1962 Plymouth Max Wedge was a midyear release. Dick made a couple of passes in one and switched from Ford. The company gave him a deal for the car and parts. (Photo Courtesy Landy Family Archives)

in addition to the work Householder was already doing. This group was led by a talented engineer named Tom Hoover, member of a company-based performance car club named the Ramchargers. This cabal soon rewrote the history of automotive performance out of Detroit.

Having made waves with a quickly built 1961 Dodge at the National Hot Rod Association (NHRA) Nationals, Hoover and his handpicked crew set about transforming the company's flagship 413 RB engine into a drag race monster that winter. The engine included a high-RPM sonic intake called the cross ram, featuring two offset 4-barrel carburetors, heavy-duty internals parts, high compression, upgraded valvetrain and cooling components, and more. This was mated to a nicely fitted suspension and capable driveline, with the new unitized body construction saving a good deal of weight compared to the fully framed competition. The midyear package release could be purchased on both Dodge and Plymouth midsize vehicles for 1962.

Plymouth Makes It, and So Does Automotive Research

Due to corporate upheaval that had placed Townsend, the former comptroller, at the top of the firm, styling was a bit off base that year, but Landy accepted the company's offer to test one of the new cars. If he decided to go with it, the deal would be actual car ownership and whatever parts he needed. After a couple of passes, regardless of what the car looked like, Dick knew it would fly, as the bone-stock model was almost as fast as his already-prepped Galaxie. He signed the contract, and a new 413 Plymouth was soon on hand.

Dick looks back at the camera as he rolls to the line with his new Max Wedge. He was one of dozens getting serious about racing then-modern Super Stock muscle cars. (Photo Courtesy Landy Family Archives)

Andy Andrews remained involved with the car as a sponsor through the autumn of 1962, but by that time Dick had already made up his mind to open his own tune-up shop. He had already garnered an excellent hands-on reputation among local racers, and the next step was a business that basically catered to performance clientele. He rented part of a building near Sepulveda Boulevard in Sherman Oaks and opened Automotive Research at 15319½ Magnolia in late 1962. This was not a Mopar-exclusive shop, and it received additional notoriety when Dick installed a 400-hp Clayton chassis dyno to give customers proven results without going to the racetrack. One of the first of its kind in Southern California, this business boomed for the Super Stock specialists, and Dick recounted that he spent a lot of 16-hour days getting the business established.

At the time, Chrysler offered two possible transmissions: the TorqueFlite automatic and the BorgWarner T85 3-speed. Equipped with the 3-speed and running in what was classified that year as Super Stock, Landy soon had the bright orange car winning in local races. He did well enough with it that he raced it at the 1963 NHRA Winternationals at the Pomona Fairgrounds when his new car was not ready yet. Indeed, a PR photo released by Plymouth showed the teams that would be at that event, all (including Bob McDaniel) in new 426-ci cars, except Landy. The 426 displacement number had been chosen

Dick stayed with the car for the 1963 Winternationals. (Photo Courtesy Landy Family Archives)

A rare color image of the 1963 in AFX trim. By this point, Dick had gone to the Mercedes DB-180 silver paint that later highlighted his early days with Dodge. (Photo Courtesy Landy Family Archives)

An early Automotive Research ad was small but effective. Landy tuned competitive cars from both Northern and Southern California in 1963, at times winning with multiple entries. (Photo Courtesy Landy Family Archives)

for 1963 production vehicles to meet a new Automobile Competition Committee of the United States (ACCUS) 7-liter (427.167-ci) limit that the NHRA and other organizations had adopted for the new year.

Bruce Kerr, writer of an "Autotopics" column in the local paper, *Valley Times Today,* noted in the lead-up to the NHRA race, "Dick Landy has accounted for 22 trophies, including six Top Stock eliminators on California strips in the past two seasons. Landy's best time, in November 1962, is an 11.99/119.20 in a 413 Plymouth Super Stock."

However, a new 1963 426 Plymouth was in the offing, again with the T85. Dick recalled that the new car arrived as a stick, but he missed a shift soon afterward and tossed a flywheel right through the side of it. There was no use in fighting that and the new reworked BorgWarner T10 4-speeds that were showing up in the latest Fords and Chevrolets, so within a week, he switched to the automatic, and he stayed with it for the remainder of the year.

Not just Dick but the Automotive Research group also did well. On one occasion, March 17, the team won three different classes at San Fernando: SS/S to Landy, J/S to Jim Wetton in a 426 Dodge, and G/S to the Bill Paul–owned 406-ci Ford Galaxie. The following weekend, the group reset the track records at Fresno: Landy in S/S, Paul in A/S, and Doug Lovegrove in an S/SA record. In late May, Dick received the aluminum parts upgrade Chrysler had released at approximately the same time he swapped to the TorqueFlite, and he promptly clocked an 11.92/117 at San Gabriel the second weekend out. Soon afterward, he towed back north to race and beat Tommy Grove for the *Drag News* number-seven spot at Kingdon Dragway in central California, resetting the track FX record to 11.89 at Fresno as well.

More Than Super Stock

Although Dick Landy was associated with hot and radically modified Dodges in the following seasons, he adapted the Plymouth to some Factory Experimental changes as well, for several reasons. First and not often considered foremost was that he tuned a lot of local racers at Automotive Research; moving into the more exclusive FX class removed him from his customers. Second, it also put him into more elite company. Dick Landy possessed the foresight to see that he could make money in drag racing as a personality; that was one reason he later let the Dandy Dick name become commonplace. Southern California was known as fuel dragster country, but local tracks noted that people wanted to see the stockers. There were days and events just for them, and the FX programs usually paid a little more than traditional Stock racing did.

This uncredited photo shows the 1963 Plymouth in action. Running in S/S and FX trim, this car helped establish Dick as a top driver and tuner in California drag racing. (Photo Courtesy Landy Family Archives)

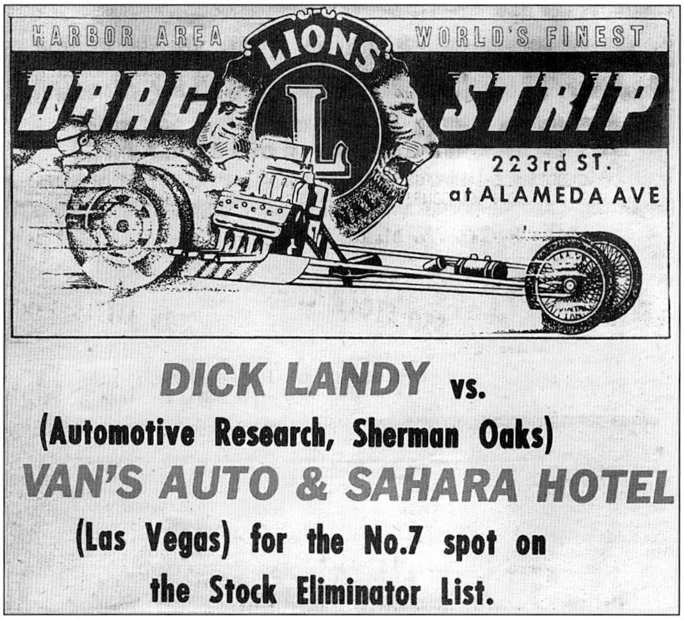

The Lions track was the place to meet. Dick was advertised for his big match against Frank Sanders's notorious 427-ci Z-11 Chevy. (Photo Courtesy Landy Family Archives)

But the biggest reason to switch was that it gave him the leeway to experiment. This included some wheelbase changes even in 1963, moving the rear axle forward. When tech people began measuring the wheelbase itself, the front wheels were also moved. Bigger hood scoops were adopted. The midnight oil burned and that Clayton dyno wheel spun furiously in the floor at the Sherman Oaks shop as Dick found out more and more about making horsepower. This facet became important as the nation's top automotive media people took an interest in Dandy Dick Landy, as his shop became a place to tune new test vehicles from Detroit.

It was noted on July 21 in *Drag News* coverage of the most recent Saturday stocker race at Lions that Dick had scored his 11th straight stock meet win and his 2nd Lions Top Stock crown in one month and had run 11.89/117.60 in his first race with new Stage II 426 equipment that Chrysler had released getting ready for the NHRA Nationals at Indianapolis.

Week in and week out, Dick continued to establish a name for himself and Automotive Research in the FX ranks that fall, culminating with Pomona Raceway's reporter Stan Adams wryly stating, "Landy takes over (to win) FX Eliminator money, others get trophies." Adams later worked as Landy's PR agent. An October 1963, the "Northern Notes" column in *Drag News* reported that Dick currently held FX records at San Gabriel, San Fernando, Long Beach, Santa Maria, and Bakersfield, plus a 1320 Standard National record at 11.80 set at Long Beach.

In the same story, Rambler dealer Bill Wright, who had clocked a 14.07 and won four trophies in three months after an Automotive Research tune-up, noted that he could have saved a bundle of money had he gone to Landy first. The year concluded with the Automotive Research Plymouth defending the number-seven spot with 11.98s over Frank Sanders in the Vans/Sahara Hotel Chevy Z11, a match race at Lions that had been heavily advertised in advance.

Also taking an interest as 1963 closed out was the Dodge Division of Chrysler. As during the Ford days, Dick was not at the top of the list at Plymouth; former GM standout Hayden Proffitt and Northern California racer Tommy Grove out of Melrose Motors received most of the Mayflower brand's ink. Frank Wylie had become the Dodge PR guy, the company had its 50th anniversary coming up in 1964, and the Los Angeles County Dodge Dealers had asked if they could sponsor him. Householder was fine with the switch. Racing executive Bob Cahill agreed, and the first Landy's Automotive Research Dodge was about to become a reality.

Where Are They Now?

One of the cars mentioned in this chapter is rumored to survive. However, according to many in the hobby, none of the cars raced by Dick Landy prior to 1964 have surfaced to date.

CHAPTER 2

B-BODY BOMBERS 1964–1970

The Chrysler B-Body, as Dick and others had proven in 1962 with the first iterations of the Max Wedge, took drag racing by storm. At the time, the NHRA had just two national events, the Winternationals on the Pomona County Fairgrounds in California and the Nationals at Indianapolis Raceway Park. Dodges had won both events in 1963, partly because of ongoing development spearheaded by individuals within Chrysler Engineering, whose racing interests had led them to found the Ramchargers team in the late 1950s. In fact, their cars had won both 1963 events. A second in-house team known as the Golden Commandos ran Plymouths, but Dodge won the Nationals again in 1964.

Thanks to its commitment to drag racing, by the end of 1965, Chrysler had released several hundred vehicles built specifically for the sport, and many of these packages were augmented with upgrades throughout the years, largely due to ongoing factory refinements. Two primary areas should be noted. First, moving the battery to the rear, lightening body construction materials, and slightly shifting the wheelbase forward made weight transfer changes. Starting on the 1963 releases, this provided excellent traction, even on the tracks of that time.

The second aspect was the understanding of ram tuning that was unique to Chrysler; this equation allowed intake runner lengths to be "tuned" sonically to force the maximum amount of air into the cylinder at a specific RPM level. This concept was transferred from the Wedge to the new Hemi Charger engine releases in 1964 as well.

Beyond these special race cars, the B-Body platform became Chrysler's most visible entry into what became the muscle car wars. With styling, options, and marketing finesse, plus visibility thanks to both drag racing and NASCAR participation, the new Charger, first released in 1966, became iconic. The Charger was one of Dick Landy's most noted and successful platforms in the late 1960s, after its first restyling in 1968. However, to help market its brawny sisters, the Coronet R/T and the Super Bee, Dick also used those platforms in both clinic work and with alternate team drivers on the racetrack through 1970. The B-Body was overshadowed once Pro Stock and the new Dodge Challengers arrived in 1970, but Dick Landy's observable efforts on the track and in the media made certain everyone knew he had been there. The big man fit the big car idea very well.

In early 1969, Dick Landy posed for this unique sunset photo with the Flyin' Wedge *Charger and his spoils of victory. (Photo Courtesy Landy Family Archives)*

The 1967 B-Body Coronet in its debut after Erik Lindberg's restoration. Dick started the year in his traditional silver scheme but soon went to this combination of multiple colors, possibly at Dodge's request for more visibility.

Landy's Dodges even appeared in ads in regional newspapers, including this one Gean Landy saved from the spring of 1965. (Photo Courtesy Landy Family Archives)

The new 1968 Charger and the 1967 440 clinic Coronet en route to a Nebraska appearance in 1967. (Photo Courtesy Landy Family Archives)

The A102 426 Street Hemi helped make Landy's B-Body promotions especially important. Without the street vehicles, there might have been less desire for clinic sponsorship by dealers.

1964: A Silver Anniversary and the First Dodges

It was significant that Automotive Research joined with the Dodge division for 1964. Dodge was celebrating its 50th anniversary, commemorating the first production vehicle effort of brothers Horace and John Dodge in 1914. That company had been joined to the growing Chrysler Corporation in 1928, allowing Walter P. Chrysler an even greater opportunity to grow his four-year-old firm into a true titan of business, becoming the last of the Big Three automakers. Decades later, Dodge was posited as the performance arm of the company, placed between the luxury Chrysler-Imperial lines and the economical Plymouth brand. From a marketing standpoint, Dandy Dick Landy was a perfect fit.

Landy's switch to Dodge was authorized by the company through Ronney Householder and Bob Cahill, both high-level members of the factory racing program. Dick later relayed that this was primarily due to the publicity available for the Dodge brand, dynamically spearheaded by Frank Wylie. It was perhaps one of the most critical choices made by the 27-year-old driver and shop owner, as he was forever after associated with this brand and its marketing.

1964 Stage III Max Wedge Hardtop

The first Dodge that Landy piloted under factory direction was also the most serious version of Chrysler's venerable Max Wedge. By then, the 426-inch RB engine block had been refined into a durable structure, topped with a set of new heads (casting 2406518) that had been assisted in part by port recommendations from Sir Harry Weslake of England. Weslake had been brought on to resolve exhaust port issues on a new hemispherical cylinder head under development at the same time, and the wedge ideas he formulated as a consultant first showed up in the Stage II head release in mid-1963. Also new for 1964 was a set of very heavy but free-flowing exhaust manifolds. As mentioned, continuing efforts by the Ramchargers, Golden Commandos, and other drag racing teams had led the Max Wedges to a fearsome level of dominance in sanctioned competition in 1963, as well as high visibility in other weekend racing events.

The 1964 Max Wedge Dodge models were referred to as Ramcharger IIIs, and their production was based on a number of possibilities. The engine could be had with either 11.0 (415-hp) or 12.5 (425-hp) compression ratios; as in the past, the engine was available across the Dodge B-Body lines, including the 330 trim, 440 trim, Polara, and Polara 500 models. For stylish association, most racers chose the hardtop body, but the Max Wedge could be had in the lighter sedan and even in a convertible that year. The factory also offered the 365-hp 426S street wedge, which did not share much with the Max Wedge other than the block's displacement. The cross-ram Max Wedge was a true competition engine and not recommended for street use.

Also offered in 1964 was the just-released New Process A833 4-speed Chrysler transmission, superseding the previous BorgWarner 3-speed offering in Chrysler's lineup. As in the past, however, Chrysler racers found dominance in the automatic ranks, where no other model from Detroit could touch them. Following his well-remembered clutch

Easily recognized, the Automotive Research logo was a noted part of Dick's personal efforts. He had a facsimile of it painted on the 1965 car.

The 1964 Max Wedge marked the beginning of Dodge's involvement with Landy. This photo from Gean Landy's scrapbook notes best times of 11.52/123.60, likely from the Pomona Fairgrounds during an early season match. (Photo Courtesy Landy Family Archives)

This publicity photo shows the Stage III Max Wedge engine and its fenderwell headers, which replaced cast-iron factory versions. (Photo Courtesy Landy Family Archives)

The Max Wedge in action against a Ford Galaxie at Riverside's first-ever **Hot Rod** *magazine drags, one of the final events where Dick drove this car. (Photo Courtesy ©TEN: The Enthusiast Network. All rights reserved.)*

Although the clinics were still two seasons away, Dick Landy, Bill "Maverick" Golden, and the Dodge Chargers exhibition team set up this display at Bill Brick Dodge in Phoenix. (Photo Courtesy Landy Family Archives)

explosion from 1963 in the Plymouth, Dick's new car was among the majority using the A727 TorqueFlite, with its dash-mounted push-button shifter.

Custom-painted in Mercedes-Benz Silver Gray to honor the 50th anniversary, Dick's new Dodge was a 440-trim hardtop, featuring the best parts and the 12.5 compression engine; the lightweight aluminum body components that Dick's car featured were offered only to buyers who selected this particular engine, according to data from researcher Greg Lane. The 1964 lightweight pieces included the scooped aluminum hood, front fenders, front bumper and bumper supports, radiator shroud, and hood-lock brace. The sound deadener, undercoating, jute carpet backing, and some panel insulation were removed, and the battery was relocated to the trunk. The high-compression models used the 1963-style 8.75-inch SureGrip differential with a 4.56 ring.

Dick took delivery of the car on January 10 and was at San Fernando on Sunday, January 12, winning the track's SX class and then the event title over the *Snorkasaurus III* Dodge of Jim Barnes. Barnes was an Automotive Research customer. Landy told interviewer Paul Zazarine years later that the team was always looking for performance advances; this was one reason he had not always been in the strong graces of the some of the engineering people. Regardless, the people whose attention he had in Detroit (Householder with his background in Indy and NASCAR and management executive Cahill) had made sure that Landy was well compensated for his efforts. At this point, however, that money was primarily for expenses and parts through the L.A. County Dodge Dealers group, whose name was lettered onto the car.

The NHRA season opened at Pomona in early February, and Dick was there with his new car. Trimmed out in A/FX with big tires the weekend before, the car had actually clocked a win at the Pomona warm-up, but it fell to eventual winner Tommy Grove in *Melrose Missile* in class and then lost in the eliminator early as well. Not often considered by Mopar enthusiasts is that both the A/FX Comets and Super Stock Thunderbolts were coming on strong during that spring and that Ford had a solid grip on the eliminators at many larger races until the Hemi cars showed up.

That did not keep Dick from winning. The Automotive Research wedge won AFX on March 21 at Lions and then took home the Street Racer class heads-up crown at Fontana on the 28th, beating Bill Schrewsberry's 427 Comet along the way.

On April 12, Dick defended his spot on the *Drag News* 1320 list. Next it was back East to Arizona with Gean for the season opener at Beeline Dragway, and the Dodge was displayed at Bill Brick Dodge with Automotive Research customer Bill "Maverick" Golden and the new Dodge Chargers supercharged exhibition team.

On April 28, in Fresno, he won the formula eliminator (on a car-length-based handicap) and noted in a period results story that he was preparing a new driver because the factory would be releasing Hemi-powered Super Stockers the following month.

Not much is listed for May beyond local races at San Fernando and Fontana. Gean Landy's scrapbooks also contain an exclusive Paddock Penthouse ticket for the

Dick took one of his earliest major titles for Dodge at this **Hot Rod** *magazine race. It was also the first major-event win for a Chrysler A864 Race Hemi drag package by any driver. (Photo Courtesy ©TEN: The Enthusiast Network. All rights reserved.)*

1964 Indy 500, and it is possible that Dick flew out for the May 30 event at Ronney Householder's request.

By now, the wedge featured nicely scalloped paint on the scoop and edges; one custom change was the addition of a third pair of taillight housings in the rear valance. Whether simply for show or to hide a little extra rear-bound weight is not known, but it was an interesting touch. Regardless, the new Hemi was soon available, and with it Dick Landy and Automotive Research moved into the national spotlight.

The team continued to run the Max Wedge car as an entry until August, when Dick headed out east for his first national tour. The wedge car held the San Fernando track record for most of the 1964 season and won a handful of events in S/SA, driven by a man referred to as Rapid Raymond in the press.

1964 Hemi Charger Business Coupe

Chrysler's new A864 Hemi engine made history in racing of all forms from its inception. Using the first-generation engine's cylinder head refinements, factory engineers adopted a new head design to the existing RB cylinder block. The primary goal was competitiveness on the Grand National NASCAR circuit, but the factory and its race engineers also knew that drag racing would be a main focus of the Hemi effort from the start. Indeed, the company quickly made the Hemi the successor of the 1964 Max Wedge drag packages at mid-season.

Moreover, the 426 Hemi engine defined the role of Chrysler in racing and on the street during the 1960s, and Dick Landy was among the most supported proponents of the technology once it was released. The 426 Hemi was created as a racing engine, but unlike many of the exotic race-oriented powerplants that came from others, it was released in far larger numbers than any competitor's race engine from its earliest days. Plus, after showing up in hundreds of race cars in 1964 and 1965, the engine was mildly reworked for street use and offered

Both cars were in the pits at Riverside soon after the Hemi was delivered. Note the unique extra taillights on both cars. (Photo Courtesy Landy Family Archives)

for that environment in 1966, losing little of its reputation when in the right state of tune.

As released in the car that Dick received, the drag racing A864 Hemi featured dual Holley 770-cfm carbs, an aluminum cross-ram intake, iron K-type heads, 12.5 compression, tubular header–type exhaust, a forged crankshaft, and cross-bolted main bearing supports in the reworked RB Hemi block. The B-platform for the new Hemi lightweight models was limited to the nondescript Dodge 330 sedan, sometimes referred to as a Polara but actually noted in the factory paperwork simply as a "business coupe." This designation was based on the fact that these cars were released with just the two front seats installed and the rear seat deleted. Polara was the more upscale hardtop Dodge, not the race package models based on the stripped-down 330.

Beyond losing the two seats, the 426 Hemi Charger (as Dodge referred to the vehicle) received all the lightweight parts noted earlier (see "1964 Stage III Max Wedge Hardtop), save the front bumper, which was now made of thin-gauge steel. In addition, these cars received aluminum doors with Plexiglas windows; these doors retained the window mechanisms and fixed vent wings. A door package released later that season for Factory Experimental cars used fixed windows and no vent wings.

The new 426 Hemi, possibly on the day it arrived at Automotive Research. The new car is still in white. This soft-focused image may be the only one of an as-delivered 1964 A864 Hemi Dodge. I believe Dick shot this picture himself. (Photo Courtesy Landy Family Archives)

On the Hemi package, the hood hinges were eliminated. The aluminum hood, with its redesigned level-top scoop, was now held in place by four large, threaded wing-nut tie-downs, which were mounted to the four corners. The chrome grille stamping was redesigned to hold two instead of four headlights, all in the interest of saving weight.

A single traverse-mounted muffler was used for the exhaust layout, fed from the new tubular headers by a Y-shaped connector between them. As in the past, these headers could be capped off at the flanges to use the

The Hemi Charger was part of Dick's first national tour. Here he races young Hank Taylor at the 1964 Nationals, where he went to the semifinals. (Photo Courtesy ©TEN: The Enthusiast Network. All rights reserved.)

Dick proudly displays the Hot Rod magazine drags trophy, one of the first competition wins for a production Hemi car. (Photo Courtesy Landy Family Archives)

The restored engine returned to a 1964-era, though somewhat unmodified, state of tune. It is not known how the engine appeared after the 180-degree headers were changed out for a more conventional design when the wheelbase was altered.

This rudimentary tach, without a redline, was used to find shift points.

exhaust, which rules mandated as "functional." Due to ongoing understanding of exhaust science, many Hemi racers found additional help by creating specific-length extensions to bolt to the header flange. Automotive Research quickly went a step further than this.

According to longtime owner Pete Haldiman, the 1964 Dodge lettered up for Automotive Research and shipped to Dick through his sponsor, the L.A. County Dodge Dealers, has VIN 614225635. By the time the factory had determined what parts would go on the new Hemi cars, it was late April. The car's scheduled production date was May 21, 1964, and it had a shipping date of May 27. It is believed that Landy's car was among the first built in the initial batch of Hemi Chargers.

Race prep at that time was similar to changes by any Hemi Super Stock racer. To be legal in S/SA, the car ran on a 7-inch rear tire, a challenge that was greatly aided by the use of the A727 TorqueFlite automatic. Big-inch stick cars required finesse and some luck to get traction. At the time, 7 inches was the NHRA Stock maximum tire width. There was no need to lighten the NHRA legal-weight body excessively, and period images show that the car ran steel wheels until late in the season. Dick had already added the unique third set of taillights to the rear panel by the time the car was on track for the first *Hot Rod* Magazine Championships the second weekend in June.

Like a number of A864 Hemi cars in 1964, the Landy car was delivered in basic white with a bright red interior. Like all 1964 TorqueFlite models, the car used a dash-mounted push-button shifter, which the driver operated with his left hand.

Initially, Dick chose to run the new Hemi in A/Modified Production, which allowed some tuning changes, the better Isky cam outfit, and a little more rear tire width. At the *Hot Rod* meet in Riverside, both Automotive Research Dodges were on hand. It appears that Landy drove both cars as well. The wedge fell to Tom Grove in round one of the actual Sunday race, and Dick recorded a class victory in A/MP at a soft 12.01/121 mph on Saturday to get the 426 Hemi its first win in open competition. The racing season was in full swing by then, and even the factory-associated drivers had a learning curve with the new engine design.

Hemi Huntin' in 1964

In addition to the *Hot Rod* Magazine Championships, the Hemi quickly proved it was going to thunder. The best time for the wedge had been 11.52/123 mph, and the Hemi had already clocked an 11.22/125 mph at Lions in a match with Dyno Don Nicholson's Comet on June 27. The following day, Dick set a new A/MP track record at San Fernando with an 11.34. In two consecutive weeks in early July at Lions, he reset the track AFX record twice (11.17 and 11.15), beat Maverick for an S/SA match race title, and then won an overall crown for all cars in the 11.01/11.75 Formula 4 bracket.

The next plan was to go east for several weeks to run Indy, and Dick had scheduled some paying match races as well. On August 1, he ran the big stocker championships at Vaca Valley in central California and broke a lot of parts, but he had repaired them by 9:30 p.m. to compete in eliminations and win the top $150 prize in open money. That prepared him for the next day at Fremont, near San Francisco, where he grabbed the track's SS/A record at a huge 11.13, plus he took Top Stock honors according to a Dodge news release.

Doug's Crazy Headers

Dick had unique headers. Although sponsor Doug Thorley had gained a reputation as a go-to guy when it came to ideas, according to Mike Landy, Dick created a set of 180-degree undercar pipes with help from old friend Vali Goelz. These were first played with on the Max Wedge design but gained more publicity on the Hemi. Because the engine had only recently become available, this experiment may have been one that Chrysler paid him to follow up on.

The idea of a 180-degree header is to use the exhaust pulse of a just-fired cylinder to create a low-pressure area at the pipe outlet when the next cylinder in the sequence is fired. In turn, this frees up power as the exhausting sequence follows each ignition sequence. To make it work requires a complicated group of crossover pipe designs. The most visible proponent at the moment Landy's set went together was Ford's small-block V-8 Formula 1 engine; the package is easily recognized because all the pipes feed into a single exhaust outlet, designed to impart the scavenging effect.

On Jimmy Clark's F1 car, however, these pipes simply hung above the engine in a spaghetti-looking pile of blackened tubing. On a factory Hemi Charger, they had to be worked in around the suspension and inner fenders of the car. It is somewhat incredible that someone actually created a set of these pipes for a passenger car application, but Dick experimented with them during his summer tour and had them on the Hemi car when the Indy Nationals hosted its first field of Hemi Super Stocks.

"Yeah, I remember hearing about those headers," reminisces son Richard Landy. "They were very complicated and a real pain in the butt if you need to take them off the engine." Dick later noted that the need to swap transmissions at the track forced the project to end; it was just too much work to remove the exhaust system to replace the TorqueFlite. The final mention of them was at the end of 1965, when a set with a forward-existing pipe was placed on the altered-wheelbase car.

Dick experimented with 180-degree header designs, seen here on the earlier Max Wedge, for several years. (Photo Courtesy Landy Family Archives)

After having trailer problems on the way to the eastern tour, Dick mounted his pit bike to the tow bar and the car was flat-towed. A Plymouth station wagon did the heavy lifting. (Photo Courtesy Landy Family Archives)

This was the leap-off point for his East Coast tour. It was a challenge, as the team somehow damaged its trailer in Arizona and ended up flat-towing the Hemi car the remainder of the trip. So it was the pit motorcycle (resting on some welded tabs on the tow bar), three guys (Dick, PR friend Jerry Gross, and Vali Goelz), tools, and parts all in the 1963 Plymouth wagon.

According to reports in *Drag News* and other papers, the big push was the grand opening of a new 1/5-mile track in Fairmont, West Virginia, called Eldora Drag Raceway, where Dick headlined the East-West Stock Car Go. Five thousand fans showed up for the two-day event, and Dick left as the victor and $500 richer.

Then it was across the Eastern Seaboard (Richmond, Virginia; York, Pennsylvania; Monrovia, Maryland; and others), culminating in resetting the track record on August 30 at sea-level Atco, New Jersey, with an 11.03 time and a trouncing of Malcolm Durham's Z-11 match-race Chevelle.

However, NHRA's annual summer blast over Labor Day at Indy the following weekend was a whole different animal. At that event, Dick ran the car as a legal S/SA entry, going down earlier than he would have liked in the tough 39-car class runoffs but qualifying well enough to come back on Monday, ready to go with his unique 180-degree sound. He won the first two rounds but met with the eventual winner, Roger Lindamood's *Color Me Gone* Dodge, in the semifinals to end the weekend.

Still, the tour had been a success, resulting in the cover of *Drag News* from a four-way race at York, several prominent magazine photos, and a pocketful of cash. Touring was part of the next decade, and this "trial by fire" had been good training.

A Wheelie Big Adjustment

After the NHRA Nationals the biggest changes to Dick's 1964 were initiated. This was at the factory behest and may have been planned for some time. An August 4 letter written to NHRA's Wally Parks by Dodge's public relations rep Frank Wiley made the argument for the use of a Dodge A100 van straight front axle in the hotter stock ranks, but Dick credited Jack McFarland of Dodge for coming up with it. Because the compact van

The 1964 car in all its glory near the end of the year. This photo may have been taken to show weight transfer issues. (Courtesy quartermilestones.com)

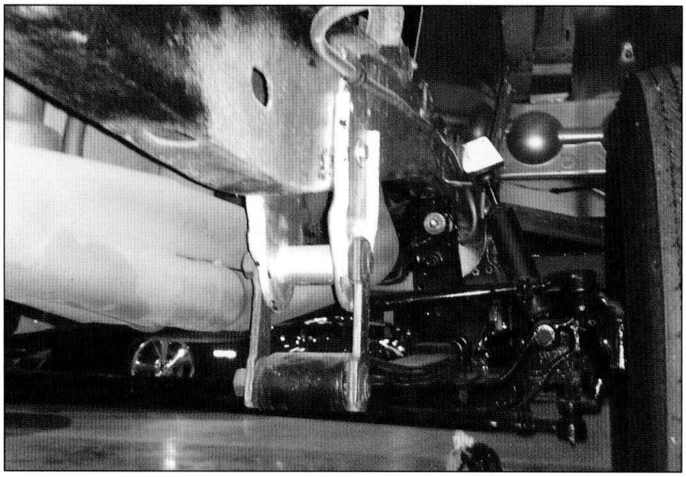

The car's unique height was created by dropping the mounting points for the new front leaf springs.

Seat belt webbing helped limit shock travel. The level of engineering may seem crude, but Landy did whatever it took to make the new conversion functional. It went almost 150 mph in this state.

was registered as a passenger car, it was technically legal to adopt this axle under a Modified Production car with approval from the NHRA. Several racers who had put Hemi engines into match race Darts had made this change. It not only eliminated the danger of the wheels toeing-out during wheel stands but also removed front-end weight, which was a concern due to the heavy iron-head engine.

A follow-up telegram on October 6 from Wiley to NHRA's Jack Hart notes that this must have been authorized because Connecticut racer Bill Flynn would be running this unit in his A/Modified Production Max Wedge Dodge the following weekend, and Landy's rebuilding was close behind.

As previously mentioned, very minor wheelbase changes had been a regular part of legal racing already, and not just by the Mopar troops. However, Chrysler's unique torsion-bar front suspension and leaf-spring differentials had made it easy to move the entire wheelbase forward beneath the body by an inch or so. By maintaining the published legal wheel-to-wheel measurement, it was possible to keep one step ahead of the technical inspectors, at least for a while. If a car went into the NHRA Factory Experimental class, a 2-percent variance from the stock wheelbase was allowed. Dick ran both Dodges in that specific trim at times in 1964, but the Automotive Research Hemi Charger soon featured far more than this allowance.

Inviting a photographer to document it for a feature in *Drag Racing* magazine, Automotive Research installed the A100 straight front axle sometime between October 15 and 30. It was bolted to the Dodge's front frame stub using a heavily modified K-frame engine support. It is possible that some of that particular change had come from the 180-degree pipe program. Regardless, the mounting featured seat belt webbing to create minor travel to the axle during adjustment, but the actual suspension now consisted of shocks and leaf springs mounted to the front subframe rails. The aluminum front fender wheel house opening was lengthened almost to the bumper but was nicely refinished, and the front wheel location could move forward a full 6 inches via a series of optional locating points.

This view shows how drastically the rear of the car was lifted in the interest of weight transfer.

The perhaps overlooked and less visible engineering occurred at the rear. The rear axle was also given new mounting points, allowing it to be brought forward as much as 8 inches. This was done by not simply reworking the spring mounting points but by cutting clearance notches in the frame and mounting jounce snubbers, which were bullet-shaped hard-rubber cones, to prevent axle windup.

The factory rear suspension design was radically reworked, and adjustable shock and spring mounts were added. This is the passenger-side tire position.

With the differential location also adjustable, the rear shocks were now positioned at a radical angle to the differential spring pad mount when it was moved forward the farthest. Perhaps the adjustability was available to allow Dick to test ideas of radically switching the two wheelbase locations, discovering how stable or unstable the car was at speed. It really was rocket science in that regard, and kudos are in order for him in being the test pilot at 140 mph or faster.

Indeed, Dick Landy became the first stocker to hit 130 mph in the quarter at his old stomping ground at San Fernando on November 22, after the conversion was done. The car already held the recent records at this track in A/Gas, A/MP, and S/SA. September and October featured a few local matches and back-to-back finishes at Vacaville and Oroville, California; friend Butch Leal's Thunderbolt was the victorious nemesis at both events. But the biggest battle was an attempt at Hayden Proffitt's number-one spot on the *Drag News* list on November 1.

This required towing all the way to Houston Raceway in Texas, right after the front axle was installed. However, that proved to be a frustrating day that left Proffitt, who was going from Plymouth to Mercury for 1965, with a trademark smile and still number one. Dick broke an axle in testing, swapped a cam in 30 minutes after the first race was lost, but burned a piston on the second shot to forfeit the race with damage. All he got from Texas was tow money, a couple of newspaper photos the next week, and a long ride home across West Texas.

When Dick visited Detroit in December 1964, he discovered that the new 1965 426 Hemi package used even more extreme measures than he had undertaken that fall. He took this snapshot of the first Plymouth mule in Chrysler Engineering building. (Photo Courtesy Landy Family Archives)

Still, the highly modified car running in the backyard of the major drag racing and hot rodding publications could not be missed. On December 5, it was used dramatically as the double-size cover of *Drag Sport Illustrated,* doing a big burnout with a 3.9 gear set after Dick had clocked a huge record 147-mph charge during the SCTA-timed half-mile drags at Riverside on November 28. There was also a color cover on *Hot Rod Parts*, an S/SA feature in *Super Stock* magazine, and most important it was featured on several pages in *Hot Rod* magazine in February 1965. Good publicity matters to sponsors, and the Automotive Research Dodge delivered it well.

Most of what Dick Landy did that fall was experimental, and the changes resulted in a package capable of pulling the front end into the air in small amounts. Although the evolving car may have been a handful at speed, it never hit a trackside guardrail or lamppost. Meanwhile, as the Landy Hemi Charger roared into the periodicals of the era, in the Structures Lab at Chrysler's Highland Park research facility, engineer Jim Thornton was building a factory-supported vehicle that featured an even more dramatic wheelbase reworking (see Chapter 3 for more detail).

As a closing note, the 1964 A864 Hemi drag package was actually the finale for the aluminum-panel efforts in Super Stock. Major rules changes enacted by the NHRA at the end of the 1964 season outlawed the panels and mandated all-steel body structures for Stock Eliminator. This fact, announced soon after the 1964 Indy Nationals, may have played a role in how radically Dick altered his still-competitive S/SA car late in the season.

At the same time, the idea of match race stockers, once the province of the southeastern United States, gained momentum nationally. NHRA-legal or not, finding a place to race and, more important, being paid, was not difficult. Dick had already been touring the East Coast that season as a booked-in driving personality, but the publicity garnered by the 1964 Automotive Research Hemi Charger set the stage for 1965, one of the most important years in both doorslammer drag racing and the legend of Dandy Dick Landy.

Where Are They Now?

The 1964 Max Wedge was likely sold sometime late in 1964; ironically, attempts to find it by major players in the collector hobby have proven to be futile, even with the three taillights. Either it is gone into butchered-up match race oblivion or it has been hidden in a garage someplace for decades. I was unable to trace it beyond the 1964 efforts of mysterious driver Rapid Raymond (last name unknown).

The A864 Hemi sedan, however, has remained quite visible, as Pete and Renee Haldiman have owned it far longer than all of its previous owners combined. After Dick sold it to Robert Runyan of Salt Lake City in the spring of 1965 as a turnkey race car, it was campaigned for two years and sold again.

Due to their ineligibility in Super Stock, a large number of the 1964 Hemi packages were radically changed into match race trim in the 1965–1966 era. This car, arguably the first true Funny Car, already featured enough adjustment by Landy that it was never more radically changed. Runyan told Pete Haldiman that the car was still running the same engine and transmission he had purchased from Landy. He noted that he had raced it in the Factory Experimental category and taken it to the 1966 Winternationals, though he did not specify whether that was NHRA's Big Go at Pomona or the AHRA (American Hot Rod Association) event held at Lions that season.

The car disappeared for about a decade; then it was purchased by magazine photojournalist Bruce Caldwell. Caldwell was aware of what it was and offered it in a classified ad in *Car Craft* magazine in May 1977, which is when the Haldimans bought it.

"The car appeared to have suffered few changes from when it was last owned by Dick Landy," Pete noted later. "The car was missing its Hemi engine and was painted white instead of silver. It appeared to have its original Hemi automatic trans and its original 8¾-inch rear end. The Dodge was easy to authenticate because of the numerous magazine photos and articles it had appeared in. The straight front axle and the six taillights were most obvious."

The Haldimans restored the car to its as-raced late-1964 condition and have displayed it at many important reunions and events during the past three decades. They sold it to noted Landy vehicle collector Todd Werner in late 2015.

Renee and Pete Haldiman have been the loving caretakers of the 1964 Hemi-Charger since the late 1970s. They displayed it at the Muscle Car and Corvette Nationals (MCACN) in 2014.

What's So Funny About That?

When Dick went 147 mph at Riverside late in 1964, he got the cover of **Drag Sport Illustrated**, *a regional newspaper. Such periodicals are rarely seen today.*

Pete Haldiman is understandably proud of the 1964 Dodge once raced by Dick Landy that he owned and has often laid out the case that it should be considered the first Funny Car. This has been a discussion of no small controversy among drag racing aficionados, coming down to a single question: What really defines a Funny Car?

For some, the supercharged-on-nitromethane engine combination of a modern body has always been the deciding factor. They point to a Comet project that Jack Chrisman built with help from Mercury in the summer of 1964 as the first Funny Car. However, those who believe the fuel is not a factor argue that the high-dollar Dodge-sponsored program using supercharged gas engines deserves the accolades. The Dodge Chargers team used custom 330-series Max Wedge sedans.

Of course, others say that it was not until 1966 when Mercury used a tubular chassis/fiberglass shell design that the first modern Funny Cars were born. But some reply, "No, those cars were injected. The real one was Don Garlits's roadster Dart II of late 1966, as it ran a supercharged Hemi fuel dragster driveline with the driver in a single-seat centered chassis!"

The origin of the term *Funny Car* was never even considered until 1965, when Chrysler brought out a string of well-publicized exhibition cars. The term has been formally credited to Mercury racing boss Fran Hernandez, who stated that his legitimate Ford A/FX cars would not be racing Chrysler's Funny Cars that spring. Those cars were not funny because of nitromethane, superchargers, or flip-top shells but because of their wheelbase changes.

And if that is the legitimate basis for the term, it becomes easy to see why the 1964 Automotive Research Hemi Charger, with its 6-inch front/8-inch rear wheelbase changes, could honestly be considered the first Funny Car. In periodicals of the day, it was often depicted as the most radical of the breed, and it looked the part with its raised stance, lightened front-end design, and changed wheelbase. I agree with Pete. Alas, even this dissertation on how it came to be will likely do little to settle the first Funny Car argument once and for all.

Although publicized to appear, Jack Chrisman and his blown nitro-burning 427 Comet were no-shows for the Riverside event. Had he made it, it would have been the first advertised Funny Car match race. This is Jack at the 1965 Pomona Winternationals. (Photo Courtesy Lynn Wineland Archive, quartermilestones.com)

1965: Leading the Charge into History

This PR image in Gean Landy's files shows the 1965 car after Dick got it running in the spring, now with the Cragar S/S wheels. (Photo Courtesy Landy Family Archives)

The wheelbase-related experiments that Dick Landy performed on his 1964 Automotive Research Dodge were specifically designed to aid weight transfer. As the year wound down, back in Detroit, at the Chrysler Suspension Lab, Engineering car 558 (featuring similar modifications taken to an extreme) was being assembled. At the start of 1964, four cars with 2-percent reworked wheelbases for NHRA-legal FX racing were constructed at Chrysler's direction. Although less than what Dick's late-year project with the A100 truck front axle had entailed, these two Plymouths and two Dodges nonetheless laid the groundwork for what transpired for 1965, and they have even been vetted by some as forebears of the first Funny Car title as well. While the wheelbase was within 2 percent of stock on the 1964 FX models, the body itself was shifted backward as well.

Jim Thornton, a calculatingly brilliant engineer and member of the Ramchargers team, had already put the finishing touches on the 1965 A990-powered Super Stock cars. Rules changes for 1965 required these cars to use all-steel bodies and also rendered all previous aluminum- or fiberglass-paneled vehicles ineligible for Stock Eliminator–type racing. (Super Stock was still part of that category.) The new A990-code 426 Hemi engine was a big part of this effort, using aluminum heads and a magnesium intake to remove approximately 100 pounds from the engine assembly. Thornton also found ways to use thinner steel for the bodies through the stamping process. However, car 558, based on a standard Plymouth Belvedere, was something else altogether.

Due to the parallel nature of the front frame rails on the Chrysler B-Body, Thornton moved the K-member engine support and suspension mount forward 10 inches, relocating it just behind the front bumper. This obviously required some changes to the front fender openings, but these were not Super Stockers, so privately manufactured fiberglass fenders worked. Longer torsion bars and reengineered control arms were also needed for this change, but it was not a hugely difficult task to adapt for this challenge either.

Next, to move the differential forward as well, the rear leaf spring mounting points were relocated in a fairly simple but radical operation. By slicing through

By the end of the 1965 season, fun and games had turned serious. Dick gets into his fire suit at Phoenix at the end of the year. (Photo Courtesy ©TEN: The Enthusiast Network. All rights reserved.)

the entire unibody floor at two latitudinal points behind the front seat and ahead of the forward axle mount locations, Thornton simply sectioned out that portion of the assembly-line floor beneath the body. With that removed, the entire rear section and floor assembly of the car, including frame rails and differential mounting points, were also cut out as one big piece and then shifted forward inside the body shell.

This left the new wheel house only inches behind the door jamb of what had begun as a 115-inch wheelbase. Because the removed segment allowed the rear axle to be 15 inches farther forward than stock and the front wheels were moved 10 inches forward, a wheelbase of just 110 inches was created. To refit the rear wheel housing for the relocated wheel, the rear quarter panels were sliced apart, the OEM sheet-metal wheel house opening was moved forward the same distance as the inner structure, and the whole thing was patched back together. With the NHRA allowing only a 2-percent variance for Factory Experimental, these 12-percent-change cars were not legal for that series, but based on what Dick and many others had found about the match race scene during 1964, the NHRA rule book was not the point.

If You Can't Beat Them, Outlaw Them

Chrysler was in a unique place in 1965. General Motors was formally out of racing and appeared to be serious about that decision. Conversely, Ford was all in for racing in every venue, from Indy car to LeMans endurance efforts, and was funneling millions into NASCAR and drag racing. Although the decisive conversations are lost to history, it is likely that Chrysler Engineering's racing program coordinator, Tom Hoover, saw the writing on the wall. Hoover competed regularly as one of the Ramchargers' engine builders. He felt that the idea was to build exhibition racing vehicles as radically as possible and not to follow the letter of the law when it came to the NHRA rules. Indeed, once the NHRA saw the prototype Plymouth on a Detroit visit in January 1965, it quickly said no to any FX legality. The cars had to run in B/Altered.

On the match race trail, however, the cars were a flat-out challenge to whomever was willing to race against them, factory-backed, NHRA-legal, or otherwise. Besides that, the alternative racing organization, AHRA, was agreeable to any factory program and traditionally found ways to make anything exciting into a showcase class. During 1965, NASCAR also had a new drag racing arm,

The 1965 season started at Phoenix and the AHRA Winter Nationals, but Dick was plagued with 4-speed issues and went back to the automatic soon afterward. (Photo Courtesy ©TEN: The Enthusiast Network. All rights reserved.)

Dick took the victory at the 1965 March Meet in Bakersfield, running amazing times in the 10.20s. This was the first big win for Dick in the 1965 car. (Charles Milikin Jr. Photo)

which also welcomed the altered Hemi program. Finally, with the construction of 200 new 1965 A990 Hemi Super Stockers on the horizon, and with Ford announcing that it would not be creating a follow-up to the now-ineligible Fairlane Thunderbolt in Super Stock (focusing instead solely on FX), Chrysler knew it could hold the line at NHRA events quite well without making a second splash in the Factory Experimental division.

Other factors also came into the decision making. Foremost was money, thanks to the NASCAR boycott. In late October 1964, Ronney Householder had called "Big Bill" France's bluff when France had stated that NASCAR rules for 1965 would exclude both the 426 Hemi engine and the use of B-Body models on superspeedways. As a result, Householder pulled the factory out of the series entirely, and a lot of former Grand National funding (and a handful of racers, such as Richard Petty and David Pearson) went draggin' in the new year.

Also, the factory already realized that drag racing as a sport was more evenly distributed than the Grand National series, which received national press but had mostly Southeastern locales. Strategically hiring drag racing teams from various areas of the nation and putting them into exciting machinery guaranteed regional exposure. Moreover, the street-based performance enthusiast (and possible Chrysler car buyer) was more likely to try out drag racing as a hobby, and the era's magazines were filled with features on better race cars and how to make modifications to go faster.

The company did not abandon circle track racing entirely; a number of racers remained busy on the Midwestern USAC, ARCA, and IMSA series. By June 1965, France had seen enough empty grandstands to make some compromises, and Chrysler, for its part, was stating that the 426 Hemi would be a street option for the 1966 model year. In fact, not well-known is that Dick Landy privately announced this fact to West Coast media friends in the late spring of the year and was referenced in those rumors. Regardless of all that, with Householder and Cahill behind him, Dick Landy's 1965 racing efforts were career changing. Assisted now with both payroll and expense account checks by Dodge, he had the funds to put the newly christened *Landy's Dodge* in front of the biggest possible audiences, first at the SoCal racing facilities and later nationwide.

Acid Baths

It had already been decided that the special 1965 Coronet and Belvedere hardtops would use fiberglass parts: front fenders, front bumpers, hoods with scoops, doors, and deck lids. Add fixed Plexiglas windows and the new A990 engine and the cars were already down near 3,000 pounds. So, very late in 1964, Dick Landy received the call from Chrysler about how to make the factory bodies to be used in the factory-altered program even lighter. After all, Southern California was the capital of the airplane and associated component business at the time, and a chemical milling tank big enough to hold an entire car body was needed. In a process called acid dipping, a metal component is placed into a balanced but highly caustic solution to remove metal thickness. It has to be done with care, as the acid can literally dissolve the metal to nothing. Dick found a place called AeroChem that could do the job. This was new ground for everyone involved. Most airplane parts were alloy or highly graded steels, not mass-produced steel like that used by Detroit to stamp out car bodies. "We dipped the first body into the tank in the middle of the day," he noted in a conversation with me in the 1990s, "and this big cloud of green smoke came pouring out of the place. After that, they did the rest of them at night!"

Depending on the amount of time in the tank, some of the cars were so thin that they were damaged in transit back to Michigan. At least one was simply scrapped in California, so racer Bill Flynn began the season racing a standard A990-type Dodge Super Stocker. The other bodies were shipped to Michigan because the factory had given the reconstruction work to Amblewagon, a local conversion subcontractor. Initially the program had called for 12 cars to be built, with 10 to be converted by this firm. Dick's was one of the Dodges.

Winter into Spring

Dick had his work cut out for him when his car came back from Michigan just weeks before the big winter events. Although Amblewagon had painted the cars in primer and what appeared to be a white base coat, next was considerable chassis work, body work, a run to the paint shop for a coat of the trademark Mercedes silver and black, and some engine tuning on the new A990 Hemi. The first event of the year was the AHRA Winter Nationals, to be held outside Phoenix at Beeline Dragway on the final weekend of January. It is likely that Dick got in only a little testing before this event, and certainly none was done in public.

AHRA chief Jim Tice and his team from Kansas City welcomed the cars and their possibilities, creating a new AHRA class with the name Ultra Stock. Ford, for its part, had already responded to the cars like NHRA had: no way. In fact, it is now thought that Mercury racing chief Fran Hernandez helped coin the name that stuck on the Chrysler machines: Funny Car.

At the start of the season, Ford actually forbade its racers to go against the radical Chryslers. The only factory-associated Ford that raced at that AHRA event was Phil Bonner's match race Falcon, but it blew an engine in time trials and had to withdraw. Dick had his own problems when the Ultra Stock class runoff occurred on Saturday; both he and Butch Leal suffered manual transmission–related parts failures, and like Bonner they could not make the round-one call for the Mr. Stock Eliminator title on Saturday afternoon. Bud Faubel's new *Honker* Dodge, a car almost identical to Dick's in appearance, took the title and fame at this event. Things went a little better on Sunday, though the Ramchargers NHRA-legal A/FX car with Mike Buckel driving won the overall Handicap Stock crown that day.

The next weekend, rain tightened NHRA's Winternationals at the Pomona Fairgrounds into a single Sunday bash. While the Fords cleaned up in the Factory Experimental category, Leal and Landy made a couple of exhibition runs late that day for the sake of the fans. Contrary to what is sometimes stated, the NHRA did not outlaw these cars entirely; they simply were not FX-legal. In fact, the NHRA confirmed this specifically to its member tracks and tech people in an open statement published in its house organ, *National Dragster.*

Testing the new wheelie casters at the shop in March. I'm guessing the cops were not around. (Photo Courtesy Landy Family Archives)

Here are the winners! Dick with engineer Tom Hoover and racing boss Bob Cahill at the 1965 March Meet. (Photo Courtesy Landy Family Archives)

Regardless, the Winternationals was one of only four national events the NHRA held that year. The other three were the new Springnationals in Bristol, Tennessee; the Indy Nationals; and a new World Finals event held near Tulsa, Oklahoma. The AHRA had its 1965 events in places like Gary, Indiana, and the Lions Club–backed track in Long Beach, California, but the next big race for Dick was actually close to home at the Patch (Bakersfield, California) for the annual Smokers Club Fuel & Gas Championships.

This event, best known as the March Meet, actually gave Dick his first big boost for 1965. Tuning on the car and chassis had begun to show results, and the month between Pomona and Bakersfield allowed the team to dial it in. This included installing a tried-and-true TorqueFlite into the car; one period race report stated that Dick had broken at least three A833 manuals at the AHRA race. After testing quietly in Fresno (but getting the AHRA F1-U/SA record there), Dick earned headlines from the effort at Bakersfield. He won the special AFX class, beating Leal in round one and then Cecil Yother, who crashed into the trackside hay bales in the 1964 *Melrose Missile* during the money round. Meanwhile, Dick was clocking an eyebrow-raising 10.26-at-138-mph performance in the other lane, which was unheard of at that time in any stocker on carburetors and gasoline. *Landy's Dodge* was nationally recognized by this feat.

Cub reporter Dave Wallace Jr. noted that the Dodge's rear bumper was torn up that first time out. This Gean Landy photo may be from that same race. The factory later forbade the antics because of breakage. (Photo Courtesy Landy Family Archives)

Next Came Moonshots

The car did not do any major wheel stands at Bakersfield, but continued experimentation had shown it was possible. Two weekends later, on Sunday, March 21, Dick showed up unannounced at San Fernando. Young Dave Wallace Jr. told what happened next in his race report entitled "Landy Turns 'Em On," printed in the West Coast race paper *Drag Sport Illustrated*.

Ed Iskendarian used this image from Lions to publicize Dick's big 9.79 performance at Half Moon Bay in May. (Photo Courtesy Landy Family Archives)

After the moon-shot efforts at San Fernando, Dick quickly issued this postcard from that day, noting his new AHRA record. The card is a rare collector's item today. (Photo Courtesy Landy Family Archives)

"I can't begin to describe what he did, I only hope ace photog Jim Kelly caught Dick's exhibition runs. As if his time of 10.42 and 136 were not enuff [*sic*] for the cheering fans, *Landy's Dodge* pulled the front wheels off the ground on three straight times, the last scrapping [*sic*] the purty [*sic*] chrome off the rear bumper! No kiddin'; to say 5 feet would have been conservative. We have never seen anything quite so sensational here at the Pond, and Dick did it for nothing today!"

California fans took to the new wheel standing immediately, and this* Car Craft *center spread showed* Landy's Dodge *to the whole nation. (Photo Courtesy ©TEN: The Enthusiast Network. All rights reserved.)

This classic image of Dandy Dick, with unlit cigar and tall 1965 injectors, showed him as the ultimate professional stock-bodied drag racer. (Photo Courtesy ©TEN: The Enthusiast Network. All rights reserved.)

Wallace noted in his similar dispatch to *Drag News* that Landy had already mounted casters beneath the car and that the Dodge was holding the wheel stands up to 50 feet. Another reporter stated that this was being done with 400 pounds of ballast at the rear. Regardless of how, the skyscraping effort received the attention of promoter C. J. "Pappy" Hart at Lions, the biggest track in Southern California at the time. Pappy booked Landy for the following Sunday, March 28, to race Doug "Cookie" Cook in the supercharged Stone-Woods-Cook *Swindler* Willys B/Gasser. After doing wheelies, Dick lost that one in two straight but then raced the MGM Hydro pickup gasser and won with a 10.41/133 effort. The weekend also included some of his most notorious runs, when he did more big wheelies the night before in front of a number of the sport's best photographers during the Lions weekly Top Fuel race.

With the Ford boycott still active, the next race was against the Shores & Hess Anglia gasser at Riverside, but things soon changed. Like Dick, Hayden Proffitt made his living by drag racing stock-bodied drag cars; he convinced his bosses in Michigan that they needed a giant killer. He was authorized to make changes to his 1965 SOHC Comet, including a straight front axle. After agreement among all parties, including Pappy Hart, the deal was a best-three-of-five against Landy at Lions. Both cars weighed 3,200 pounds. Seen at Pomona's weekly racing program in late April testing this combination, *Landy's Dodge* ran 10.60s but still made MPH readings above 133.

The event was in mid-May as part of the first annual Lions BOMP (Best of Modern People) Nationals. In the meantime, Dick had a chance to go to Puyallup, Washington, and Woodburn, Oregon, for a quick Northwest tour and more wheelie demos. By then the car had settled down, but the promoters were clamoring to see repeats of the earlier wheels-up efforts. Even this early, *Landy's Dodge* was quickly proving not just popular for its exhibition qualities but feared as a top-performing race car. Hayden Proffitt used that to his advantage.

The BOMP weekend started with Dick racing Tom Jacobson driving Tom Sturm's Chevelle on Saturday evening in testing; tuned for the next day's big race, the Hemi ate a cam on its only pass, meaning a thrash for Sunday's race against Proffitt. In testing and prerace trials, the Comet recorded times at the top of the 10-second bracket, while the Dodge was consistently in the 10.60s. First round, red light for Proffitt; second

The package was greatly aided by design changes made by Chrysler engineers. This is Dick and journalist buddy Jerry Gross, who went to work for Chrysler during the clinic era, from the summer of 1965 Eastern tour. (Photo Courtesy ©TEN: The Enthusiast Network. All rights reserved.)

round, ditto; and again, third round. Proffitt had lost all three runs on this technical error but had managed to show the Comet leading the race in every single photo that was shot! Hart actually fined him for doing this, as the track was packed with fans wanting to see the first actual Mopar–Ford battle of 1965.

Dick ran quicker every run, clicked off a fast 10.50 in the third match, and then stripped the weight off the car and posted a final 10.25/135-mph single to prove he was king of the stockers in Southern California.

Injection Is Indeed Nice

The BOMP event heralded another big first: Hilborn had just given the new Hemi injector layout to the factory racers, and Dick and his crew swapped this onto the car during the two-day effort and made some shakedown runs with it, clocking 10.70 times. This had been something Chrysler engineers had been playing with since late 1964, and it had been on the 558 mule at its only competitive race, the AHRA Winter Nationals. Continued testing had resulted in exacting tube lengths to allow the ram effect found in the cross-ram Race Hemi intake to work with injectors. This in turn allowed the use of nitromethane.

The ram effect was a critical part of why the Chrysler Hemi was so dominant in racing. During testing with the A311 Indy car Hemi engine in the 1950s, engineers had learned that if you could create a resonance to the inbound fuel charge, you could get it to fill the cylinder more completely. This was no small thing; calculating the amount needed for this to happen at an optimum RPM point was worth upward of 20 hp with no other changes. So the length of the intake runner from its high-pressure area at the inlet (either the opening in the intake valley or the top of an injector bell) to the back of the valve was very important. The longer the runner, the lower the RPM where the sonic effect occurred.

The ram effect occurred as the incoming air/fuel charge hit the back of the closing valve on the combustion cycle, momentarily bouncing back up the runner toward the inlet opening's high-pressure end. The charge then sonically rushed the opposite way through the lower-pressure intake runner just as the valve opened, grabbing whatever additional air/fuel was available as well.

The calculations required for this were a highly guarded secret for years at the company, but it worked. The specific lengths of the new Hilborn injectors were specified based on whether the car was a 4-speed or automatic. Ronnie Sox and his Plymouth showed how well this had been established when he clocked a 9.98 at York US 30 Dragway in Pennsylvania in late April, the first normally aspirated stocker to ever go under the 10-second barrier.

Photographer Bob Martin captured a series of images of Dick at Fontana Drag City on May 20 doing a series of tests with these units on the car. It took Dick only a short time to dial them in, helped in large measure by a series of racer-only factory notes on baseline tune-ups and possible problems. The Ramchargers clocked a 9.83 at York the weekend after Sox went 9.98.

Dick went to Half Moon Bay on the California coast on May 23 for a regional championship race. He left with the winner's money, a solid 9.79 best at 140 mph, and a featured photo in one of Ed Iskendarian's camshaft ads. Another trip to the Northwest occurred over Memorial Day Weekend, and Dick beat Cecil Yother driving the newest *Melrose Missile* three straight at Pacific Raceways in Puyallup.

June was a quick month, as Dick and his brother Mike, fresh out of high school, started east for a long summer tour as soon as the big Hot Rod Magazine drags at Riverside had been completed. In the interim, Frank Wylie of the Dodge News Bureau suggested that Dick add the twin headlight design seen on the production Coronet. This was simple enough, and the actual headlights were also replaced with spun metal discs at this time, further lowering the nose weight. The Plexiglas windows were also tinted blue.

"We did everything we could to get the car lighter," Dick recalled in another conversation with me years later. "We went so far as to see where we could snip out edge corners, even to save just a few ounces." Thick, square-channel bracing for support allowed the suspension to act alone without damaging the paper-thin body. During the car's restoration in 2014, Ed Strzelecki found several places where Dick added bracing to support the acid-eaten metal, possibly even before its first paint job. Nonetheless, Dick noted in a late 1965 interview with photographer "Diamond Jim" Kelly in *Drag Sport Illustrated* that the car was down to an amazing 2,646 pounds at the end of the season.

Dick recorded an unheard-of 8.47 time at Riverside in the warm-ups for the Hot Rod meet, but this was done with a running start, meaning the car was moving and under power before it started the timers. On June 13, this major event also was previewed on the front page of the *Los Angeles Times* sports section, with *Landy's Dodge* as its

With a large crowd present for the BOMP event, Dick and his team installed the new Hemi Hilborn injectors at the track for the first time, running some mild times in test runs. (Photo Courtesy Landy Family Archives)

Brothers Dick and Mike Landy at work in the shop. Note the multiple makes present and the 1965 Dodge in the back bay. Mike was still in high school at the time. (Photo Courtesy Landy Family Archives)

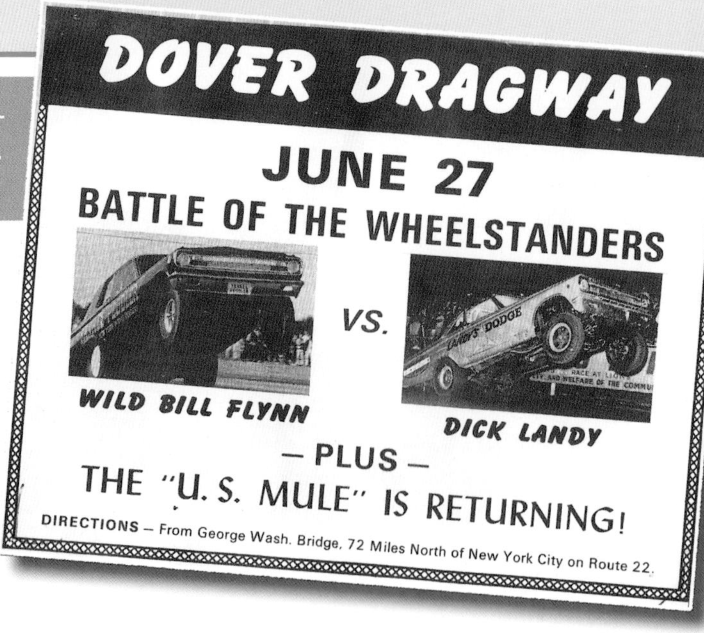

Engineer Dale Reeker had said "no more wheelies," but this was how the event was advertised. (Photo Courtesy Landy Family Archives)

focus, once again proving that Dick's prowess for good PR was never lacking.

For the race, Dick was classified in a special exhibition eliminator and lost on a red light in round one. He also raced Jack Chrisman's supercharged Comet as an exhibition, again drawing the foul. Nonetheless, this effort was a crowning touch to its California spring as the team headed east on Sunday night, with everything needed loaded in a new 1965 Monaco station wagon. A tool box and the pit bike were with the car on the tagalong trailer.

The Eastern Tour: Summer of 1965

The life of a touring racer was fairly grueling. For one thing, the tracks were often located in the middle of nowhere. Dick told writer Eric Dahlquist in a feature article titled "Dodge County," which ran in the June 1965 issue of *Hot Rod,* that he was booked solid once he left California. Not all the results of those races were recorded in the weekly racing newspapers, but it is likely that Dick ran at least two times a week; he noted to Kelly that he had made 31 match race appearances between mid-June and Labor Day. The motels were dingy and small, the track food not always up to par, and the demands of the promoters sometimes onerous. If the promoter wanted to show all five races as scheduled (meaning two wins per car), somebody usually red-lighted in at least one of them.

Then there was the issue of breakage: transmissions, axles, engines, suspension parts, and more. Indeed, regarding the latter, in early June Chrysler engineer Dale Reeker sent a telegram to each of the major racers, stating that they needed to quit doing wheel stands immediately due to this situation.

"At first they gave us a lot of trouble about wheel stands, but that was only because it was something new and the guys were breaking the parts," he told Kelly that December. "It's very scary when you take an $18,000 to $20,000 race car and start breaking the front end coming down. After the fellows do about 10 or 20 wheelstands, they get used to it; they learn to back off and it is just like going down the course. Now they are not bothering us about it because nobody is breaking parts anymore."

Following the NHRA 1965 Springnationals at Bristol, things between Ford and Mopar had thawed enough that the factories' drivers were back in battle against one another on the match race circuit as well. Part of this involved setting up agreed-upon rules before a match began; a second part was creating new class breakdowns. This might mean a class in which all racers had to weigh 3,200 pounds on gasoline (32G) or 2,800 pounds on fuel (28F). In this way, a promoter hosting large or open events could run both class races heads up and then use some form of handicapping to run a final overall eliminator to conclude the event. It was not perfect, but it helped.

Among the recorded events from 1965 were Dick's all-Dodge match with Bill Flynn at Dover Drag Strip in New York on June 27 (Dick won three straight), on July 4 at Pocono Drag Lodge against Ed Schratman (Dick won three straight), and on July 5 at Numidia, Pennsylvania, against K. S. Pittman (Dick took two of three wins). At

Dick in a match race ad with Bill Flynn. The film was sent to him from fan Paul Shiffer, who worked at the track and appreciated the time Dick spent talking with him. (Photo Courtesy Landy Family Archives)

East Coast photographer Charles Milikin Jr. caught Dandy Dick making another fast lap at the little track in rural Numidia, Pennsylvania, during the summer of 1965. He was racing the K. S. Pittman Willys. (Photo Courtesy Charles Milikin Jr.)

Pocono, the text of *Eastern Drag News* noted that the crowd was screaming, "We want wheelies!" After the promoter and Dick discussed it, apparently some money changed hands and the Dodge was up on the back bumper. It is possible that part of this included Dick asking that no photos be taken for submission to the magazines due to Reeker's recent telegram, as nothing dramatic was ever published.

The same thing happened two weeks later, on July 18, at Cecil County, Maryland, where *Landy's Dodge* carried the nose a full 1/8 mile on an exhibition. Again, competition was the feared K. S. Pittman Willys, but Pittman was having his own unintentional wheel stand problems, and Landy won two nights straight over K. S., both there and the evening before at 75-80 Dragway near Monrovia, Maryland.

Like Proffitt, "Dyno Don" Nicholson was now reworking his car, and one of the biggest match races of the tour was a four-abreast five-race ruckus at York US 30 in Pennsylvania on July 10. This featured *Dyno's Comet*, *Landy's Dodge*, Tom Sturm's big-inch Chevelle, and Bud Faubel in a station wagon that he had recently received from Dodge. This was the former Cotton Owens/David Pearson *Cotton Picker*.

In round one, Faubel won; round two was canceled by foul starts; in round three, Dick was third, at 10.46 and Faubel won; Dyno was the winner of the fourth and fifth matches. The text in *Drag News* noted that Dyno's main goal was to keep Landy from getting another victorious headline; a tie with Faubel was okay with him.

The Dodge went progressively faster though. On July 25, Dick raced Joe Wies driving Hank Hankins's supercharged *Trader* Plymouth at Richmond, resetting the track record to a 9.64/141.43. Writer Jerry Gross, who was on the tour with Dick, noted that this was the second weekend that *Landy's Dodge* ran nitromethane, and

At the All-Hemi Reunion in 2007, the Unlimited finalists from the 1965 Super Stock Nationals (**Landy's Dodge** and the Al Eckstrand-driven **Golden Commandos** cars) stand side by side.

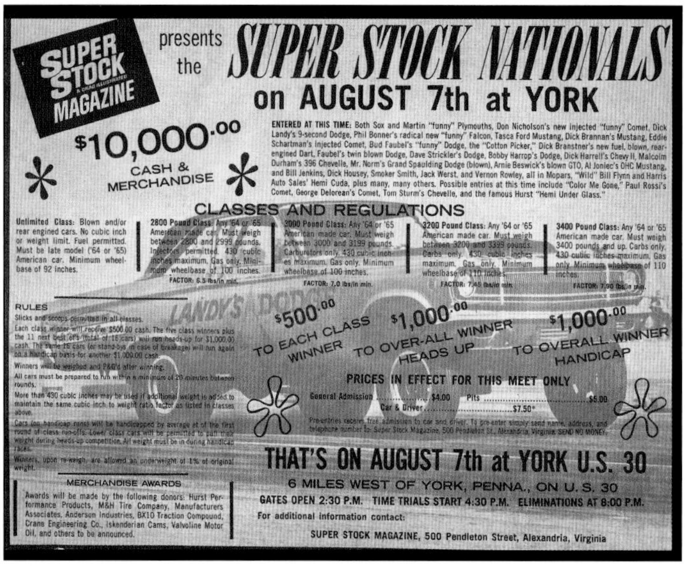

A color newspaper ad for the 1965 Super Stock Nationals used Landy's Dodge *as its background. The design was published in several magazines.*

he raced against Arnie Beswick's blown GTO at Capitol Raceway near Baltimore on August 1. The factory had just released a new set of even larger-diameter injectors. Still, all of this was a prelude for what was coming on August 7, 1965, the Super Stock Magazine Nationals.

Super Stock Nationals

In the annals of drag racing, certain events stand as spectacular; the Super Stock Nationals at York US 30 Dragway was certainly one of them. The publishers of *Super Stock & Drag Illustrated* had worked for months to promote this one-day race in the magazine, even using *Landy's Dodge* as the background in the advertising. It had quickly become the most popular periodical for fans of match racing and stock-bodied drag cars.

Twenty-five thousand fans overran the little country airport that Saturday night, eventually causing the organizers to make it a free event. There were no killings, no destruction, but crowd control was impossible, and here was almost every major name in the sport, running to clock his best performances as the people stood almost the full length of the unguarded track surface. Like the Woodstock music festival, everyone in attendance knew this was history making.

Running on a load of nitro, Dick was the class of the field in the Unlimited category, which consisted of two GM cars (Dick Jesse's GTO and Pete Seaton's Chevelle), one Plymouth (the Golden Commandos driven by Al "The Lawman" Eckstrand), and five Dodges (Landy, Bob Harrop, Bud Faubel, and two cars out of the Mr. Norm Grand Spaulding Dodge stables, one blown and one injected). In round one, Dick got Jesse's goat. He then clocked a huge 9.52 (his best run to that time) to beat Jim O'Conner in the Mr. Norm ex–*Color Me Gone* injected Dodge. He followed that up with a 9.58 in the class final, but Al Eckstrand took the victory on a starting line advantage, running a slower 9.67 but crossing the finish line first.

At 2:30 a.m., when the call went out for the overall heads-up eliminator, Bud Faubel won the first round over the silver Dodge. Dick admitted in a results story that he had simply run out of jet sizes to get any more fuel percentage into the engine and that everyone had really "tipped the can" that night.

The rest of August was not recorded, but the big AHRA race at Lions the weekend before Labor Day was. This event, more than any to that time, helped put stock-bodied drag racing on the map in California. Jim Tice of AHRA and C. J. Hart had decided to break the national event field into two weekends, one for stockers and one for dragsters; the latter was over Labor Day Weekend as was the NHRA Indy Nationals. As a result, under factory direction, a large number of the Ford-backed drivers left the East Coast for California in the middle of the month and dominated the stock weekend in front of 18,000 fans over two days.

It is not known whether Dick came back over Labor Day at the behest of Hart, of Chrysler, or simply because his tour was over, but he became a headline part of the dragster weekend. What showed the writing on the wall was low attendance at this meet, though some of it could be accounted for by rain. Regardless, it was not a cheap return, as Dick, running fuel and trying to run for the record book, blew one TorqueFlite, broke an axle, and tossed out two driveshafts before running 9.87/138.90 to

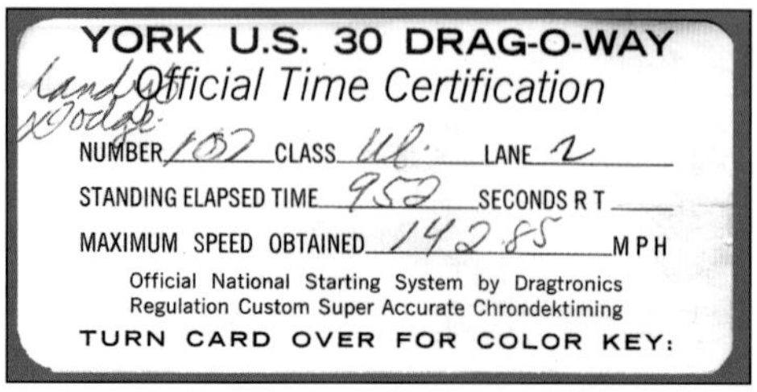

Big numbers at York on August 7, 1965. Dick later admitted that he had pushed as hard as he could to make the car faster that night and had simply run out of additional injector jetting. Bobby Harrop won the overall title in a similar factory-assisted Dodge. (Photo Courtesy Landy Family Archives)

grab the track's stock-bodied record. After some runs at San Fernando, plans were made to go one last tour of 1965, which crowned a memorable season.

The Landy Dodge Coronet after being restored by Mike Guffey. It was perhaps the most significant vehicle of Chrysler's wild foray into Ultra Stock.

West Coast Racing Series

As soon as Lions had its AHRA stocker blowout, West Coast tracks recognized that it was time to get on the moneymaking program. Promoters flew to San Francisco for a caucus hosted by Clark Marshall of Seattle. The operators came up with a plan to run a series of Saturday-night East versus West big-money open-class stocker races during October. These started in Washington State and ended in Southern California. Cash payouts, which totaled between $20,000 and $30,000 for the series, included guaranteed tow money for pre-entries, round money, and win money for each event. Because many of the West Coast guys had been touring the East all summer, and a number of the East Coast professionals would have a chance to make inroads and garner some year-end notoriety, everyone was interested. It was a win-win situation.

So on Saturday, October 2, Dick was again in Puyallup, Washington. As at the Super Stock Nats, there was an Unlimited class, plus other breakdowns based on weight and fuel. The class runoffs paid $300 to the winner and $100 to the runner-up. The two eliminators (handicap and heads-up) paid $600 to the winner and $200 to the runner-up. *Landy's Dodge* was considered the car to beat, but among the others on tour were the two Sox & Martin Belvederes; Butch Leal's two *California Flash* cars; Malcolm Durham's Z11 Chevelle; a number of factory Ford pilots, including Proffitt, Bonner, and Les Ritchey; and some fierce locals at each stop. Running Unlimited that first night, Landy won the heads-up title and left with that, plus enough round money to gross $1,000. In Spokane, Landy won the handicap eliminator plus round wins to pocket another $1,600.

The next stop was Fremont, near San Francisco, with more than 5,000 paid admissions. Dick was in rare form, clocking a personal best of 9.33/145.16 to dominate the event, winning both handicap and heads-up eliminators plus the Unlimited class title over Hayden Proffitt. That was worth $1,500 more.

Western fans had their first taste of major stocker action during the fall of 1965. This is Dick at Phoenix in December. The car has been repainted since the summer tour, with larger lettering, probably due to needed bodywork. (Photo Courtesy ©TEN: The Enthusiast Network. All rights reserved.)

A cast of thousands in the pits at Woodburn, Oregon. This wild tour, which Dick won, established stocker racing popularity on the West Coast. The car is surrounded by fans in the center, with the Monaco wagon to the left. (Photo Courtesy Landy Family Archives)

By this point, the weeklies were paying attention, and the rosin-based wheel stands were taking their toll on many cars. Landy had noted in interviews after the Super Stock Nationals that he often adjusted tire pressure and sometimes swapped tires based on the changing traction conditions, even increasing air pressure to allow for a little less grip. The result in that late-night final of heads-up racing at Fremont was a near-best 9.38/144.46.

Then came Lions. Eight hours of action on Saturday, October 23, left 11,000-plus paid admissions hoarse from screaming. Malcomb Durham, Phil Bonner, Doug Thorley, Al Vandewoude, and Jim Liberman all suffered serious front-end damage with monster wheel stands caused by the edge-to-edge gold-dust rosin on the Long Beach track surface. The Unlimited final was again Proffitt and Landy. Hayden's Comet got a jump, but *Landy's Dodge,* wheels hanging a steady 2 feet off the track under power, had power to spare and clocked a 9.42 for the win; the SOHC ran 9.67 in losing.

In the heads-up eliminator, postponed one night due to the mechanical carnage and the already-extended noise curfew, Cecil Yother beat Landy for the overall crown, but Dick's total winnings for the night again topped a grand, and that $1,100, coupled with the previous races, netted a gross of $5,200 for the tour, huge money in 1965. Second-place Sox took home $2,900 in the two-car team, and Shirley Shahan was third at $1,400.

The car made its final 1965 public appearance at Lions on December 18, testing another set of 180-degree headers, similar to what had been on the 1964 car, with one exception. The front pipe came straight out from under the bumper. Dick proved it was a runner with a 9.50/144 single, but that appears to have been the end of the experiment with the 180 package. He broke an engine on a 9.94 second pass.

The final test of the 180-degree headers, shot at Lions. The car was on nitro, but no action photos could be found. (Photo Courtesy ©TEN: The Enthusiast Network. All rights reserved.)

The Dodge was noted in *Super Stock* magazine to have received more publicity than any other car in the country. After the West Coast tour, Dick won two more big events that winter: Mickey Thompson's 200 MPH Club dragster meet at Fontana in Unlimited Super Stock and the title at the Western United States Super Stock Championship at Beeline. On October 29, *Drag World*'s Terry Cook editorialized in *FX Foothold* that although the SoCal dragster contingent verbally looked down on Funny Cars

1966: What a Droptop!

As most people know, Dick Landy raced a fuel-burning Dart in 1966. However, one B-Body of note showed up in late 1965 at Automotive Research. This was a 1966 A102 Street Hemi Coronet convertible pilot car, later serving notice of Dick's tune-up when *Hot Rod* magazine showed images of it literally airborne during road testing. Although other B-Body models were tuned in 1966 as well, Dick finally returned to the larger cars in the latter part of 1966 to prepare for 1967.

This 1966 Hemi Coronet convertible was a test car for* Hot Rod*; Dick dyno-tuned it in October 1965.

in general, they secretly paid a lot of attention to local boy Landy and his winning efforts. There is no question that the 1965 Chrysler Funny Cars had put stocker racing on the map, and there is no question that Dick Landy's efforts that season played a vital role in it.

"The most amazing thing back East was the proof of our effort to promote the personality," he summarized in the "Diamond Jim" Kelly *Drag Sport Illustrated* interview. "In the morning, when we would get up to leave the motel, there would be maybe 50 people around outside and they didn't want to see the car. They wanted to see me or they wanted to see Leal, or Strickler. Not the car, the personality."

Unlit cigar and all, Landy was now a superstar in drag racing.

Where Are They Now?

The 1965 Landy factory-altered was perhaps the most celebrated of the 1965 Funny Cars; although a number of these cars were destroyed in the following seasons, Dick's first went to fellow California racer and former Automotive Research customer Jim Wetton, who campaigned it primarily on the West Coast the next season as *Studio Dodge*. Dick actually did some early 1966 racing with it before delivery. Ironically, Wetton came to work for Dick for a while in 1967 as the clinic program began.

The car eventually went to Ohio and then in 1977 to Iowa, where racer Toli Polowick used it as a weekend warrior out of his stable of Mopar racers. Polowick deserves a great deal of credit, as he saved many of these cars long before anyone else cared. From Toli, it ended up with noted collector Mike Guffey of Indiana. At the time, in the early 1990s, a Midwesterner had been attempting to pass off an A990 clone as *Landy's Dodge*.

Dick was none too pleased about dealing with that situation legally, so when Guffey contacted him saying that he had the "real" car, Landy stated that he would not verify anything until he saw the car personally. With Dick booked into a special personal appearance at Atco, New Jersey, Mike towed the unlettered Dodge from Indiana to the Atlantic shore. There Dick did some quick checks and declared it to be legitimate, in part due to a broken taillight lens that had never been replaced.

Guffey later sold it as part of a multicar deal to investor Ralph Whitworth, who was building a large collection of cars in Nevada. When Whitworth needed to liquidate, the car ended up with Nick Smith of Florida. Ed Strzelecki performed a full restoration on it back to its May 1965 configuration. It was featured on the cover of *Muscle Car Review* magazine in 2015.

Friend Jim Wetton bought the 1965 car and ran it as Studio Dodge in 1966. Dave Peters's illustration shows it in the shutdown area. (© Print illustration painted by David Carl Peters, Courtesy DragRacing-Artist.com)

The 1965 Landy's Dodge as it looks today. The car was restored to its May 1965 appearance. (Ed Strzelecki Photo)

The home-made structure under Landy's Dodge likely stabilized it but also allowed for Dick's suspension tricks. (Ed Strzelecki Photo)

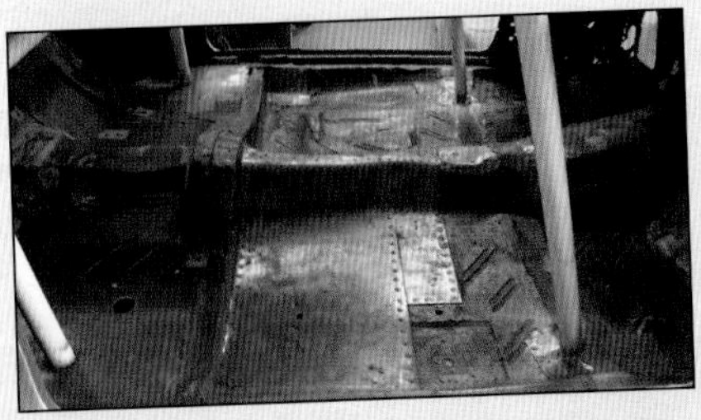

Although all Dodge factory race cars had acid-dipped floors, the chassis and patch fixes were unique to the 1965 Landy's Dodge. They do not show up on any other surviving factory-altered-wheelbase car. (Ed Strzelecki Photo)

1967: Coronets, Clinics and the Advent of Super Stock

Marketing became a big part of how Dodge promoted its model line. Dick is seen here at the 1967 Winternationals, where he debuted the new Hemi Super Stock Coronet. (Photo ©TEN: The Enthusiast Network. All rights reserved.)

After the season with the fuel-burning Dart (see Chapter 3), Chrysler chose to refocus its promotional emphasis away from the category it had actually spearheaded, which could be loosely termed "unlimited experimental." The self-supported teams from Detroit, the Ramchargers and Golden Commandos factory engineers, continued to push the developmental envelope in their Funny Cars and dragsters for the new season. Meanwhile, the racers most actively sponsored by Chrysler's marketing programs, Dick Landy for Dodge and Sox & Martin for Plymouth, were back in production-based cars. There were several important reasons for this.

Dick appears in a Dodge PR advertising poster that he displayed at clinic events. Note that the car shown is not an R/T. (Photo Courtesy Landy Family Archives)

The first and foremost was the exploding muscle car market. The high visibility of Landy's Automotive Research Dodges of 1964 and 1965 may have helped sell some sporty 426-S wedge-powered Coronets during those years. Conversely, the radical 1966 Dart, depicted in the national media, probably did not sell a lot of new Darts. This included even the short run of high-performance 273-ci D-Darts. Nor was it likely that people went out and bought new Hemi-powered Coronets and Chargers after seeing Landy's radical Dodge Dart in action that first year of the Street Hemi. The image association between winning on Sunday and selling on Monday was no longer evident.

However, having seen the way General Motors positioned image vehicles like the 4-4-2, GTO, and Chevelle SS, executive Bob Rodger and other men in Chrysler management decided the company would begin offering similarly styled package cars, created to sell to performance car buffs. Rodger especially understood this, as the legendary Chrysler 300 of 1955 had been his brainchild. The muscle car idea was simple: Put a powerful street engine into a two-door body, with extra add-ons that gave the car additional performance and curb appeal, and sell excitement. So in its second year, the 426 Hemi became the engine option in the new Plymouth GTX, based around the Sport Satellite, and Dodge's top Coronet 500 became the basis for the Dodge Coronet R/T.

The Street Hemi was still in the Charger as well, but the budget specials such as the Coronet Deluxe and 440 trim sedans were now gone. A major reason for the change was the hope to increase per-unit profitability on Hemi-equipped street cars. This decision had unintended consequences as it priced many younger buyers entirely out of the marketplace. The bottom line for 1967 was that Dodge's relationship with Dick Landy was to heavily push the performance B-Body R/T models.

Super Stockers in Action

The second thing that contributed to Chrysler's refocusing of priorities was the advent of Super Stock as a stand-alone eliminator in the NHRA. From the Ford days of the early 1960s through the summer of 1964, Dick had been part of the Stock classes. However, he had fully embraced the exploding match race and unlimited stocker scene immediately after that. Fellow racer Hubert Platt laughingly said that the era was "run whatcha brung and bring all you got!" Dick truly enjoyed this type of racing. The Dart's supercharged experimentation toward the end of 1966 was actually the natural evolution of these cars, but safety and the heavily altered appearance of the cars now created problems from a sales standpoint.

So at the end of 1966, due to the number of new performance cars being formulated and sold, the NHRA decided that the former Top Stock division (which had consisted of S/S and A/S cars in Stock Eliminator) would now be its own eliminator called Super Stock. The B/S and lower cars that had made up Junior Stock now became simply Stock Eliminator, for the so-called little guys. The fact that so many racers were now more adept at reworking stock-equipment cars for better performance played a role in this, as the NHRA already knew about the extent of factory involvement. The answer was to separate the latest, hottest cars into this new category, which was to consist of 10 classes on 5 weight categories based on a weight-to-estimated-horsepower rating, also new.

This estimated, or factored, horsepower rating was a new formula for the stock-bodied classes, as the NHRA had previously used Automobile Manufacturers Association (AMA) numbers released by each company to arrive at horsepower figures. Aware that some of this was deliberately underestimated by Detroit, and based on the more liberal internal engine changes the new SS division allowed, the NHRA created its own arbitrary horsepower figure for each powerplant. The weight of the car (without driver) was then taken from AMA paperwork to classify each vehicle. Engineering-minded racers and corporate race directors quickly figured out which factored engine/vehicle combinations fit best into the new eliminator's five automatic and five stick classes.

Another 1967 promotion was the "Good Guys in White Hats." Dick sometimes wore the apparel even at the track that year. (Photo Courtesy Landy Family Archives)

The team arrives at Crocket Bros. in Fresno, California, for a display and TV promotion. This was early in the season, and the clinic ideas were brand new. (Photo Courtesy Landy Family Archives)

This was not all fine and dandy for Dick Landy, however. Mike Landy notes that Dick hated handicap racing, and this was unfortunately the big deal in Super Stock. The NHRA spent the next three seasons attempting to formulate level playing fields, sometimes with quite draconian measures on record setting and break outs. The breakout rule was used for those going too quickly, resulting in losing. This was the amount of elapsed time by which a racer exceeded the performance estimate, index, or class record.

Therefore, any new record-setting number was critical to everyone in that particular class, as it was the difference in starting line advantage given to the slower car during final eliminations. As a result, during those three seasons and beyond, the major factory players (management and drivers) were also actively involved in manipulating win results during qualifying. For instance, smoking tires from locked-up brakes at the finish line often told this story, as drivers tried to save the index or records going into eliminations.

This was one reason the heads-up class win in Super Stock held so much significance during those early years. Advertisers often used these victories when showing Dick's success. However, as Landy's effort progressed with the stock-appearing cars, his personal focus moved more toward Modified Production. Here, against the gassers and altereds, classification was made on a simple weight-to-displacement basis, so more serious engine and vehicle changes were allowed. As a result, drivers other than Dick often piloted the Dick Landy Performance Clinic vehicles that the team fielded in the Super Stock and Stock Eliminator ranks during this time.

Clinical Effort

A parallel but hugely significant change occurred as the Landy operation "moved down" in performance from supercharged fuel into Super Stock. After

The latest models are posed inside the original 1920s showroom at D. E. Stetler & Sons in York, Pennsylvania. (Photo Courtesy Landy Family Archives)

discussions among Bob Cahill, Dick Maxwell, and other members of race management at Chrysler, it was decided that the two most visible drag racing competitors, Landy and Plymouth's Ronnie Sox and Buddy Martin team, would also visit auto shows and select dealerships to help market the new high-performance models. The benefits were obvious: The race team could arrive earlier in a regional location, perhaps one close to a track hosting a racing event, and showcase performance. They displayed the race cars and made personal appearances, coupled to demonstrations and discussions about Chrysler cars and performance products. The press releases announced, "These classes won't be a drag!"

The latest engine in Chrysler's RB line up, at 440 ci, had debuted in full-size cars in 1966; in code A134 4-barrel performance trim, it was now the standard engine in the R/T and GTX. The Hemi was the only other engine option in those models. Whichever engine was chosen was backed by either the 3-speed A727 TorqueFlite or the A833 New Process 4-speed, which in turn pushed power to the limited-slip SureGrip-equipped differential. These heavy-duty driveline pieces were standard on the models. Also standard were select exterior trim items, upscale interiors with bucket seats, and performance-type tires, all which made the cars fairly expensive.

Paperwork in the Landy family archives reveals that the clinic program in all likelihood greatly exceeded what the factory had hoped for. However, this came at a cost for the teams. Unlike in previous years, when tours meant having time to work on the cars between events, Dick was now racking up frequent-flyer miles while his brother Mike, young son Richard (during summer), and crew members such as Willie Honsberger took on the vagabond existence of near-constant travel. This included overnight drives to the next location, cleaning cars, pre-event preparation, and setting up the clinic displays. If not on the tour, Dick handled whatever fresh business needs arose at the California base and flew to the event on a Chrysler expense account. He did the clinics, and then it was off to the dragstrip for either demonstrations or actual racing.

"For 10 years, I spent three months every summer on a truck with the race cars," recalls Richard. "I did plenty of changing oil. All the motors had to be broken in. If you wanted to do that, back home we went out in the desert and drove the car in the middle of the night, open headers, and loading it back before the cops showed up. We sometimes built motors on the road. We did some of those break-ins back East on four-lanes, but it was harder to do that.

"What I remember was we had something going on basically every weekend. I would set up the projectors, staple up the posters, bring in the parts racks on the A-frame displays, the PA systems, whatever they needed. Yeah, like slave labor."

At the end of the weekend or planned time, the race cars were cleaned up, everything was packed up, and it was down the highway for the next event after taking Dick to the airport. This went on for the entire season, with Richard touring in the summer. Writer Jerry Gross had moved to Detroit and gone to work on Dodge's payroll, and he and Mike Dobtin now worked as PR people for the Landy operation.

The clinic program got underway at Daytona Beach, and in the family slide reels are a handful of shots taken right on pit road at the 1967 Daytona 500. Whether Dick took these pictures or they came from the camera of Jerry Gross is not known, but they provide ample evidence that the focus of the clinic effort was far more than simply drag racing.

"We always tried to tie [the clinics] into a real race in the area," Dick told me for a story on the program years later. "We wanted to do the clinics with those dealerships that were most aggressive in selling the performance car line; it wouldn't make much sense to go through the effort if the dealer wasn't selling those cars.

The first clinic decal was rudimentary, with block lettering. The 1968 Scat Pack designs were still a model year away.

Richard Landy grew up fast on summer tours with the team. (Photo Courtesy Landy Family Archives)

"It was work for the dealership too; they would have to do the prepublicity work with our PR man, and they would have to get ready for the clinic to happen. We would forward audiotapes for radio use, and our man would go in ahead of time to get things ready. Dodge News Bureau did a lot of that stuff, and we would work with their regional office. It was expensive for the company to support the program, and the company wanted it to go to those dealerships who could justify that expense through their sales.

Richard Landy on his pit bike. He remembers the summer tour of 1967 as when he learned what work was really all about. (Photo Courtesy Landy Family Archives)

Richard, age 12, and Willie Honsberger during a stop in Ohio. Note the clinic posters; the car was a loaner from Frederick Dodge. (Photo Courtesy Landy Family Archives)

These five heavy 1967 clinic displays showed aftermarket parts for the latest Dodge performance cars. They were assembled and disassembled at each location. (Photo Courtesy Landy Family Archives)

"If the race was on a Saturday and Sunday, we might do it on Friday night. We would always try to do it beforehand and have a radio disc jockey come out with the popular music to help promote the event. Sometimes, not often, we would do them on Mondays after the race, but the best night was Thursday. We did them in the evenings, because that was the time when the people we were trying to reach were not working. The factory concluded that the customer [was] an average of 26 years old. They did a lot of surveys and they had figured it out pretty close."

Most buyers also sought to personalize their new cars, and this was one area where the clinic idea proved to be even more beneficial to all involved. Both Dick and Buddy Martin knew a lot of people in the performance aftermarket, and Gross's industry connections were as deep if not deeper. As a result, both teams inked their own sponsorships for parts and accessories.

With Landy, these parts were displayed on five large boards for 1967, along with factory performance pieces. The boards were set up with the cars being displayed, and during the clinic program these possible aftermarket changes, all which could be added to a new or currently owned car, were promoted as well. Manufacturers sent samples, giveaways, and door prizes; paid to have their decals displayed on the cars; and promised associated mentions in advertising campaign exposure. Everybody benefited.

In conclusion, the clinic program launched with great success in 1967; it was one of the best promotions of any company during the supercar era, and other Detroit firms followed the formula in succeeding years. For Dodge, Dick Landy was always the primary torch-bearer in the effort, and it can be honestly stated that his involvement in this particular matter sold a lot of performance Dodges.

Dick and parts magnate George Hurst are seen with what was probably a loaned 1967 Coronet R/T during Speedweeks in Daytona. Dick used Hurst products in many of his cars and was featured in Hurst advertising on occasion. (Photo Courtesy Landy Family Archives)

1967 Clinic Cars

For 1967, the team was in hardtop Coronets. The first car is actually one of the most unusual in Landy's career, at least as far as Hemi collectors are concerned. In the breakdown of production, nearly all the 1967 Hemi Dodge Coronets were R/T models, and officially this was the only body the engine could be purchased with, aside from the later run of WO-code race cars. Although there were no four-door versions as in 1966, a handful of non-R/T examples were built. Just one was a 440-trim hardtop body with a Hemi/4-speed driveline; that car went to Dick in late 1966 and was the actual prototype of the later SS/B program according to *Hot Rod* magazine.

Still, Hemi body shells were heavier than standard bodies that year, due to torque boxes and other strengthening components. Engineer Tom Hoover, who played with a 1966 Hemi Coronet on Detroit's Woodward Avenue, noted in my book *Hemi: A History of Chrysler's Iconic V-8 in Competition* that the 1966 and 1967 Chrysler Hemi cars posed a real challenge to meet the published AMA weight. Nonetheless, perhaps in an effort to get the first Super Stocker down to that number, Dick's new 1967 Hemi stocker was not an R/T. Painted silver at first, this 4-speed car was actually lettered with "R/T" on the rear quarter panels but lacked the metal R/T trim pieces and grille; these were added later.

Although Dick and Mike shook down the cars at Pomona with little success; once they had been painted identically, their first real race occurred at Carlsbad Raceway near San Diego. Dick raced Rick "Boss Joe" Lee, a radio personality, turning 11.30s in the Hemi; Lee was given a handicap start to take the 440 car to the 12.40s.

The second car was a standard production Coronet R/T powered by a 440/automatic driveline. It served as the clinic program demonstrator car and could be raced in the SS/EA or B/SA category as well.

Therefore the clinics had a car representing both R/T models and options. Usually, the race cars were moved into the showroom along with the parts displays and projection equipment for the slide or film show. Often one of the dealership's own new Coronets or Chargers was put on the team's trailer outside for display.

That first year, Mike was often the pilot of the 440 car if there was an event or the need for another driver. The man who had bought Dick's famed 1965 Coronet, Jim Wetton, toured with the team early that year as well, driving the truck and the extra car as needed. Of course, Dick piloted the non-R/T Hemi 4-speed machine at the major events in 1967.

"We had a spare car, actually a car that was closer to stock than the cars we raced, and we would bring that so that the guys like a disc jockey could drive it," Dick recalled later, regarding the 440 package. "We would set up a handicap race at a track nearby, and the people loved it. We might run at one o'clock and another one later in the afternoon and race one of our real cars against the extra one we had. The big dealers would actually use that car as a sales tool and bring out their salesmen and give them a chance to get up to speed on the latest equipment."

Cleaning the cars was very important. This was one way to make sure they stayed that way during highway travel. (Photo Courtesy Landy Family Archives)

The two cars at Pomona for the Winternationals. The Hemi car, in silver, is on the ground, and the new 440-powered R/T is on the trailer. (Photo Courtesy Landy Family Archives)

WO Package Cars

In February, Chrysler built a run of special cars just for Super Stock racing, as it had done between 1962 and 1965. However, with rule changes and the reality that many Chrysler racers were still in the superbly designed 1965 models now classed in SS/A (stick) and SS/AA (auto), these new models were not Race Hemi cars. Rather, the 55 WO-code Dodges (and 55 RO-code Plymouths) made use of a mildly modified Street Hemi engine with a unique in-line intake manifold. Factory reengineered, each intake had been hand-milled for greater intake plenum efficiency by Plymouth-sponsored racer "Akron Arlen" Vanke under contract to Chrysler. The Vanke intake and a set of slightly changed Street Hemi Carter AFB carbs, plus transistorized ignition, were the only major engine changes. The company knew the racers would install the cam and headers of their choice, so they were left stock as delivered. A heavy-duty 4-speed or automatic driveline backed this all up.

The new WO package components were on the car at the Hot Rod *magazine drags. Dick made the most of them before the day was over. (Photo Courtesy Landy Family Archives)*

At Riverside for the 1967 Hot Rod *magazine meet, after the two cars had been identically painted, sometime before the clinic tours started that spring. (Photo Courtesy Landy Family Archives)*

***Hot Rod* publisher Ray Brock personally wrote Landy this note, which was found in Dick's office files. Brock noted all the stock accessories on the 440 car he would be driving at Riverside and chided him accordingly. "Professor Landy" is depicted in a graduation cap in some early 1967 Dodge PR images.**

A helmeted "Professor Landy" appears to be giving pointers before the racing gets underway. The student is Ray Brock. (Photo ©TEN: The Enthusiast Network. All rights reserved.)

The hardtop body was all steel, void of frills and undercoating, and featured a low-profile hood scoop and steel wheels. All of them were painted code WW1 White with black interiors and heater/radio delete. For weight transfer, the battery was moved into the trunk as with previous package cars. Similar to the Plymouth GTX and Dodge Coronet R/T, hardtop bodies were selected, so these special cars were available only in that configuration.

Furthermore, the shipping weight on the new race cars was left at the standard AMA amount as stated for the street models. Letters between the NHRA and Chrysler Product Planning's Dick Maxwell shed light on this, as Chrysler wanted to be sure it did not end up with these cars in SS/A, the same Super Stock class as the 1965 models. Heavier and even without Race Hemi parts or compression, they ended up in SS/B, just one class lower. Most notably, the as-manufactured body still made use of the heavy Hemi-specific substructure, even without the undercoating and so on.

Mike Landy laughs now, "You know, we knew right away that we were the professionals here; those tech guys were mailmen who were working for a weekend. So we made an effort to do whatever we could to make the cars work better. Part of the process was to know what they looked for and what they didn't."

The first and biggest title for Landy that year came on April 9 at the *Hot Rod* magazine meet at Riverside, right after Mike had installed the WO-type Hemi scoop on the car. Dick dominated Super Stock, clocking an 11.61 over Bill Ireland's Fairlane for class honors, then taking home the eliminator on Sunday by beating Len Kennedy's Buick GS.

As mentioned, the cars were weighed without the drivers, so anything that could get them closer to the minimum 3,686-pound legal weight was done. Even today, Mike only smiles when asked about some of those changes, but later that season, Dick decided to take all the new WO parts and swap them and the Hemi/4-speed driveline into the 440-powered R/T. In return, that car's 440 engine and automatic driveline were moved into the heavier 1967 440-trim Hemi body. This change took effort but ended up saving close to 75 pounds, which was important because Dick's big footballer frame weighed more than 200 pounds. At least the overall car weight was now a little closer to what distaff Dodge pilot and 1966 NHRA Winternationals champ Shirley Shahan had in her new *Drag-On Lady* Coronet. Even the VIN tags could conveniently be switched as needed because these were not street cars.

Mike was in the A134 440-ci R/T during the Hot Rod magazine race and drove during clinic work. He also helped maintain both cars. (Photo Courtesy Landy Family Archives)

Heavy weights in a Lightweight World

Due to the legality issues in Super Stock, car prep was not overly extensive that year, beyond the tricks mentioned above. This work included blueprinting the engines, making the allowed parts swaps such as the camshaft, and Dick's changes to the suspensions, including looser shocks and stiffer rear springs. Chrysler offered a slick-shift 4-speed transmission for quicker shifting, which Dick used. Even some minor leeway was made to the fenders to move the rear wheelbase slightly, still notable on the surviving car.

The aforementioned sponsors helped, of course. Cragar contributed its noted S/S-type chrome wheels, Goodyear supplied tires, plugs came from Champion, and Valvoline contributed cases of oil. Other major product sponsors that year were Hurst and Doug's Headers. As mentioned earlier, these companies not only paid for the right to be part of the racing effort but also agreed to place the team's cars in print advertising, which increased exposure even more. For their part, the teams agree to promote only a handful of sponsors.

Early on, the 1967 clinic program included a promotion to allow a local radio personality drive against Landy or Sox on the dragstrip. This ended after an inexperienced disc jockey ran a Plymouth dealer demo off the end of a track. Dick noted in one interview that the company carried $5 million in liability insurance on the program.

Ray Brock, Linda Vaughn, and Dick Landy in the Riverside winner's circle, where Dick picked up another cool trophy from this event. (Photo ©TEN: The Enthusiast Network. All rights reserved.)

Premium parking near the starting line at the NHRA U.S. Nationals did not help the team win there in 1967. Although Dick trailered Bill Jenkins in a match race during early August, Jenkins won this event. (Photo Courtesy Landy Family Archives)

A car was rumored in a recent Chrysler-oriented magazine story to be a lost R/T that Dick was given as a street car, but the family deemed this tale to be false. In 1967, Dick and Gean used a C-Body Monaco for personal driving, and the team's 1965 station wagon was still being used as well.

The biggest highway change for 1967 was the new extended-cab D700 truck and tagalong trailer, as the team now had two cars on tour. And tour they did. After an uneventful trip to the final NHRA Springnationals in Tennessee, Dick and Mike went north to the 1967 Super Stock Nationals, held at Cecil County Dragway that year. Dick won SS/B-class honors on Saturday and took three round wins on Sunday in handicapped racing before meeting up with the Camaro of eventual winner Dick Arons in the semifinals. Arons was guaranteed a soft index in SS/EA when Mike's Coronet broke a cam in the previous day's class final. Even Dick's best-to-date 11.11 was not enough to overcome Arons's handicap (nor was Sox's 11.01 in the final).

Landy did get some revenge against the Bow Tie guys when he beat Bill Jenkins in a match race at Englishtown in early August. The truth was, the big B-Body models were at a disadvantage in weight and the win at the *Hot Rod* magazine meet was the season highlight for Dodge in general. Although he did not win at the NHRA Nationals, a new 1968 Charger from that event went West for him.

NHRA's first Super Stock World Championship, which had a huge $10,000 season-ending purse, was won in Tulsa, Oklahoma, by a 1965 Plymouth driven by Ed Miller. The year finished with some local clinic appearances, but by then Dick Landy was already looking ahead. The year 1968 brought new race cars, bigger racing events, and the advent of Dodge's legendary Scat Pack. Exciting new horizons lie ahead.

The "Spare" Car

Although Dick mentioned a spare car, the photographic record shows just the two cars for that year. Whether the Landy team received a third R/T or an actual complete WO car is not known. At Dick's direction, Mike swapped the WO Hemi parts that had already been installed on the early Hemi body onto the real R/T. Dick might have resold what was no longer needed; if that included assembling a complete 1967 car from parts on hand, that record has been lost.

Action (and big bucks) was the big deal in Super Stock in 1967. This is the restored car.

Where Are They Now?

The A102-powered, Street Hemi Coronet is probably considered a true gem in its restored form, and it would be just as significant as a race car. However, it is believed to have been sold with the 440 driveline and may well have not survived the ravages of time. There was no record of its resale in the Landy paperwork, and it is almost certain that the VIN number was interchanged with another to get the car past Mike's "mailmen" at tech. After all, there would have been no plan to ever return it to a street car.

Meanwhile, the A134 440 Magnum Coronet R/T with the Hemi driveline installed was later sold to White Bear Dodge in Minnesota and raced for some time after 1967. Restorer Erik Lindberg located it and uncovered why the Hemi body had disappeared. This car was subsequently brought back to the condition that Dick likely would have run it in during late 1967, and Erik worked closely with Richard Landy in its spectacular renewal. Today it resides in the collection of Greg and Kathy Mosley.

As for the rumor that there was a third car in the Landy paint scheme during 1967, it could not be verified, and experts are torn about its existence. If this car had existed, it would have been a clinic demonstrator only, with very little modification. Alas, I found no photos showing three 1967 Landy Coronets together, and no record of a third car, and I contend that only two raced as a *Landy's Dodge* in 1967.

Members of the Landy family (Gean, Richard Jr., daughter-in-law Peggy, and Robert's daughter Jasmin) with the car restored by Erik Lindberg. It is now in the collection of Greg and Kathy Mosley.

The restored 426 Hemi as seen in the 1967 Coronet R/T today. These were not much different from standard A102 Street Hemi models.

The Coronet in its debut at Mopars in the Park. From behind, it is easy to see how large it was. This was the only season Dick drove the Coronet model in regular competition.

The Hurst shifter with its reverse lock-out design was usually part of Dick's personal race car fleet after 1966. The heavy 1967 Super Stockers needed all the help they could get.

When Dick Landy began making plans for 1968, it is unlikely that he realized just how complicated things would become that year. He certainly understood that he would have a lot of clinic travel. In late-1968 correspondence between Dick and Bob "Crusher" McCurry, a former Michigan State football captain who headed up Dodge's sales division, Dick noted that he hoped to give away a free Charger R/T from the clinic incentives in front of the masses at the 1968 NHRA Nationals over Labor Day Weekend. McCurry adamantly replied that the car could not be presented before all 40 clinics were finished, so this did not happen until the 1969 Winternationals. In 1967, Dick had done 70 individual clinics; that number almost doubled for 1968.

Beyond all that, 1968 was a big year for Dodge Division, which introduced the bumblebee–themed Scat Pack for its performance cars. This promotion was meant to orient interested buyers toward a select group of models whose purpose was power: the Charger R/T, the Coronet R/T, the Dart GTS, and later the Coronet Super Bee, which was a midyear introduction. The Dart played a pivotal role in race-day decision making at midseason as well (see Chapter 3). For the B-Bodies, however, the start of the new season was a big deal.

The Chargers

Dick had his first 1968 Charger delivered in a unique way. The redesigned model had taken the press by storm, and the public responded by purchasing more than 90,000 of them during 1968. Streamlined by the stylists with swelling fenders, a deep-set grille, paired panel indents on hood and doors, and a flying buttress rear window, the Charger now had a truly unique design, unlike the prior fastback Coronet. It looked swoopy, and this powerfully rendered design fit Dick Landy and the Dodge Performance Clinic perfectly.

Where things have become confusing from a research perspective is looking back at the period. There are no PR images showing two race Chargers together; it is possible

With fresh cars, Mike and Dick were ready for the new year in October 1967. This photo from Gean Landy's archive beautifully displays the team's new paint schemes, done by Nelson Carter. (Photo Courtesy Landy Family Archives)

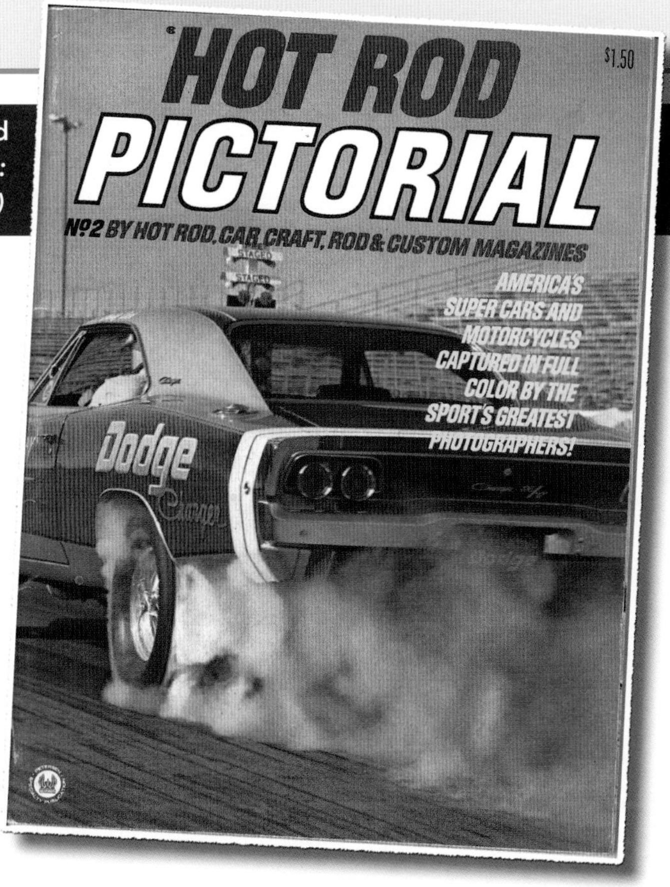

The Charger, which ended up on the cover of the 1968 Hot Rod Pictorial, *was a coup for the team and for Dodge. (Photo ©TEN: The Enthusiast Network. All rights reserved.)*

that Dick had one single example that ran first in SS/B and later ran in the NHRA A/MP with minor changes, in AHRA's new heads-up SS/Eliminator with more changes, and then rotated as needed between the two combinations on one chassis. Once the new Hemi Darts arrived, the Hemi Charger took a backseat to the quicker, smaller models, regardless of the Charger's curbside appeal. Nonetheless, based on research and the recollections by those involved, there remains a possibility of two Chargers in 1968.

Charger 1

The factory brought a 440-powered 1968 Charger R/T to the 1967 Indy Nationals, which took place as the new models began production that August. This may have been a pilot car (hand-built to test assembly line effectiveness and parts fit), but it was built very early in the 1968 production cycle. It was turned over to two young men from the Rods, Inc. car club of Indio, California, Don Solt and Gordon Jensen. They were flown to Indy, where they met Dick, watched the races, and then drove the car 2,500 miles back to California as a tester for *Car Craft* magazine. Interestingly, the car was a radio-delete example. According to magazine reports filed by Jerry Gross, once Dick had it, the car was first tested with a Hemi from one of the 1967 cars and then quickly painted in Dick's new and now-legendary scheme. Set up in SS/B trim, this car and the 1967 Coronet were loaded up and taken to Nebraska for a Dodge clinic appearance in late September and a debut at a Cornhusker State track.

A full story on this Charger and the accompanying 1968 440-ci "clinic" Coronet R/T for Mike to drive was featured in *Car Craft*'s January 1968 issue, in a story called "Landy's Rebellion." Thanks to staffer Terry Cook, who covered the car's buildup to that point, the results of that first September appearance were 11.50, 11.46, and a solid 11.22 after a fuel-line kink was found. The NHRA SS/B record was 11.16, so this was not bad for a simple swapped engine and transmission. It was noted that soon after that the car had run down into the 10.90s in testing at 3,675 pounds. A second benefit was added weight in the rear due to the flying buttress body structure.

The next major appearance of this Charger was at the Los Angeles Auto Show, where Dick displayed the car with the new Charger III concept, cutaway engines, and Joan Parker, the spokesgirl for McCurry's new "Dodge Fever" ad campaign. At this point, Doug's Headers was still lettered on

From the grandstands, somebody in the Landy entourage took this image of Dick doing his big burnout with the Charger.

The stylish Landy boys and the new cars. Mike would soon be in army green. (Photo ©TEN: The Enthusiast Network. All rights reserved.)

the car, but that changed to Hooker when the 1968 race season started.

However, the plan to run in legal SS/B trim at the NHRA Winternationals was curtailed when the new 440-ci Darts being offered by Norm Krause's Grand-Spaulding operation were legalized by the NHRA for that event. Because those cars fit into SS/EA, where the new Ford Cobra Jet Mustang was classified, Dick raced that A-Body design in Super Stock instead.

Charger 2?

If a second Charger was built in late 1967 or early 1968, it was the more radical example that ran in NHRA's Modified Production category. Both the NHRA and AHRA had MP classes, but with different rules. The NHRA rules mandated an American-manufactured engine (any make in any passenger car body), carbs, gasoline, and production-number OEM heads. The body needed to retain the stock front suspension, could not

The Charger makes a pass in Nebraska, where Dick came for a scheduled appearance and clinic. The new car impressed everyone. Few had seen a 1968 Charger, and none had seen a 1968 Charger race car. (Photo Courtesy Landy Family Archives)

The Charger, a cutaway Hemi engine, and the clinic boards are shown in the spacious Dodge display at the Los Angeles Auto Show. (Photo Courtesy Landy Family Archives)

This is the only image I found of the two-panel dealership poster, which would be a rare collector's item today. This picture was taken at the Holiday Inn in Bristol, Tennessee. (Photo Courtesy Landy Family Archives)

use fiberglass or lightened body parts, and had to have a 98-inch-minimum wheelbase.

In the AHRA, rules for modified cars were much more open, but Dick's focus and notoriety there were instead on a brand-new heads-up class for 1968 called Super Stock Experimental, or SS/E. A short piece in the January 1968 issue of *Hot Rod* noted how Dick had lengthened the stock wheelwell by 3 inches just before paint went on the car to fit an 11.0 x 16 slick underneath it. In AHRA legal trim, this Charger clocked an incredible 10.49/132 mph at Lions on January 28.

AHRA versus NHRA SS/E

It needs to be noted that AHRA SS/E and NHRA SS/E and SS/EA classes were entirely different, but they have created large controversies among fans who mistake the lettering of one for that of another in old photos. The AHRA SS/E formula was simple: Get a 1966 or later body, meet a minimum weight at 430 cubes max, bring gas and carbs, and have at it racing heads-up. It was the formative version of Pro Stock in that regard.

Conversely, NHRA SS/E and SS/EA classes in 1968 were for cars that met all NHRA-legal Super Stock requirements and weighed 8.70 to 9.49 pounds-per-factored horsepower; they ran heads-up only in class. The 428-ci Cobra Jet was left by the NHRA at the same 335 hp that the factory rated it (the same rating that Chrysler gave the new 383-ci Super Bee). Although the weight factor for NHRA E-class cars occasionally moved slightly in following years, these were never outrageous cars.

Editor Terry Cook also wrote a big story on Modified Production in the May 1968 issue of *Car Craft*. He said that the Charger that Landy ran at Pomona was the same car he had reported on in the January issue. Based on what was required by the NHRA, that is possible. The car received a hood scoop that was probably formed from sheet stock; this was narrow and tall, leading one to assume that the car was using the in-line A102 intake. Bottom line: It worked well enough that Dick won the A/MP class title at Pomona with a 10.89-at-130-mph, an extra feather in his cap with Super Stock–class wins, which Mike won as well. Even ABC Sport's announcer Keith Jackson took a ride in the Charger for television fans before eliminations began.

However, when AHRA's Winter Nationals occurred at Lions the following weekend, the Charger that Dick drove was more radical. It used the 1965-style A990 Race Hemi scoop and also ran that very quick 10.49 in AHRA's first SS/E final, beating Ronnie Sox's Road Runner to give Landy's Charger its second big win in as many weeks. The car earned Dick one of his most famous publicity stories, with a wheels-up run in the gold dust on the cover of *Super Stock* magazine's April issue.

The full story, likely written by Gross under the pen name

Replace the nose with fiberglass and the chassis with a 1965 A990 Hemi, and the front wheels come off the ground. Result: the first-ever heads-up SS/E champion at AHRA Winter Nationals at Lions. (Photo Courtesy Landy Family Archives)

Jerry Cahill, states that the car was specifically built to run AHRA S/SE, whose 8 pounds per cubic inch meant 3,408 on a 426-ci engine. Dick put a worked 1965 A990 Hemi in the car, with aluminum heads and magnesium intake. This car had fiberglass fenders, hood, and deck lid, none of which would have been legal in the NHRA, but author "Cahill" said that this was a good combination for NHRA MP as well. The story even had a couple of photos of the Charger from NHRA's event.

Dick could have pulled the 200 pounds off this car with fiberglass and the lighter engine, but removing almost 300 pounds, especially with the full interior it featured, may have been more of a challenge. The story noted that the car had a stainless-steel K-frame, 6-cylinder torsion bars, and a small radiator as well, but it is likely that this body was acid-dipped during the buildup if indeed it was being focused toward the AHRA race division. This of course was never reported, and Jerry Cahill (aka Gross) had been at the game long enough to know how to massage the text. The bottom line was that some people who have chased the cars believe there were two 1968 Chargers, while others think there was only one.

The Landy handout card for the year shows the sheet-metal scoop in NHRA-legal trim as Dick runs toward victory. Note the lack of front brakes. (Photo Courtesy Landy Family Archives)

Dick took home the Winternationals crown with the Charger running A/MP in 1968. He also won SS/EA class in the 440-ci Dart. (Photo Courtesy Landy Family Archives)

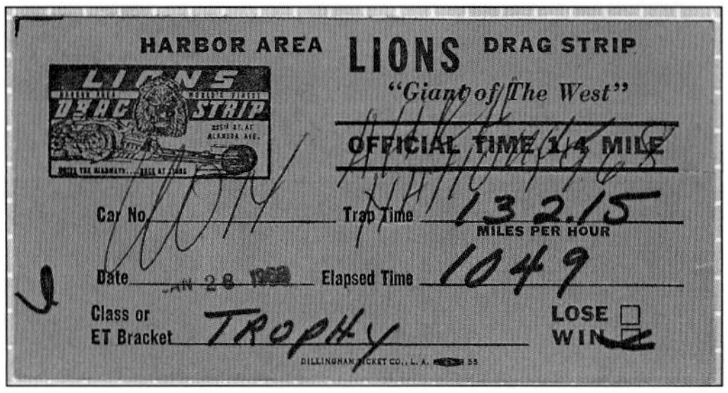

Dick Landy won the first real heads-up Super Stock Experimental race in the Charger, beating Ronnie Sox's Road Runner with a fast 10.49 at Lions. (Photo Courtesy Landy Family Archives)

The Coronets: Big Boys of Scat City

The Dodge Coronet remained a big part of the clinic program. Butch Leal drove the team's 1967 Hemi Coronet at the 1968 Winternationals in SS/DA trim, going to the semifinal round on Sunday before meeting eventual winner Al Joniac in his Cobra Jet Mustang. Dick drove this same 1967 car for the final time at the *Hot Rod* magazine meet, taking over from Mary Ann Foss (née Jackson) when the new Hemi Dart was disqualified on Sunday morning.

Restyled for 1968, the newest R/T still featured a flush grille, plus a mild hood blister with chrome trim and a wraparound rear body stripe. As the car best suited for clinic demonstration work, the 1968 Landy Coronet probably toured more than the Charger and Dart, yet it appears to have been raced less. The 440-ci example the team raced in 1968 was actually acquired in the fall of 1967, probably in late September. Photos from Orange County showing both cars were taken soon after the two were painted, and this same group of images was used for most of the 1968 press photos early in the year. There was no Landy Hemi Coronet for 1968.

The R/T was a premium model for the Dodge brand. It could be had in hardtop or convertible form, and it featured nicer interior and more brightwork compared to the base versions of the car. As a result, the R/T was actually priced out of the range of many young buyers. That changed when Plymouth tackled a similar sales problem for GTX. It used off-the-shelf parts to build a hotter 383-ci engine, put it into the base version of the two-door Belvedere, and made a deal with Warner Brothers to market it as the Road Runner, using the cartoon character. Plymouth

Landy fan and artist David Carl Peters captured Dick's heads-up victory at the 1968 AHRA Winter Nationals. (©Print illustration painted by David Carl Peters; Courtesy DragRacingArtist.com)

Another look at the Charger at the auto show in Super Stock trim, late 1967. (Photo Courtesy Landy Family Archives)

Building a Charger the Landy Way

Considering how little track time it saw as a Super Stock entry, possibly changing to a Modified Production before the 1968 winter events, the 1968 Landy Charger was very well documented in several magazine features. Thomas Voehringer at TEN: The Enthusiast Network located some amazing never-before-published images detailing the Charger from an October 1967 photo shoot. This is how a car was prepped back in the day, a far cry from what we see in the class today.

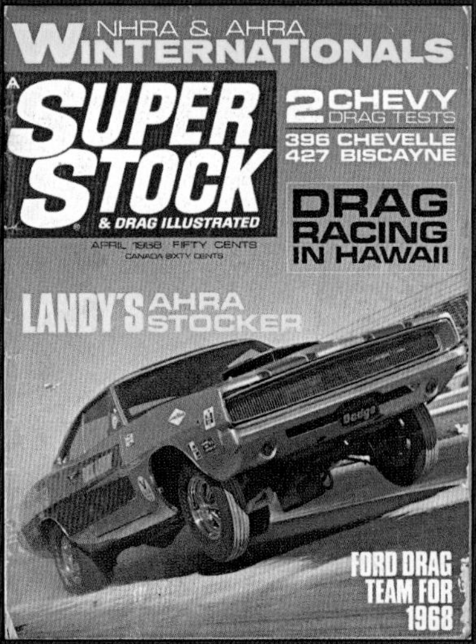

Beautiful artwork of the Charger on the cover of Super Stock & Drag Illustrated.

Dick Landy in the Charger. Note the shifter positioning and glove.

The tach was driven off the distributor, and the oil filter was remounted for easy access.

The homebuilt 1968 deep-sump pan with baffle doors and swinging pickup.

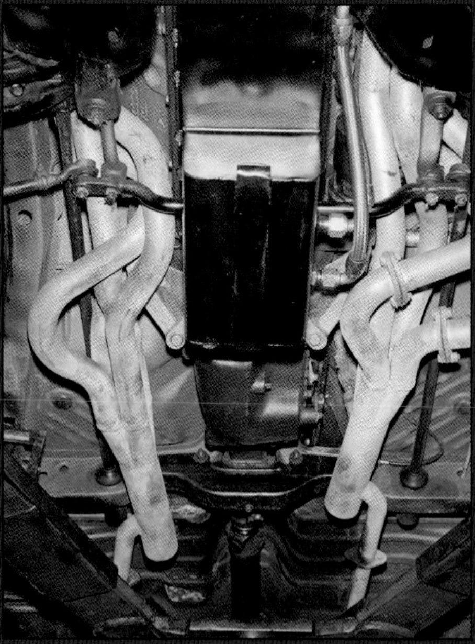

Note the sump size and header positioning.

The rapid changeover was a little rough; note the K-frame mods.

A high-capacity electric fuel pump was bolted to the frame near the gas tank.

Note the height extension on the pinion snubber to limit axle movement under power.

Adjustable mounting points for the rear springs helped the crew set up for track conditions.

Super Stock required mufflers; Dick complied. Note the fuel pumps.

The office was Spartan: Hurst T-handle, face-adjusted tach, radio delete, and minimal safety equipment.

Where Are They Now?

A newspaper "For Sale" advertisement adds a little more mystery. Three Landy Super Stocks were being offered for sale through Bob Lambeck, who came on as a driver in 1968 after Mike Landy was drafted. These cars included the 1967 R/T with a Hemi, now equipped with an automatic, as Leal had run it at Pomona (the car that went to Minnesota); one of the 1968 Hemi Darts (the automatic example that Lambeck had driven during 1968); and the 1968 Hemi Charger 4-speed, just as it had been raced at the Winternationals.

Unfortunately, this ad is undated, but it presumably came from the second half of the year. If there were two Chargers, this could show where one of them went, but things are not always what they seem. It is strongly believed that the more radical AHRA-legal entry was reconfigured to become the new 1969 *Flyin' Wedge* entry the following season.

This ad ran sometime in 1968, but it is not verified whether the cars sold. Lambeck ran the SS/BA Dart in 1969. The Charger is believed to have become Flyin' Wedge with new sheet metal. (Photo Courtesy Jeff Husk)

thought it might make 2,500 of them, and Dodge decided to pass on a similar market entry. By late 1967, with Plymouth on its way toward selling more than 50,000 Road Runners in 1968, Dodge needed to get into the action and fast. The result was a midyear release called Super Bee.

Interestingly, it does not appear that the Landy team ever built a 383-ci Bee for the demo program. (The only engine option for the model in 1968 was the Street Hemi.) However, it stands to reason that if the team's Coronet was on display, the dealer in question would likely have had a 383 Super Bee in stock, and Dick could posit that the changes made to the RB-engine series 440 worked just as easily on the lower-deck B-series engine.

In terms of racing history, the new Coronet R/T was driven first by Mike and then at a number of events by new driver Bob Lambeck, but again the bigger car soon took a backseat to the Darts in terms of visibility. On leave from the army, Mike won the SS/FA class at Pomona in this car and fell to Dave Wren in round one. Bob then won class at the *Hot Rod* magazine drags with it before the team began racing a second Hemi Dart in SS/BA trim. This clinic 1968 Coronet also raced at the 1968 Super Stock Nationals, where Dick won the SS handicap eliminator both nights, thereby making this driver one of Landy's most successful 1968 Super Stock entries in open competition when coupled with the aforementioned class wins.

The 1968 Coronet R/T at the 1968 Super Stock Nationals. Dick drove this car to wins in the handicap eliminator on both Friday and Saturday nights. (Photo Courtesy Landy Family Archives)

The transporter had a lot of miles. Regardless of what was on the truck, the Coronet R/T was almost always on the tagalong in 1968. Here are Mike and Dick Landy soon after the new cars were finished. The truck is a 1967 D700. (Photo ©TEN: The Enthusiast Network. All rights reserved.)

The 1968 Landy clinic decal followed the new theme Dodge had introduced as its latest marketing ploy. The cars now had a wraparound rear stripe. This little stinger was transformed in a cartoon and used in various promotional campaigns.

Where Are They Now?

The 1968 440-ci Coronet R/T has been researched by many enthusiasts. It's believed that after it was sold, it was converted to a wedge-powered Stock Eliminator entry lettered *Alley Oop*. Later pictures show a car like this with a Six Pack hood scoop and filled-in side marker openings running in SS/HA. Its whereabouts today are unknown. Crew member Greg Renkenberger gave Landy researcher Jeff Lamars some additional data, as he had worked on the car back in the day. Jeff put this information on his "Dandy Dick Landy" Facebook page, which explains what was different on this car when it was new.

Renkenberger told Lamars, "Jeff, about the '68 R/T wedge car; it's starting to come back after all the years... [As] I remember, the first thing we did was exchange the factory rear springs for the factory race replacements, two electric fuel pumps were added on the right side of the fuel tank. We might have replaced the fuel pickup in the tank and ran a larger fuel line to the front of the car; the old fuel line was a restriction. Like I said before, we replaced the brakes with the smaller Dart brakes.

"If you notice on the magazine pictures a cool can was added along with the battery moved to the right rear of the trunk. The transmission was a B&M trick unit with a shift kit; B&M built that. I can't remember what the stall speed was in the converter. Super Stock would only allow a 7-inch tire so with the Goodyears we had to shave 1/4 off each side. [T]he shocks were replaced along with a few suspension parts. I just don't know what rear gear was used. The car was really very stock. We only did a few wedge motors a year. They just didn't require a lot of maintenance, but the heads had a little extra work."

I was not able to identify this clinic location, but note the hand-painted advertising in the office windows and the youthful onlookers viewing the 1968 Coronet. (Photo Courtesy Landy Family Archives)

1969: Dodge Fever Continues

The 1960s were winding down in more ways than one. The year 1969 found Dick Landy busy touring with the clinic program. Driver Bob Lambeck was running two A-Bodies (the 1968 SS/BA Hemi Dart and the SS/EA 440-ci model) on the Western Super Stock circuit tour, and Dick primarily pushed into the unfolding realm of what became Pro Stock with his match-race NHRA A/MP and AHRA SS/E Dart. So it seemed the B-Bodies took a backseat. Ironically, once again the Charger proved to be the best PR thoroughbred in the Landy stable, and the Coronets were back this year as well.

Flyin' Wedge: Charged Up Again

If I continue with the possibility of a single Charger from 1968, it would have been fairly easy to convert the well-tuned 1968 model into a 1969 version with trim and sheet-metal changes. The focus for the Charger at the start of 1969 was not racing but was instead coupled to Dick's being voted onto the 1968 *Car Craft* magazine All-Star Team. These accolades were given for Super Stock Engine Builder of the Year by reader ballot, and once again the crew at Petersen Publishing made the most of it. Soon after, Dick was given the chance to build a 440-ci street engine, giving pointers and recommending parts, using a 1969 Charger. Most interesting is that the A/MP-winning hood from 1968 is in one of the parts photos, so it possibly was not sold, as shown in that "For Sale" ad. As a result, *Flyin' Wedge* was a big deal that garnered another national magazine cover for Landy, on *Car Craft*'s February 1969 issue.

Dick garnered more fame at the NHRA Winternationals on the Pomona Fairgrounds, and he did it this time by winning the entire Street Eliminator title. The winning car was the same *Flyin' Wedge* Charger, now featuring a factory Six Pack scoop, which had not been formally announced at the time. After temporary Landy driver Herb McCandless bested the Sox & Martin Road Runner for the B/MP class title using this Charger, Dick took over the car on Sunday morning, having been eliminated in the A/MP Dart. He then hammered through five rounds of competition and claimed the first of his NHRA Nationals eliminator crowns.

Driving flat out as the rules allowed in the final round, Dick ended up resetting the B/MP record by .45 to a blistering 10.80; he had just missed the 11.25 breakout index in a number of prior rounds. The *National Dragster* results story claimed the car was wedge powered, but Terry Cook and his *Car Craft* insiders noted Hemi power

You can almost hear the roar as Dick shocks the tires and launches Flyin' Wedge. *Thomas Voehringer, researcher at TEN, located this long-lost and misfiled image. (Photo ©TEN: The Enthusiast Network. All rights reserved.)*

The photo ran on the cover of Car Craft *in early 1968. (Photo ©TEN: The Enthusiast Network. All rights reserved.)*

A dramatic image, taken during a private sponsor photo shoot in early 1969. (Photo Courtesy Landy Family Archives)

at Pomona. Indeed, based on later reports, engine swaps may have been a regular part of the actual races even if the car stated "Flyin' Wedge" on the rear quarter panels all season. Herb, for his part, was not overly happy.

Flyin' Wedge *in early 1969. Note the small number of sponsor decals, part of the agreements made with those companies. The factory had not released the Six Pack cars yet, but the latest scoop design was now on the Charger. (Photo Courtesy Landy Family Archives)*

"Yeah, that race was a sore subject for me," recalls the man dubbed Mr. 4-Speed. "I had been hired to drive that Charger, and on Sunday, Landy, [Dick] Maxwell, and [Tom] Hoover came over and told me I would get paid what I would have made, but Dick would be driving the car. Gale [Mortimer] and I had done a lot of work on it right after the AHRA race in Phoenix, and it was fast. After I went to work for Sox & Martin, Gale actually came to work for them as my crew chief."

After its exposure to the public via race victory and magazine coverage, this car was used as both a clinic machine and to run in either Modified Production or one of AHRA's Formula classes. The wedge engine package, which had used a modified Edelbrock CH4B intake and Max Wedge heads, was upgraded to a Six Pack package once those parts were released by the factory, again with follow-up in *Car Craft*. Very little is known about how

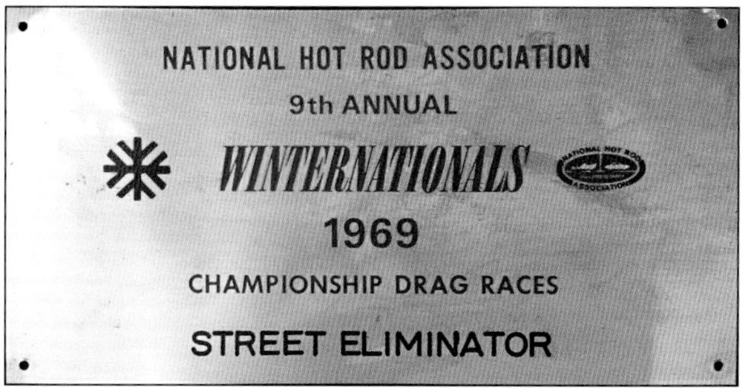

The Street Eliminator title at the 1969 Winternationals was Dick Landy's first NHRA national-event win. The sanctioning body had just four national events at the time, so this was a big deal. (Photo Courtesy Landy Family Archives)

much this car traveled with the wedge engine installed. Regardless, it likely proved to be a very good clinic car, as it aptly demonstrated a level of modifications with the parts and sponsors that Dick promoted.

In June, trimmed to F1 FS (Formula 1, Factory Stock), the Charger won the overall 1969 AHRA Top Stock Eliminator title at Bristol, as well as set a new AHRA record there. Again, it appears to have had a Hemi under the hood for that event. At NHRA races that summer, including the Indy invasion, it remained in B/MP trim.

There were at least two Chargers at Indy that summer, this one again in B/MP and a more legal Hemi/4-speed version in SS/F. Debuting in the spring, the latter had already won class at NHRA's Springnationals in Dallas in June and was also at the Super Stock Nationals, held at York, Pennsylvania, that year.

Three Chargers were mentioned in a magazine feature when Dick was asked about his cars in late 1969: *Flyin' Wedge* with a Six Pack, the B/MP Hemi, and the NHRA-legal SS/F stock entry; the latter two had won class titles at Indy. However, all facts seem to indicate that *Flyin' Wedge* and the B/MP entries were actually the same car, changeable as needed based on the sanctioning body or clinic/media needs.

Larry Carrier packed the stands at Bristol for Dick and the AHRA. He left there with a victory in Top Stock, using Hemi power and Flyin' Wedge *in a Formula Stock classification. (Photo Courtesy Phil Smith Archive, quartermilestones.com)*

Then there was Gean Landy's driver that year. This silver Charger R/T featured a worked 440 with a Six Pack scoop and was on hand at a corporate photo session at Irwindale with the 440 Dart and *Flyin' Wedge*. Although the Six Pack track development had been done by engineer Bob Tarozzi using a Charger model, the notable scoop designed by John Bauman was never offered on a factory Charger. Ever aware of media possibilities outside the automotive press, Frank Wylie sent a photographer to take candid photos and Dodge did a formal press release on the Landy family car, with Gean stylishly posing with it.

"That car was very powerful, and loud," Gean laughs now. "I can still remember actually taking the kids to school in it. One day I went around a corner too fast and accidently splashed some kids with a big puddle. They knew it was me. That was embarrassing."

Final Tunes Played on the Coronets

Dick noted in the late-1969 story mentioned above that there were still two Coronets in the stables: a 1969 Hemi Super Bee and the 440-ci clinic Coronet. Little is known of the latter car. The Hemi Bee, however, was being driven by Bob Lambeck by this time and was classed in SS/EA. Although he occasionally traveled when needed, once his army business was over, Mike Landy played a more supporting role at the new shop and admits that he did not really enjoy the driving aspect of the sport. This was especially true under the caustic scrutiny of the Detroit bosses. Gean further recalls that Mike was not really able to work full-time in the shop until he returned from his stint with Uncle Sam.

The bottom line was that in this final year of the Landy Coronets, Lambeck's Hemi Super Bee was the least expensive Hemi model available in the Dodge lineup. Lambeck was able to put this car into the winner's circle later that season in the Division 7 Super Stock Jackpot series, which competed across southern and central California. He switched between it and the SS/BA Hemi Dart as needed and finished second overall in points in that group. There were no national event crowns for the Bee, however, though it did win SS/EA honors at Indy that

I am not sure which sponsor is with Dick, but this is the 1969 B/MP class winner's circle. The cast was the result of a midsummer motorcycling accident. (Photo Courtesy Landy Family Archives)

year. This was in part due to the car's weight disadvantage against the onslaught of Ford and Chevy competitors arriving in the same class. Nonetheless, the team raced this Hemi Bee into the 1970 season, and Bob drove it at the 1970 Winternationals as well.

As for Mike, he had stepped away from the fame of acceleration after being in the army. "At the clinics I drove a bunch of cars," Mike recalls. "Sometimes I would drive them at the track to break the cars in. I drove the clinic cars after the radio personality thing ended too. So I drove at the shows, but after a run at Pomona when I red-lit, I got out of the car, threw my helmet on the ground, and said, 'That's it; I'm never driving again.'"

"The only engines we worked on regularly were the Modified Production engines," he continued, regarding the Sportsman years. "The Super Stock engines we rebuilt maybe once a year; they weren't set up to break records. The MP engine was for the one the boss drove, so we had to keep him happy. For the MP engines, we changed and cut the manifolds, port work, that type of stuff."

The Dodge Super Bee was already notable in 1969 and became even more so once the actual Six Pack models arrived. As the car itself had been in 1968, this was a midyear release. Featuring a newly refitted 440 Magnum with crank and cam changes, the Six Pack was named for three Holley 2-barrels atop an Edelbrock intake and was rated at 390 hp. It was available from Dodge that year in a special package car that featured a lift-off hood, big tires, and a Hemi driveline as standard. Parts procurement became a real problem for these Bees, and members of the performance development group later noted that they would have sold a lot more Six Packs had the standard-equipment pieces, such as wide police car rims, been more available. Dodge was busy with a lot of things that year, notably the new Daytona NASCAR special and the upcoming release of Challenger, so the company sold as many Super Bees as it had parts for, and that was the end of that.

Despite a broken leg, Dick raced in Super Stock with a Hemi-Charger in SS/F. He is seen here on Monday against Bill Tanner, who won the round. (Photo ©TEN: The Enthusiast Network. All rights reserved.)

During class at the 1969 Nationals, Flyin' Wedge *won B/MP with Hemi power and is seen here in Monday's first round. (Photo ©TEN: The Enthusiast Network. All rights reserved.)*

Never missing an opportunity to have Landy in the spotlight, Dodge released this press photo of Gean's Charger and a bunch of school chums. (Photo Courtesy Landy Family Archives)

The family Charger was also at Irwindale while the crew did a cam swap on the Lambeck-driven 440-ci Dodge Dart. (Photo Courtesy Landy Family Archives)

The Coronets played a big role in the Landy effort for many years, starting in 1965. Here is Bob Lambeck at Indy in 1969. (Photo ©TEN: The Enthusiast Network. All rights reserved.)

Although the cheesecake PR angle was part of the era, Gean really did drive this car, taking the Landy kids to school in it. An unnamed photographer gave this 8 x 10 as a gift to the Landys. (Photo Courtesy Landy Family Archives)

Bob Lambeck and the Hemi Bee get underway at the Big Go in 1969, the final Indy Nationals of the decade of the American supercar; things changed quickly in the early 1970s. (Photo ©TEN: The Enthusiast Network. All rights reserved.)

Although the B-Body of choice for 1970 was an SS/EA Hemi-Charger, the team had the Super Bee running at the 1970 Winternationals. (Photo ©TEN: The Enthusiast Network. All rights reserved.)

Still, Dick Landy was called on to do publicity for this car. He is thought to be in an advertisement for this model that ran for just one issue in several car-enthusiast magazines that summer. A formal press release also showed the filming of a TV commercial, with a photo caption stating that Dick was trying out the new vehicle. However, there was no formal record of him ever campaigning a Six Pack Bee, nor are there pictures of one with a *Landy's Dodge* paint scheme, perhaps because, one, the Hemi example was already running well enough, and two, the model's promotional value was cut short by the aforementioned lack of parts. Besides, the team already had two Chargers and at least one 1969 Coronet, and Dick certainly was in the loop on the upcoming Challenger. The broken leg Dick suffered that summer from a motorcycle accident over the July 4 Weekend did not make things any simpler, and driver Joe Fisher joined Lambeck in helping out crew members Greg

This might be the car that became the SS/EA Super Bee in 1969, but it is not certain whether it started out as a Hemi model. (Photo Courtesy Landy Family Archives)

Renkenberger and young Richard Landy at Indy, though records are absent as to who drove what.

Not counting as a racer but of interest to many is the prize 1969 Charger presented by Landy, McCurry, and Wally Parks to one lucky clinic attendee at Pomona in 1969. This was via a drawing from names submitted during the 1968 clinics, and the winner was not present for the drawing. If it exists, provenance on this car would be required for it to be valued higher than an identical 1969 Charger. Although modified by Landy for performance, it was likely a 383-powered model, as it does not have a scat stripe denoting R/T.

Where Are They Now?

White pants did not stay that way when adjustments had to be made at the racetrack. This is Flyin' Wedge running in Modified Production. (Photo Courtesy Landy Family Archives)

Flyin' Wedge *was the Landy team's most successful Charger. (Photo Courtesy Landy Family Archives)*

Flyin' Wedge was notable for its accomplishments and was chased by several car locators to Moose Parrah, the Louisiana operator of a well-known dragstrip in Baton Rouge. The car was raced hard and then pushed to the side like others when Moose brought in something else to play with. It reportedly ended up being sold with a number of other vehicles (including the remains of Sox & Martin's long-missing Superbird) and was eventually moved to a local salvage yard. One eyewitness stated that he saw the carcass of *Flyin' Wedge* stacked up on a pile of junkers headed for the crusher; nobody is saying if it ever got there.

The Hemi Super Bee is believed to have ended up in Texas; several attempts at locating it have proved to be futile to the guys who do that sort of thing, but it may still be out there. Dick himself is thought to have looked for this car during the 1990s without any success. The other B-Bodies from 1969 are all unaccounted for as well: the second Hemi Charger that ran in Super Stock during the mid-season, the 440 clinic Coronet if it was new and not the remodeled 1968 version, Gean Landy's silver driver with the Six Pack hood scoop, and the Six Pack Super Bee that Dick drove for the advertising campaign.

"I have a side note to where the Chargers went," Robert Landy told me. "One of the 1969 cars actually showed up on a street corner in a local Dales Jr. grocery store parking lot about 1979/1980 or so (with the lettering rubbed off) as a street car and for sale. It wasn't really that old at the time, and we just kind of laughed about it. I surely wish one of us had seen fit to buy it back!"

And that was before *Dukes of Hazard* filming swallowed up a lot of the remaining Charger bodies in Southern California; we can only hope it is tucked away.

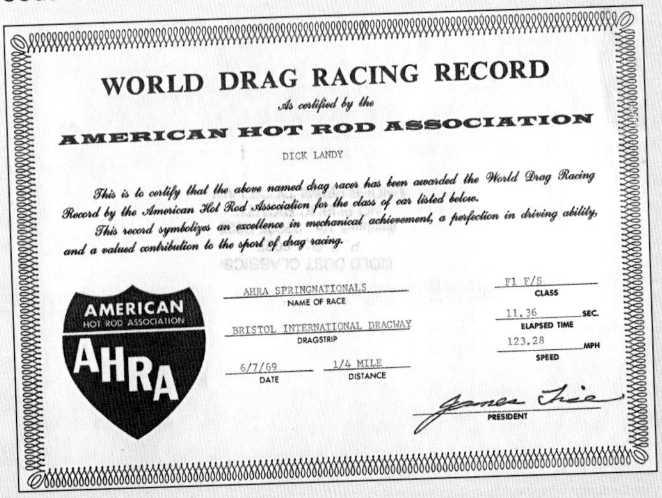
WORLD DRAG RACING RECORD

As certified by the

AMERICAN HOT ROD ASSOCIATION

DICK LANDY

This is to certify that the above named drag racer has been awarded the World Drag Racing Record by the American Hot Rod Association for the class of car listed below.

This record symbolizes an excellence in mechanical achievement, a perfection in driving ability, and a valued contribution to the sport of drag racing.

AMERICAN HOT ROD ASSOCIATION AHRA

AHRA SPRINGNATIONALS — NAME OF RACE

BRISTOL INTERNATIONAL DRAGWAY — DRAGSTRIP

6/7/69 — DATE

1/4 MILE — DISTANCE

F1 F/S — CLASS

11.36 SEC. — ELAPSED TIME

123.28 MPH — SPEED

PRESIDENT

The AHRA record from Bristol was reset to 11.36/123.28. (Photo Courtesy Landy Family Archives)

1970 Grand Finale: One More Charge into History

Things became quite different in 1970. For one, the noted hijinks of Super Stock racing began to wane, as most of the noted factory and professional-level drivers moved up into the new Pro Stock division. For Dick Landy, this was a huge change, as he was now the point man for the Dodge Division in the class. There were literally dozens of other Dodge racers who made this change as well. Although the factory continued to be involved in Super Stock, the huge amount of time and money needed to run Pro Stock competitively precluded Dick (who hated index racing regardless) from participating in Super Stock anymore. Although Dodge's early 1970 advertising featured Dick showcasing the restyled Coronet R/T, it is believed that he had no direct involvement in one of these cars until *Hot Rod* staffer David Frieberger showed up at DLI for an engine swap story with a street model in the 1990s. The last Landy team B-Body was a Charger that Dick rarely drove.

As mentioned, Bob Lambeck was in the 1969 Hemi Super Bee at the NHRA Winternationals in Pomona, and Dick took the B/MP Dart to a class title and victory circle there, his second consecutive event victory there with cars classed into Modified Eliminator. When it came time to replace the 1969 Super Bee soon afterward, a new 1970 Hemi Charger arrived. The Charger was in its third and final year of this body style, and with the team busy with other projects, the car became the de facto touring clinic car for about seven months.

The Charger was delivered to Dick with a certificate of origin rather than a title, though longtime car owner Ron Sites notes the vehicle was a true Hemi body. Dick received it in late March 1970, and some time was spent turning it into a pretty trick race car before it showed up formally in June. The steel nose and bumper reportedly went to AeroChem for processing, leaving them quite thin. The standard Landy suspension changes were made, and a Hemi with blueprinting was added. Set up to run both stick and auto, the rest of the car was set up for NHRA-legal Super Stock /EA.

Toward the end of the season, the car simultaneously held national speed records in both SS/E (125.00

It is certain, thanks to Ron Sites's paperwork, that the 1970 Hemi-Charger was brand new when Dick first got it. The 1969 SS/EA entry raced at the 1970 Winternationals. (Photo ©TEN: The Enthusiast Network. All rights reserved.)

The Sites car was raced during the early 1970s and then parked. Ron bought it in 1979 but never had the opportunity to race it. (Photo Courtesy Sites Family)

Ron and Roseanne Sites of Maryland shocked the Mopar community when they unveiled this almost original 1970 Landy Super Stocker. (Photo Courtesy Sites Family)

Mike Landy and young Richard on the road. Racing was a way of life for a decade. (Photo Courtesy Landy Family Archives)

The Landy kids (Richard, Danette, and Robert) sit on the tire rack during a test day at Lions in 1968. Robert worked at DLI for most of its existence. (Photo Courtesy Landy Family Archives)

at OCIR in September) and SS/EA (122.95 at Fremont in June), but its only major claim to fame was as runner-up at the final NHRA Springnationals at Dallas International Motor Speedway on June 14, with Bob Lambeck driving. A number of major players (notably Ray Allen, Jack Werst, and John Tedder) were in SS/EA that year, likely giving the Landy crew a bit of frustration on race day. Still, Lambeck took the 1970 Division 7 Super Stock title as well and drove this car for that. He and Dick won both the Pro Stock and Super Stock crowns in a single day at the Bonneville dragstrip in September. When the clinics were curtailed for 1971, the team stayed busy with the Challengers and Darts, and Bob was soon out on his own; the Charger was sold in October to dealer Sam Pannuty.

It raced around the Northeast during the 1970s, and Ron and Roseann Sites bought it from its fourth owner in 1979 with an intention to race it with a fresh Hemi. When work and family responsibilities took over, that program never materialized and the car was simply placed in storage for more than 25 years, basically preserving it. The family made huge waves in the Mopar collecting hobby when they exhibited the unrestored car at Carlisle in 2006, with Dick personally viewing and giving the car his approval at the event, less than a year before his passing.

The Sites car is the only second-gen Landy Charger known to still exist.

A last look at Flyin' Wedge*; the 1960s and sportsman racing were ending. (Photo Courtesy Landy Family Archives)*

CHAPTER 3

A-BODY ACTION 1966–1979

The venerable Chrysler A-Body had not been designed as a racer, though it did do that almost from the start. The Hyper Pak 6-cylinder effort that Tom Hoover and the factory engineers put together for the Valiant when it was first introduced made a big splash in circle track racing (to the extent that NASCAR subsequently eliminated the class). Some years later, the A-Body played a starring role in many racing seasons for Dick Landy.

Consider the following facts. The A-Body was actually the fastest car Dick ever drove, when the supercharged nitro-burning Dart was used in 1966; that car pushed toward the double-century mark before testing was suspended. The Dart was also one of the winningest cars that Team Landy ran between 1968 and 1970, when both he and driver Bob Lambeck raced the second-generation models in both 440 and Hemi trim to victory. Finally, the A-team gave Landy his most noted season-long honor when he returned to the new fastback Dart Sport in 1973, going all the way to the AHRA Pro Stock World Championship that year. Conversely, he had his most serious accident in this design when he hit a trackside obstruction in 1975.

Many agree that of all the A-Bodies that sported the Landy name, the most notable was the 1968 Hemi package built by Hurst. Even with the new Charger in the spotlight, Dick had two of these cars, happy to get away from the heavy B-Body Coronets of 1967. He took a class title with a rare 440-ci Mr. Norm version of this body before the Hemi cars arrived. What is not as often noted is that the Hurst Hemi package helped initiate the formative era of Pro Stock. After Dick upgraded one of the 1968 models to 1969 trim, he won B/Modified Production class and then the overall Modified Production Eliminator title with it at the NHRA Winternationals in 1970. Frankly, he was more disgusted than many other drivers with the arbitrary rules used by the NHRA to level out Super Stock. He found the MP categories more to his liking. He was on hand for a meeting after the 1969 Nationals at Indianapolis to help form the rules for Pro Stock.

This 4-speed Dart was one of the team's most famous cars, raced by both Dick Landy and Bob Lambeck to event victories. It is now in Todd Werner's collection.

In that class, the fastback A-Body became the natural successor to the E-Body Challenger for a number of reasons after 1972. When Dick formally retired from driving, he took a year away from racing and then decided to go to the even smaller import models that were beginning to populate Pro Stock. Sons Richard and Robert Landy both fondly recall a Dodge Demon that was the go-to car for the shop for a number of years. Of course, changes in the overall marketing program for Dodge promoted the A-Body in those later seasons, but by then Dick Landy was pretty much on his own in terms of racing. The Landy A-team thundered for almost a decade.

This uncredited advertising photo shows Dick sitting on the back of the truck with the Winter-nationals-winning 440-ci SS/EA Dart in the back-ground. (Photo Courtesy Landy Family Archives)

Dick drove his restored 4-speed Dart in exhibition racing during the 1990s, when Ed Vandersnick owned it.

Apparently created by a local painter, this original artwork for the 1966 Walker Dodge sponsor proposal for the Dart Funny Car is still part of the Landy Family Archives. (Photo Courtesy Landy Family Archives)

The 1976 Landy race car, built by DLI for by Larry Huff and raced by Dick following a wreck of his own car, was later found by Dean Klein and restored by Erik Lindberg. Marco DeCesaris owns it today.

For Dick Landy, 1965, with the altered-wheelbase Coronet, had proven to be the most eventful season of his career to date. It certainly established him among the most visible players on the national drag racing scene. However, things changed radically going into 1966: Chrysler put the A102 Street Hemi onto the boulevards, and drag racing took another leap forward.

Historically, Al Turner and Fran Hernandez at Mercury have been credited with initiating the modern Funny Car era. With their factory entries, driven by Dyno Don Nicholson and others, looking far less like the showroom models by the end of 1965, the company had gone to a chassis design that supported a much more stock-looking one-piece fiberglass Comet shell. These cars bridged the "funny" look to something more akin to a traditional stock car appearance, and the design became very effective as it was refined during 1966. The result was a source of ongoing frustration for Landy and others, who stayed the course when the New Year began with modified stock vehicles with at least some OEM body components.

Part of the rapid 1966 evolution of the category were the opposing pushes of technological advances and outright showmanship. In addition to the Comets, which were powered by fuel-injected SOHC Ford engines, a number of competitors had gone to superchargers. Some were one-off machines, including AMT's *Piranha* and Gene Conway's *Destroyer Jeep*. After their steel supercharged 1965 Dart was wrecked in June 1966 in Detroit, Don Garlits and driver Emory Cook debuted a blown Hemi Dart roadster that was simply one of Garlits's dragster chassis shortened with a higher roll cage. It ended up topping 200 mph before the end of the season and formed the basis of what all Funny Cars were like by 1970, when the NHRA created a season-long points division for them.

"Showmanship" at this time ranged from giant wheel stands to bogus grudge fights to slapping a pie in the face of a starter. Considering that the cars were capable of potentially fatal speeds, some of these antics were short-lived, but they gave the match-bash Ultra Stockers an identity crisis. This semicircus changed as the class phenomenon became more driven by mere performance than sideshow acts. Of course, the mystique of laying down long trails of gold dust, or dance floor tack, for traction was also part of the exhibition process. However it was billed or executed, the spectator turnstiles spun in 1966 for Funny Cars. Promoter C. J. Hart and the gang at Lions Drag Strip even played real calliope music when hosting a big Funny Car match race that season.

Landy's New Dodge

The 1966 season had found Dick to be the last man standing for Dodge when it came to true factory sponsorship. Things had thawed with NASCAR. The factory had finished 1965 with a number of big names already returning to the Grand National series. David Pearson won the 1966 NASCAR season title for Dodge, and the money that had been available for drag programs in 1965 went back into stock car racing.

Landy's professional appearance, noted wheel standing publicity, and match race win record likely played into him getting Dodge's only fully backed deal for the new season. What that deal entailed is no longer known, but it was enough that Dick noted to *Rod & Custom* magazine that he had $20,000 tied up in the racing rig and now had a full-time mechanic (brother Mike) working solely on the car. Indeed, in late spring, the formal

The fuel-burning Dart eventually became the fastest car Dick ever drove. This is at Englishtown against Phil Bonner's Falcon in the summer of 1966. (Photo Courtesy Landy Family Archives)

The 1966 Dart was completed just before the big winter events held by the NHRA and AHRA in Southern California. Dick made just one lap at each event; he was still sorting out the car. (Photo ©TEN: The Enthusiast Network. All rights reserved.)

announcement was made that Automotive Research was closing and that the Landy operation had moved into a Van Nuys business park, across from Don Alderson's Milodon company, to focus solely on racing.

The factory engineers, led by the Ramchargers, released a blueprint set to construct an altered-wheelbase 1966 Dart using commercially available fiberglass parts and a steel body shell. This model was selected over the just-introduced Charger simply because it had less frontal area and a smaller body size. Besides, the Charger was already being promoted on NASCAR speedways; the Dart put a different model into the limelight for the public. The Ramchargers had one, as did 1965 AHRA race winner Bud Faubel and others; young Charlie Allen and his new *Atlantic Dodge Flyer* Dart ran matches all over Southern California.

According to stories that ran in *Super Stock & Drag Illustrated* (*SS&DI*) and in *Hot Rod*'s *1966 Yearbook*, the

The new Dart is shown here under construction. This picture may have been taken at Race Car Specialties, owned by chassis builder Woody Gilmore. Dick is near the rear wheelwell of the car. (Photo ©TEN: The Enthusiast Network. All rights reserved.)

As always, the Dart drew a crowd. Dick is either pulling the spark plugs or making injector pill adjustments in this snapshot from the Hot Rod *magazine race at Riverside. (Photo Courtesy Landy Family Archives)*

Although classified into A/XS, according to new NHRA rules released in April, Dick instead chose to compete in Sunday's Hot Rod *magazine race in Unlimited Stock against the supercharged cars of "Jungle Jim" Liberman and Jack Chrisman. (Photo Courtesy Landy Family Archives)*

basis of the 1966 *Landy's Dodge* was an OEM steel unibody that had been acid-dipped. Editor Terry Cook noted in one of his January 1966 *Drag World* newspaper columns that a "well-known factory sponsored racer who shall remain nameless" had destroyed a brand-new body during a dipping process. If the next *Landy's Dodge* was being referred to, it would help explain why the Dart was late in getting finished. Dick and Dyno Don Nicholson ran a January race at Beeline Dragway in Arizona in their 1965 cars, as Nicholson's flip-top Comet was under wraps until the AHRA season-opening event at the new track in Irwindale, California. The same newspaper article said that Landy had won 39 of his past 41 matches; he won this one as well.

The Dart's floor was made of .060 aluminum, and the cage was 2 x 3 rectangular steel channel stock that was extensively drilled for weight lightening. A roll bar of .125 2-inch-diameter pipe was welded to this. The hood, fenders, and deck were all fiberglass, with Plexiglas windows all around. The Spar brothers at B&M had been involved with the construction of the car, as had Woody Gilmore of Race Car Specialties (RCS). Gilmore helped build the chassis for the new Ramchargers Dart, but the extent of his involvement in the 1,800-pound Landy project is unknown.

What is known, based on the *SS&DI* story by Jerry Gross, is that RCS did provide the straight axle and that Dick had begun this project where he had left off with the 1964 package, using a multipoint adjustable wheelbase. The factory 111-inch stock wheelbase was increased to 112 by moving the rear axle 10 inches forward and the RCS front axle (equipped with Dodge truck spindles, American mags, and no brakes) 11 inches forward.

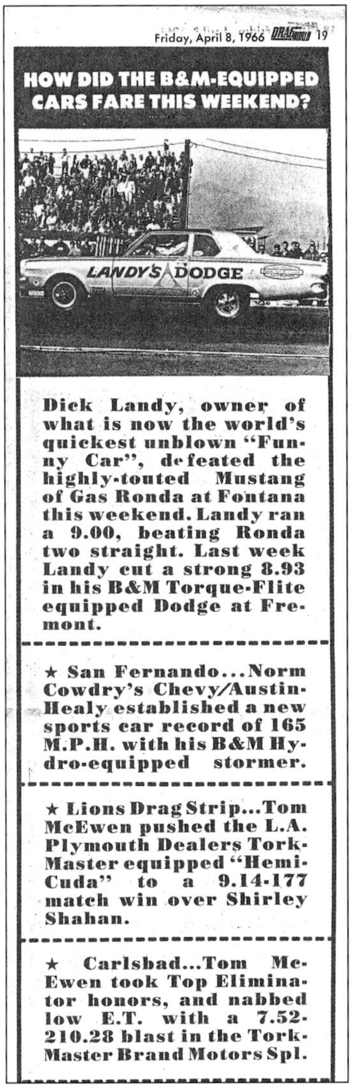

Friday, April 8, 1966 DRAG WORLD 19

HOW DID THE B&M-EQUIPPED CARS FARE THIS WEEKEND?

Dick Landy, owner of what is now the world's quickest unblown "Funny Car", defeated the highly-touted Mustang of Gas Ronda at Fontana this weekend. Landy ran a 9.00, beating Ronda two straight. Last week Landy cut a strong 8.93 in his B&M Torque-Flite equipped Dodge at Fremont.

★ San Fernando...Norm Cowdry's Chevy/Austin-Healy established a new sports car record of 165 M.P.H. with his B&M Hydro-equipped stormer.

★ Lions Drag Strip...Tom McEwen pushed the L.A. Plymouth Dealers Tork-Master equipped "Hemi-Cuda" to a 9.14-177 match win over Shirley Shahan.

★ Carlsbad...Tom McEwen took Top Eliminator honors, and nabbed low E.T. with a 7.52-210.28 blast in the Tork-Master Brand Motors Spl.

B&M used the Dart to highlight its advertising after Dick clocked an 8.93.

Fans cheered Dick on at the huge BOMP event at Lions. There he earned yet another Drag Sport Illustrated *cover.*

That was augmented by adjustable chassis points in the rear to allow for adjustments of 6 inches horizontally and 3 inches vertically. Hand-built heavy channel torque arms and special coil springs were used, with rear-facing shocks. The factory Dart leafs were simply for support, and a Terramaster rear end with quick-change 4.30 gearing was now in place of a Chrysler unit. The front axle swap was primarily for weight savings and, as in 1964, used the gasser trick of short front leaf springs, which made 4 inches of horizontal axle movement possible. Brakes were by Airheart and only at the back; a parachute was added to that.

Power at first was a stock 426-inch Hemi with a blueprinted C&T Stroker Super Stock crank; Dick stuck with the Isky 550 cam he had used in 1965. Indeed, the injected combination was little changed from the previous year. Because Dick was staying with an automatic, the Hilborns featured the large 2⁷⁄₁₆-inch throttle bore with a tall 16-inch length. He told Gross that the technique was to get the car to launch at 1,800 rpm to prevent torque converter failures. A B&M reworked TorqueFlite was behind that, complete with a push-button shifter remounted near the driver-side door, where he could punch it easily.

Never neglecting style, the Dart GT's wooden steering wheel was the tiller inside. Paul's Body Shop in Sherman Oaks did the black and silver paint. The car also had chrome Cragar S/S rims with M&H 10 x 15 tires. Still, the 28-year-old father noted at that time that the car was being created with safety in mind. He told Gross that he hoped the car would be good for 8.60s at 160 mph and that he did not believe supercharging was the answer.

Flights of the Featherweight Dart

Dick remained almost solely in unlimited-type heads-up racing; he did not move the car's classification around to slow it down. The Dart made its formal debut to the public on February 6 at Lions Drag Strip during its big United Drag Racers Association (UDRA) dragster race. The UDRA was an independent group of fuel dragster pilots and owners, a pseudo union pushing for better purses and track safety that Dick may well have joined. As part of the show, Landy raced against Dick Brannan, a well-connected Ford racer from Detroit who also had a new modified stocker, a lengthened Mustang. The Dart went 9.21/144 in a time trial but slowed to a 9.27/123 with engine breakage in the first round of the match to lose and was retired for the evening.

The following two weekends might have entailed more testing, but two one-shot public runs were made, one at the aforementioned AHRA Winter Nationals at Irwindale with a 10.20/149 shakedown pass and then a fast 9.35/154 blast at the NHRA Winternationals in Pomona that stood as the best run of all the Funny Cars on hand. The NHRA still did not know what to do with them and classed the blown nitro doorslammers into CC/FD, where a lone dragster won the class crown, and it used C/FD for injected-fuel burners like Landy's. At Irwindale, Nicholson's new Comet flipped its top, literally. As a result, Dyno could not race against Dandy for the top position in the East-West Stocker Championships held at Lions at the end of February. Landy's Dart raced a gasser truck instead, running 9.63, 9.69, and 9.71, again the best times of the evening and the only car to consistently be in the 9-second bracket.

Meanwhile, March brought the first trip to Beeline Dragway in Phoenix for the AHRA track opener. A 9.54/134 in a Saturday handicap run found the 112-inch Dart off the track and in the dirt without damage, but Dick came back on Sunday to run Unlimited Super Stock Fuel, beating Gene Snow with a 9.51/150 to start the day. In round two, he clocked a 9.37 and used a holeshot to beat Ronnie Sox's new *Baccaruda* (which clocked a blistering low-ET-of-the-meet 9.18 loss), then stepped up to a 9.32/149 to beat Dick Harrell in the final. Pictures exist, but no times were recorded for Landy during the March Meet at Bakersfield, and it is possible the car broke early on there. The month finished with a trip to Kingdon Dragway near Lodi, California, where NASCAR's drag racing division held sanction for a short time; there Dick beat Cecil Yother's *Melrose Missile* and Al Vander Woude's *Flying Dutchman* for the race crown.

But the real reason for this trip occurred at Fremont, south of Oakland, California, on March 27. Butch Leal had beaten Landy's vaunted 1965 car for the *Drag Racing Magazine* number-one West Coast spot in early January, and this was the rematch. The new Dart downed Leal's 1965 altered-wheelbase *California Flash* in three straight and officially broke into the 8-second zone for the first time at 8.93/156 in the final, though the Dart's hood flew off at speed.

April 3 found him against Gaspar "Gas" Rhonda in a highly billed match at Fontana Drag City. Rhonda was considered the toughest West Coast Ford, and fans packed the place. By this time, the Dart had begun to change. For one, it had a new nose, with the wheel openings moved much farther forward. This change had been first seen in primer on the car at the Kingdon meet and was now painted. The replacement hood after the "Leal lift" a week earlier was still two-thirds as long, open across the back around the set-back engine to relieve air pressure.

Landy shut down the Ford with a 9.00 in round one and a 9.11/155 in round three to become the most notorious unblown stocker in Southern California. He was against Hubert Platt's new Mustang at Sacramento on April 17 for a booked-in race that was covered in the drag papers as well as *Speed and Supercar* magazine. This meet found Landy both beating strong crosswinds and "Hu Baby's" legendary starting line antics to take that crown as well. The subsequent text in the magazine called Dick "the undisputed king of the exhibition match bash, King Landy."

Speed Kills, Speed Thrills

Not long after this, Ford factory ace Les Ritchey was killed in an accident at Fontana. The cars may have been funny looking, but their primitive construction and short, ill-handling wheelbases were a dangerous trend. As a result, a big Saturday-night rematch with Gas Rhonda at Lions was called off as the factory Fords went back to Holman-Moody for a checkup. At that event, the latest KFWB radio BOMP, Landy showed he was still boss with a 9.08/150.50 without any rosin, the second-quickest unblown stocker time ever (behind his previous 9.00) at the legendary racetrack. What amazed the press was that the 12,000 or so fans, there mainly for a big top fuel race, gave the Dart the biggest cheers. Now stretched out to 116 inches, the car made the two-page cover of *Drag Sport Illustrated* the following week.

Artist David Carl Peters made this portrait of Dick in the Dart. Note the position of the push-button shifter in the window area. (Photo illustration ©David Carl Peters. All rights reserved.)

David Carl Peters painted this image of Dick racing the colorful "Jungle Jim" Liberman in Lew Arrington's Brutus *GTO at Fontana Drag City in May. (Photo illustration ©David Carl Peters. All rights reserved.)*

One writer noted something else. If a spectator had questions about his street car or Mopar race car, Dick was always willing to talk to that person and give advice. The efforts of Automotive Research paid off when Dodge released a short batch of high-performance 273-inch Darts in late spring. Again, friend and *Hot Rod* magazine associate Eric Dahlquist came to Landy's shop for tuning tips on this D-Dart, and Dick got the car into the 14-second zone with mild changes. A story ran in the August 1966 issue.

Closing the Doors at Automotive Research

Automotive Research closed its doors in May 1966. Few people recall that Dick still worked on other makes, even for racing. Perhaps his best-known outside customer that year was Paula Murphy. The sports car racer and future Funny Car star had Automotive Research prep a new W30 4-4-2 for her for the winter meets. In "The Hook" gossip column in *Drag Sport,* it was noted that Dick had prepped five cars for the AHRA race at Irwindale and won all five classes and that Murphy took home class honors at Pomona in the Olds as well. Perhaps a call from Cahill or Maxwell had been part of closing the shop for a while. Besides, the East Coast tour soon started, but not before a couple more shots for the press in SoCal.

On May 29, the Dart beat Lew Arrington's feared the *Brutus* GTO, piloted by "Jungle Jim" Liberman, two of three at Fontana, with a 9.21 in the final, and had the rematch with Rhonda on June 11 at Irwindale, which Dick again won two of three, going 9.48 in the final. However, the Dart was still showing a bad propensity to wheel stand off the line. Often, by doing multiple rosin burn-throughs, the driver could get a sense of traction, but too much bite meant going up instead of forward. Gas Rhonda got his revenge at a race in Puyallup, Washington, in June, as Dick had "wheelie" problems and the Mustang won two of three. Then Jungle Jim went to the final against Jack Chrisman's GT1 Comet roadster at the event that had likely kept Landy on the West Coast: the *Hot Rod* magazine drags at Riverside International Raceway. In fact, *Landy's Dodge* was the only unblown car in the S/XS class. It won round one over Jim Davis with a 9.25 and beat Jungle with a 9.19 but blew an engine and could not return, so *Brutus* was back under the break rule and went to the money round, where it was trounced by Chrisman's factory-backed Mercury.

A Word from Our Sponsors

After Automotive Research closed its doors (Dick kept the building just in case), a proposal went to a local dealership, Walker Dodge, for some associate backing. Walker had been racing a yellow 1965 273-inch Dart Charger (a special California edition). The dealer agreed to pay to have its name on the rear quarter panels of the Landy Dart just above the wheelwell, and it remained there for the rest of the season.

For the Landy kids, however, it was an unmentioned sponsor that had the biggest impact. Ironically, the Wham-O Wheelie Bar probably generated more exposure for the Dart and Dick Landy than any drag racing event did that season (see sidebar).

Back East

As June became July, the team began touring the East Coast, taking in some of the larger events and match racing. One popular match was between the Dart and a Falcon raced by Phil Bonner. Dick also raced friend Malcolm Durham on a number of occasions, including the Dart's first big East Coast appearance at the 1/8-mile track in Manassas, Virginia. The car won over Bonner at Aquasco, Maryland, in three straight, again running an 8.99 best, but it dropped three straight to Nicholson's rebuilt Comet the same week, again with wheel-standing issues.

Wham-O Wheelie Bar

The Wham-O toy company is well known for its popular products: the Frisbee, the Hula Hoop, and the Slip 'N Slide among others. It came up with the Wham-O Wheelie Bar, a roller wheel that could be mounted on the rear of a Schwinn Stingray-type bicycle. The company wanted to use a wheel-standing car for advertising; both Landy and Bill Golden, in *Little Red Wagon*, were featured. Dick actually even rode the bikes for a number of demonstrations, cigar in mouth and wearing white sneakers. The PR images ran in magazines like *Popular Science*, and a TV commercial was filmed on the street near the shop. It showed the car doing some of its monster launches.

"The Wheelie Bar was really cool," recalls daughter Danette (Landy) Satenstein. "We all got new bicycles and rode them all over." Richard recalls that they got hundreds of Super-balls, Frisbees, and other products as well. Although the Wheelie Bar never took off like many of the company's other toys, it was a great nonautomotive sponsor for drag racing. Dick Landy was again on the cutting edge.

Who says you need four wheels for fun? Dick was always a motorcyclist and dirt bike rider. He seems to have mastered the Wham-O Wheelie Bar quickly, as this PR photo shows. (Photo Courtesy Landy Family Archives)

The Wham-O Wheelie Bar never caught on like the new Frisbee did, but it gave Dick a lot of ink in nonautomotive periodicals. A commercial, showing the Dart wheels-up, was filmed on the street near the shop. (Photo Courtesy Landy Family Archives)

The Dart from behind during the summer tour. Note the sponsor's names on the deck lid and how narrow the Dart actually was. The lack of a rear deck spoiler is . . . terrifying. (Photo Courtesy Landy Family Archives)

Part of the mystique of 1966 was the use of hydrazine as a fuel additive to nitromethane. "Yeah, we played a lot with that stuff," Mike Landy recalled recently. "It is the most powerful nonnuclear explosion you could make, but you have to dump and clean the fuel tank out right away. It ate the pistons alive, and we only had the parts we could carry in the station wagon, so we were careful. Some of the tracks were rough; there you had to aim the 1966 car. You couldn't really drive it."

Whether the volatile mixture was in the tank on July 29 is not known. However, the car ran a huge number against Ronnie Sox's *Baccaruda* at 75-80 Dragway in Monrovia, Maryland, going 8.69 at 161 mph, but it literally came apart at the top end, with its Plexiglas windows shattering and the roof buckling. It skipped the rest of that evening's activities. It was quickly rebuilt, and the team headed back to Cecil County on July 30 only to lose three to Tasca Ford's Bill Lawton. There, the Dart clocked the event's low ET/top MPH with 8.76/160.42. Truth be told, the Ford program had made some real progress that summer, and now any race wins required stepping up hard on fuel and hurting parts.

Super Stock Magazine Nationals

The first weekend in August, at the Super Stock Magazine Nationals at New York National Speedway, Dick dropped below the 8.50 zone for the first time at this event, going 8.46/166 in qualifying to get the best performance of any racer there on Saturday. However, the Dart did not fire for the first round of the 2,000-pound Fuel class that evening. Dick then decided to go all out and moved into Unlimited Fuel with the blower cars for Sunday. He won round one, repaired a head gasket, and then beat Arnie Beswick's Tempest with an 8.79/159 in round two. In the final, he lost to Don Gay's GTO with a piston-melting 8.77/161 pass, which put the car out of contention before the big Mr. Super Eliminator program began that evening.

Breakage continued to be the issue through August and September; it cost Dick another final-round chance at Cecil County against the Ramchargers, as well as at Alton, Illinois, and Gary, Indiana, both times against Nicholson. He did win the rematch at 75-80 against Sox, running a track-record-setting 8.63/163, and he claimed a three-of-five victory at Capitol Raceway near Baltimore over Nicholson that included an 8.55/172 single. The overall best recorded time for 1966 was from Rockford, Illinois, on September 5, when the car recorded back-to-back 8.38 and 8.37 runs to set the track record, both at more than 170 mph.

One news story noted an even better 8.24/175.50 for the car, but this number was not recorded by Dick; nor was it in Gean Landy's scrapbook file. The bottom line was that Nicholson's Comet had now touched into the 7-second zone at a race in Milan, Michigan, and something drastic needed to change once the team got back to California.

Before returning to California, the Dart won several fall events, beating *Seaton's Shaker* in Kingston, North Carolina, in late September, topping Phil Bonner's Mustang at Yellow River's 1,000-foot track on October 2, and taking home a nice $1,000 prize at an open event at Grandview International Raceway near Beckley, West Virginia, over Bruce Larson's Chevelle on October 11. Back in the Golden State, old rival Hayden Proffitt was now in a topless Corvair,

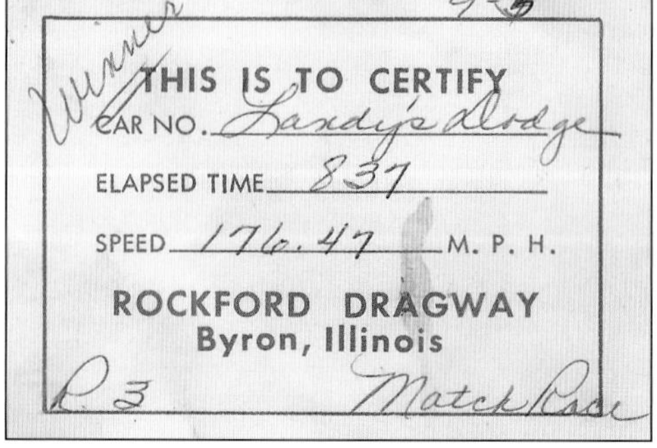
Winner 9-5
THIS IS TO CERTIFY
CAR NO. Landy's Dodge
ELAPSED TIME 8.37
SPEED 176.47 M. P. H.
ROCKFORD DRAGWAY
Byron, Illinois
R 3 Match Race

Big numbers at Byron. This 8.37/176 time slip marks one of the quickest passes for the 1966 Dart. (Photo Courtesy Landy Family Archives)

Dick recalled that the car proved to be a real handful with the supercharged combination, as the chassis was not set up for the level of power it created. (Photo Courtesy Landy Family Archives)

and the Dart raced him at Irwindale on October 22, winning two out of three. Paula Murphy's new supercharged STP Mustang, tuned by Fat Jack Bynum, was now competing as well. Dick beat her with a 9.30 at Fremont while testing was ongoing with the new blower combination.

Blower Bomb

The easiest way to play catch-up is to leapfrog over the injected Fords and move into a supercharged combination. To aid this, the Ramchargers dragster group sent a complete unassembled blown-fuel Hemi to be built for the car in early October. This combination would be finalized and then used as the basis for anything the factory might authorize as a blown Funny Car. In the meantime, Buddy Martin researched what the 1967 chassis would consist of and had the cars built.

"I ran it a few times, and it hauled, but we had a lot of problems just working out how to stage it," Dick recalled later. "It was completely different from a fuel dragster, clutch in and out, and we were trying to do burnouts through rosin and things like that. I ended up redesigning the barrel valve with Enderle so the idle circuit didn't pressure surge. The blower thing was all [Chrysler engineer] Dale Reeker's idea."

Dick also recounted that the testing was done at the little track in Fresno for three weeks. The car responded to the package fairly well, but even the tough B&M-built TorqueFlite was not able to handle the power. On one run, the transmission blew up and the car caught on fire; Dick received some burns on his leg. At trackside, executive Bob Cahill saw this and decided right then that the factory needed to reconsider the program. He did not want to be responsible for the potential injury or worse. Corporately, Chrysler chose to go in a different direction for 1967, but the supercharged combination remained on the car for the rest of the time Dick raced it.

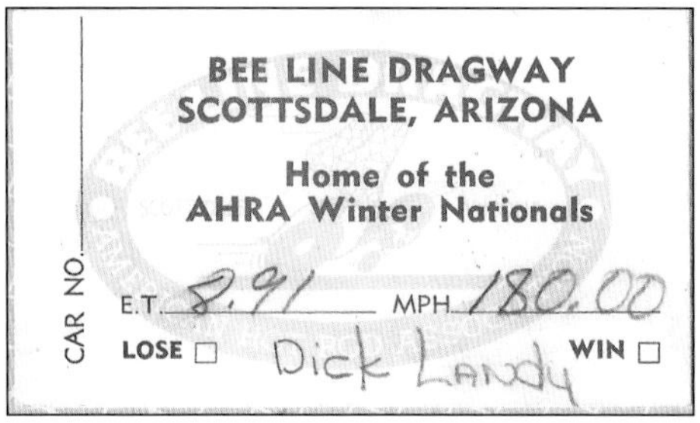

Dick put the car on the top of the charts during qualifying with this blistering 8.91/180. (Photo Courtesy Landy Family Archives)

The first race with the blown engine was a big Funny Car race at Irwindale on November 12, but the car was bogging badly off the line. Dick ran an 8.76 at a top speed of 177.16 only to lose both matches on holeshots. On November 26–27 at the Lions huge East-West Stocker Championships, it was more of the same: big wheelies, engine breakage, and running over the staging equipment to lose to Gas Rhonda in round one. The car was fast, no doubt, but very unpredictable. In its final appearance under Dick's control at the December 3 Western States Super Stock Championships at Beeline Dragway, it ran a wheel-standing 8.91/180.00 best in qualifying only to fall to "Dyno Don" Nicholson in round one with another nose-up 9.06 at "just" 174 mph. Had research continued, there is no doubt that Dick and Mike would have sorted it out, but big changes for 1967 meant that their Funny Car summer was over. A new Hemi Coronet 440-trim car was already in the shop, and the Dart was parked for another day, one that never came.

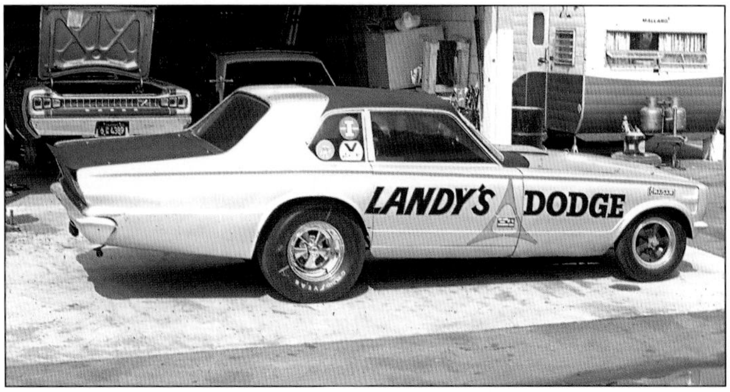

The Dart on the day it was sold, in September 1967. The factory's effort to go to Super Stock that season had proven to be successful enough that Dick did not race it again. (Photo Courtesy Landy Family Archives)

"I don't think any of us really wanted to go back into Super Stock," Dick admitted. "I mean, we could still match race, even with the stockers, so we made money, but I really didn't care much about the big meets, with all the handicapping going on and all that stuff."

The Funny Car era ended for Dick Landy when he made his last pass in the car for new owner Gene Kidder the week it was sold in late 1967.

Where Is It Now?

Dick kept the Dart until late in 1967. The new 1968 Charger and 1968 440-ci Coronet were in the garage the day it was sold to racer Gene Kidder. Dick took it to Irwindale that night and made a fast 8.80 clocking for Kidder's approval, then sold it to Gene without the engine.

After leaving his bank job in 1968, Gene raced the Dart on the Midwest's UDRA injected-fuel circuit for some months as the *Sacoman Dodge Fever* entry. However, with so many competitors going to superchargers that summer, Gene decided to step up as well. He contacted Dick, who still had the blown Ramchargers combination engine tucked away at the shop, and bought that engine. Because the army had stationed him in Texas, Mike drove home and delivered the engine to the Kidder team, and this power put the car back up into the 180-mph range. One fateful day that November, at a match race in Palm Beach, Florida, the car cut down a back tire and rolled over several times.

In 1993, Gene handwrote a letter to Dick, recalling the car's history and eventual demise. "Thanks to you (chest belt and all), the car held together and I am alive. I salvaged the engine, but souvenir hunters ripped off all the fiberglass body parts at the track while I was being checked out at the hospital. Later, I traded the chassis for shop equipment."

It is likely that these images were shot during the evening before the Dart was bought by Gene Kidder. That's when Dick made his last demonstration laps in the car at Irwindale, before the engine was pulled out. (Photo Courtesy Landy Family Archives)

This photo shows what the car looked like in early 1968, before Kidder bought the supercharged engine for it. (Photo Courtesy Landy Family Archives)

One last look at the Dart on Gene Kidder's truck on its way to a new home in late 1967, and its eventual destruction. The durable construction saved Kidder's life, but the car was no more. (Photo Courtesy Landy Family Archives)

For many, the 1966 Dart is considered Dick Landy's most radical race car of the 1960s, and in terms of performance and sheer danger, that is true. However, the end of the 1960s found Dodge Darts again playing a huge role in Dick's racing career and visibility. The year after that final Funny Car, Dodge redesigned the model into a more sophisticated package. The new car featured crisp lines, wider frame rail and track dimensions, upgraded options, and, of interest to this narrative, the ability for larger engines to be installed on the assembly line. In mid-1967, the announcement came for the Dart GTS, which had a 383 B-series engine under the hood.

That car was the result of the efforts of "Mr. Norm" Krause and his crew at Grand-Spaulding Dodge in Chicago. Mr. Norm had noted that the new Barracuda had already received the big-block, so they shoehorned the B-engine into a new Dart at their shop and took it to Detroit to show the bosses, who put it into production. This option also fueled the fire that led Norm to create the first of the Super Stock Darts that ran out of the Landy stables.

Fighting Cobras in SS/EA

The NHRA's Super Stock class structure changed slightly for 1968, adding SS/F and making SS/E the former SS/D numbers, 8.70 to 9.49. Ford had announced the Cobra Jet, a new Mustang with a 428-ci engine, and it would be fitted into the E class. Krause and Chrysler talked in late 1967, and Norm agreed to buy 50 1968 Darts that had the larger 440 Magnum engine installed; this quantity legalized it for Super Stock. These cars were built under a special order to a subcontracting facility that Hurst Industries owned near Detroit, and Norm sold the small batch of Darts fairly quickly. Based on how the NHRA factored the horsepower on the engine that year, the 440 Darts (all automatics) ended up in the same class as the new Mustangs.

At this point, Dick had the 1968 Hemi Charger, which had appeared in a number of magazine stories as well as in his publicity info for 1968, stating plans to race it in SS/B. With the Darts made legal by the NHRA after Krause's operation submitted an owner list to the sanctioning body in January, Dick was instructed to race the new SS/EA 440 Dart at the NHRA Winternationals the following month. It is not certain if a car was quickly shipped to him turnkey-ready or if the Landy shop did this conversion.

At the 1968 Winternationals at Pomona, Dick drove the SS/EA 440-ci Dart to a class win and a first-round victory over Gas Rhonda's Cobra Jet. (Photo ©TEN: The Enthusiast Network. All rights reserved.)

The first 1968 Hemi Dart on a pass at Orange County, from original film in the Landy family's collection. This photo was taken during the early days of testing this car, probably in April. (Photo Courtesy Landy Family Archives)

The 440-ci Darts were the prelude to the Hemi versions that debuted less than 90 days later. This press release photo taken at the 1968 Winternationals shows Dick racing against one of the Cobra Jets for class. (Photo Courtesy Landy Family Archives)

The team works on the 440 SS/EA Dart during a 1969 Irwindale test and photo session for Chrysler. (Photo Courtesy Landy Family Archives)

Regardless, the car was ready to go for the event in early February, and Dick made the most of it.

Ironically, it was former Funny Car rival Gas Rhonda at the receiving end of the Dart's success, as Dick beat the noted driver's brand-new Cobra Jet Mustang in both the EA-class final on Saturday and again in the first round on Sunday. Dick singled in round two but came up against his own solid qualifying performance to break out in round three against Dave Wren's Plymouth.

This Dart actually remained part of the stable the rest of the year and into 1969 and was a real winner. New driver Bob Lambeck piloted it on several occasions to victory across Division 7 that summer and fall, not only winning the 1968 division crown but amassing 3,400 points, more than any other Super Stock pilot in the nation.

Then the Bomb Dropped

At the same time Mr. Norm was selling every 440 Dart he could build, Dick came out to Irwindale to take a look at a new Plymouth. This was not just any car; this was a Barracuda built at the Woodward Garage, Chrysler Engineering's little skunk works off the legendary Motor City Boulevard, and it had a Hemi. This car was the prototype of special Plymouth and Dodge A-Body models that would be going into limited production soon afterward, announced simultaneously by the two divisions in late February.

After the 1967 package cars had proved to be not quite what the Super Stock ranks needed, factory-racing coordinator Tom Hoover decided to build a true beast.

In 1993, Dick stands with the automatic version of the Hemi Dart, restored to its as-raced 1968 configuration.

The same changes that had created production line 383 Darts and Barracudas also made a Hemi swap more feasible into the A-Body. With SS/B at 6.00 to 6.49 pounds per factored horsepower, a fresh 500-hp (NHRA factored rating) Race Hemi similar to the 1964 design offered good possibilities. The tooling for the 1965 A990 aluminum heads was no longer available, so the engine used Street Hemi heads. The expensive magnesium intake was cast aluminum instead. A just-designed and -tested hood scoop covered this layout. The only option on these cars was a choice of transmission: either the slick-shift modified A833 4-speed or the manual valve body–equipped A727 TorqueFlite automatic. This in turn dictated the differential type (Dana 4.88 or 8-3/4 4.86, respectively).

For the first time, cars built by Chrysler for drag racing were not street-legal, and a signed disclaimer noting that fact was required from buyers. In addition, conspicuous warning decals were placed on the car and under the hood. Paint was standardized (gray primer), with the new fiberglass parts (the hood and front fenders) left in black gel coat. Using techniques perfected in the early 1960s packages, light-gauge steel was used for stamping out the front bumper and the doors, which lacked window mechanisms and instead used a strap of seat belt webbing to open and close thin Corning windows. Weight was added in the back through a large truck battery, and engineer Bob Tarozzi's favorite change was a set of computer-aided rear springs, created specifically for this car, that gave it excellent traction. Hooker made the headers, eliminating the need to squeeze cast-iron manifolds in the tight engine bay, and as mandated by the rules that year, a rudimentary exhaust system of pipe and glass-pack mufflers was added. This ended just forward of the rear axle.

Although dressed casually, Dick had no problem digging in if the job required it. He is seen here doing a collector change on a header. (Photo Courtesy Landy Family Archives)

As with the 440 Darts, Hurst Performance was the subcontractor, and it received these cars right from the Hamtramck assembly plant as partially finished 383 models, unceremoniously brought in by a hook-type wrecker to a special rebuilding shop about 8 miles away. Here the Race Hemi engines were installed, with some special changes to the brakes and engine bays; the fiberglass and lighter steel pieces were added; and, for the Darts, some rear wheelwell reworking was done for clearance. Seeing the prototype Plymouth being tested, Dick was likely well aware of what was transpiring even as he ran the 440 Dart at Pomona.

With parts procured, Hurst began building these new cars in March, and one of the first ones came to Dick in a unique way. The *Hot Rod* magazine drags were still a big deal. Dick had ordered two Hemi Darts, one a stick and one an automatic. According to Daryl Klassen, who once owned the 4-speed model, it was VIN-tagged as an automatic and was shipped via cargo jet to Dick without a driveline installed. It is even possible that the already-built race engine from the 1968 Charger, painted black, was intended to go into this car.

Backed with an automatic in the interest of time, he came to Riverside the second weekend of April with

The Hemi engine in the first Dart soon after it was running. Note the writing on the air horns for valve adjustments. Black paint helped heat dissipation and hid little details. (Photo Courtesy Landy Family Archives)

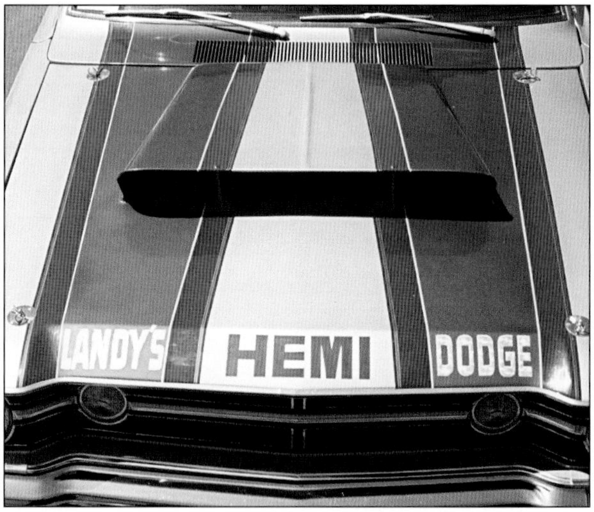

Scientific Chrysler Engineering hood scoop research had begun in earnest by 1966. The result was this immense unit centered over the cross ram on the 1968 package cars. (Photo Courtesy Landy Family Archives)

In Super Stock, the NHRA required cars to have functional exhaust systems. The cherry bomb mufflers and little turndown exits are seen here near the differential. (Photo Courtesy Landy Family Archives)

Sunday morning at Riverside. Dick is about to get the news that the NHRA is not going to let the Dart race in eliminations because Chrysler could not prove that it had sold 50 units by then. The W in the window is from the class win on Saturday. (Photo Courtesy Landy Family Archives)

this vehicle for the race and easily won the BA class title, getting the big W sticker on the windshield. On Sunday morning, racing politics showed up and the NHRA told him the car would not be allowed to compete in the overall eliminator, as Chrysler could not prove it had already sold 50 examples of the model. Dick then took over the team's old 1967 Hemi Coronet, which Mary Ann Foss had been brought in by Dodge to drive in SS/DA, but Dick had no luck repeating his winning 1967 efforts at the popular race. It was a less-than-stellar beginning for the A-bomb.

Bob Lambeck: Man with a Cause

Dick Landy occasionally had other drivers in his cars during earlier seasons, but with brother Mike being drafted and the cars becoming ever more sophisticated, he needed somebody with real talent in 1968. Following the introduction of the three Darts plus the already-on-hand B-Bodies, he picked, with Dodge's blessing, a young transplant from Michigan named Bob Lambeck. Also a resident of Sherman Oaks, Lambeck had already established himself as a feared competitor in Junior Stock racing with his Powerpack-equipped 1957 Chevy. He quickly proved to be a great asset to Landy's efforts.

During the following three seasons, Bob became the most visible member of the Landy team on the West Coast, as Dick's clinic schedule kept him on tour much of the year. In addition to match racing efforts, Lambeck aggressively pursued NHRA World Championship Series points in Super Stock for the team, resulting in his great Division 7 showings those seasons, often driving multiple entries each year. With a pleasant personality and professional appearance, Lambeck also met the standards that Dodge required in a representative, and he was tagged to drive the new Dart Swinger Pro Stock when the class was introduced.

At the end of 1970, Bob determined that it was time to strike out on his own, and with Dick's blessing, he took possession of a used 1968 Hurst Dart (not a Landy team car, however) and converted it to look much like Dick's 1969 A/MP car. A serious accident at Orange County in a Duster-based Pro Stocker during the 1973 season perhaps slowed his professional career, but he returned very successfully to sportsman racing soon afterward, first with Chryslers and later with Chevrolets. Lambeck and his son Doug, now driving, posted several event victories in the ensuing seasons, including back-to-back Super Stock titles at the NHRA U.S. Nationals in 1998–1999. Today he remains close to the Landy stomping ground through the operation of Bob Lambeck Enterprises, his engine-building service in Northridge, California.

With Mike in the army, young Bob Lambeck became a member of the Landy team. He drove cars primarily on the West Coast and continues racing today. (Photo Courtesy Landy Family Archives)

Bob Lambeck's name was stickered into the Dart's windows in 1968. He had the misfortune of losing the first round at the NHRA World Finals in Tulsa after gathering the highest points in the nation in Division 7 Super Stock racing. (Photo Courtesy Landy Family Archives)

Furthermore, it is believed that this same Dart was test-driven for a *Motor Trend* story by Eric Dahlquist just before the shop installed the 4-speed combination. This vehicle was Dick's personal race car for the rest of 1968. The automatic car arrived, was completed by the shop, and then became part of the West Coast cars that Bob Lambeck took responsibility for driving. During the rest of 1968, Bob drove it in addition to the 440 EA model while chasing his big-sum NHRA World Championship Series (WCS) points, but he likely regretted having decided to use the Hemi instead of the wedge when he came to Tulsa for the World Finals that October. The only Landy team car on hand at the NHRA season finale, Bob red-lit in the opening round to get a long quiet ride home as his sole consolation. That's drag racing.

Bristol rolled out the carpet for the Landy team, with this marquee at the local Holiday Inn. Dick also did clinics during this trip. (Photo Courtesy Landy Family Archives)

How SS/B Becomes S/SE

One unique feature of the second-generation A-Body Dart that came about in 1967 was its easy interchangeability of parts. Among the VINs found in Dick's files was one for a 1968 318 Dart. This vehicle could well have been bought to replace one of the SS/B cars simply in pieces; John Dianna mentioned in a 1970 article on Dick's new Challenger Pro Stocker that one of the Darts had to be completely rebuilt in 1969, as it was worn out. The effects of the pinion snubber against the floorboards, especially on a 4-speed car, could literally toe in the frame rails of the unibody models. Regardless, when Dick and the crew showed up in 1968 for the AHRA's newly acquired Spring Nationals at Larry Carrier's Bristol International Dragway in June, they had the 4-speed Dart ready for the special heads-up SS/E class, which was part of Saturday night's big show.

Indeed, a number of teams attended. These included the Bob Banning guys (doing double duty with a Funny Car), Sox & Martin, and a handful of Brand X guys, including Bill Jenkins and 1968 NHRA Winternationals winner Al Joniac in a NASCAR tunnel-port Cobra Jet Mustang. Among Gean Landy's resources are a number of slides showing the car taped up for SS/E, but victory was not to be. Sox won to become the first national event titlist in a Hurst-built Hemi car that evening.

The heads-up Charger was left at home after Lions in 1968. Dick raced the Dart in AHRA's next SS/Experimental eliminator during Bristol's newly resanctioned Spring Nationals. (Photo Courtesy Landy Family Archives)

Ronnie Sox poses on the Sox & Martin hauler in front of the 1968 Barracuda and one of the B-Body cars. (Photo Courtesy Landy Family Archives)

Here is the Hemi Dart running at the 1968 NHRA Springnationals, held that year at Englishtown, New Jersey. Bob Lambeck went to the semifinals at this event in the 440-ci Dart before falling to winner Ronnie Sox. (Photo ©TEN: The Enthusiast Network. All rights reserved.)

The Super Stock Magazine Nationals returned to New York National Speedway on Long Island in 1968. Although Dick was frustrated in competition, wheels-up launches were becoming part of the program, as seen here. (Photo ©TEN: The Enthusiast Network. All rights reserved.)

Once blueprinted, the Hurst cars were a very easy fit into this heads-up category, as well as in NHRA-legal SS/B and SS/BA form, but Dick Landy was frustrated by a number of factors while driving these cars in Super Stock during 1968. Most notably, it seems the Barracuda models were more efficient in class racing at first; in fact, they won almost every national title in Super Stock from Indy 1968 until Ron Mancini took a Dart to back-to-back wins in 1970 at York and Indy. It should be stated that Bob Lambeck did very well in Division 7 with his example, but the team's meticulous prep at the new shop played a big role in that.

Nonetheless, Dick won a couple of match races with the Dart that season, and his best was one of his last of the 1968 season, a big wheel-standing win over Bill Bagshaw's new *Red Light Bandit* in late October at Orange County,

By the time the Super Stock Nationals rolled around, the Hurst A-Bodies were in abundance. Here is Dick in staging between an unidentified Dart and Bill Stiles's Barracuda. (Photo Courtesy Landy Family Archives)

Four young men take a look at the Landy team rig in the hotel parking lot near the big event at New York National Speedway. (Photo Courtesy Landy Family Archives)

where he also set low ET and top MPH at 10.46/131.19. Regarding the new Lions class for super stockers that subsequently resulted, colorful Lions Drag Strip operator C. J. Hart informed a *Van Nuys News* reporter the following month that "weak sisters, sandbaggers, and journeyman handicappers had better stay home; we're running heads-up racing here!" Because Dick had been asked by Chrysler to focus more on Modified Production, he was already heading in that direction. Following the Street Eliminator win at Pomona in the *Flying Wedge* Charger in early 1969, he spent most of the season in MP with the Dart, preparing for what became Pro Stock.

A late-season charge saw Dick on the cover of Drag News. The Dart was now getting some big air under the front end for the new heads-up class at Lions. This antique issue is Dick's personal copy, making it a one-of-one artifact. (Photo Courtesy Landy Family Archives)

Dick proudly wore this jacket after being named Super Stock Engine Builder of the Year by Car Craft readers in late 1968. (Photo Courtesy Landy Family Archives)

1969: Call the MPs; Pro Stocker Forerunners

The Chrysler factory had no interest in following the Darts and Barracudas with new models in 1969. There had been little change in the design, and the cars remain unchallenged as the best of the Super Stocks, even with the arrival of cars such as the all-aluminum 427 ZL1 Camaro and Boss 429 Mustang. For Dick, this sort of racing became even more mundane because the class structure now went down to SS/H, allowing the many small-block entries big head starts in eliminations. The Hemi Darts continued in the Landy racing program for the new season, but like the *Flyin' Wedge* Charger, they were often in Street Eliminator when Dick was on the loud pedal.

"I raced Ronnie at the big races for class a few times, and the factory said, 'Look, this isn't going to work,'" Dick told me years later. "You had to win class to get into the final eliminator; it didn't help the program when we're knocking each other off, so I got the ticket to go run Modified like Street Eliminator, and Ronnie stayed in the Super Stock class. That way there were cars in the different eliminators, and we got a lot of magazine coverage out of that, even though we didn't run for Stock class any longer."

Making the car legal for A/Modified Production did not require a host of changes. There was more leeway in the engine mods, and suspensions could also be upgraded, though Dick showed that he worked primarily with minor adaptations to the Chrysler-designed package. The real issues were weight balance and lightening changes, sometimes sending pieces to AeroChem for chemical milling, sometimes using research to create undetectable lightweight replacements for standard trim parts.

"Kent Fuller helped rebuild one of the 1968 Darts, and Dick sold the other one," says Mike Landy. "It was still a good car, and Dick just got the money out of it. He did that when stuff was just laying around; Chrysler was very nice to Dick, and we had lots of stuff; they were okay with him letting it go when we were done with them."

As a result, wheel-standing efforts became even more visible, and AHRA's basic formula of heads-up Super Stocks took the nation by storm. That year several independent events staged head-ups doorslammer classes, notably SS/X (Experimental) at the Super Stock Nationals. The AHRA found the formula to be so popular that S/SE was now part of each event.

A photographer from Petersen Publishing captured Landy in the office of his Dart at the 1969 Nationals. Note the cast and toes on his right leg. (Photo ©TEN: The Enthusiast Network. All rights reserved.)

Because it was not running in Super Stock, the 4-speed Dart was given a 1969 nose, which became another source of confusion for fans, especially when the car was marked S/S or S/S-E in AHRA trim. The new grille was released with little change from 1968 so this was a simple swap, and it was also legal for NHRA MP racing. Relettered with a new font for 1969, this upgrade gave Dick a current-year configuration to race and show at clinics, and Sox & Martin did likewise with their Plymouths not restrained by Super Stock legality.

Pomona

The A/MP Dart was the one Dick drove the most in 1969, and it would have been the most likely candidate to receive pieces from the 318 model

Original artwork for a never-published advertisement. The graphics show components from 1967 and 1968, perhaps something that Champion considered, based on the headline.

Tommy Erwin captured this image of the SS/E Dart at the 1969 AHRA Spring Nationals at Bristol. These vehicles were the direct predecessors of Pro Stock. (Tommy Erwin Photo; University of South Carolina)

Dick at the peak of his career prior to the advent of Pro Stock. The consummate professional, he had become a statesman of the sport. (Photo ©TEN: The Enthusiast Network. All rights reserved.)

The Dart was no longer being used in Super Stock and wore the 1969 panels in A/MP. Dick raced this car in class at Indy and ran the Charger in B/MP. (Photo ©TEN: The Enthusiast Network. All rights reserved.)

Herb McCandless talks strategy with Mike and Dick during the 1969 Nationals. Herb was working full-time with Sox & Martin by the time he won Pro Stock here the following season. (Photo Courtesy Landy Family Archives)

if it needed rebuilding. The possibility of a third Hemi Dart has been posited, but is actually unlikely.

In terms of actual racing, the year began with the team taking four cars to Pomona; Butch Leal was in the 1968 440 SS/EA Dart. As noted in Chapter 2, Herb McCandless started the weekend as driver of the *Flyin' Wedge* Charger with a Hemi installed. Bob Lambeck was in the team's normally automatic SS/BA Dart but was running here with one of B&Ms ClutchFlite transmissions in A/MP, while Dick was in the 4-speed Dart, also in A/MP. When he lost the final round to Sox in that car, he took over for McCandless in the B/MP Charger on Sunday and then won the entire Street Eliminator crown.

The A/MP Dart went to the winner's circle for Landy's second victory in three weeks when he took the Las Vegas National Open title later in February. He won a heads-up match race with the car at Detroit Dragway in April and won a similar race at Union Grove, Wisconsin. Racing the Charger as well, Dick had little time off due to the multiple clinics on many weeks that summer, and disaster struck when he broke his leg in a motorcycle accident during the July 4 holiday. The accident kept things quiet during the midsummer months for the cars he drove. When Dick showed up at Indy, he had a cast, crutches, and backing from *Motor Trend* magazine for eliminations.

While all this was going on, Bob Lambeck continued where he had left off. For 1969 his name was added to the sides of the cars, now reading "Landy/Lambeck," and again he ran primarily West Coast circuit races. The spring Division 7 Super Stock Jackpot Circuit took him all around California, and he finished in the runner-up spot behind the Ed Terry Ford team in that series with a final-round showing at Fremont in the Dart and a win at Half Moon Bay in the Hemi Super Bee. The summer found additional success for him: wins at Irwindale, Carlsbad, and, in late September, the points meet in Amarillo, Texas.

Indy

When Indy took place over Labor Day Weekend in 1969, the Landy entries were an invasion. Two Chargers, two Darts, and at least one Coronet appear to have been

The B/MP Charger won class, but the 1969 Nationals were otherwise uneventful for Landy's army and the A-Bodies. With racing done for the weekend, the crew loads up the cars to head down the road after the Big Go. (Photo Courtesy Landy Family Archives)

Although the factory released a fresh 1969 440-ci Dart package, Bob Lambeck continued with the version from 1968, shown here at an Irwindale test day. (Photo Courtesy Landy Family Archives)

on hand. Because Dick was not competing here in the higher echelons of Super Stock, the racing politics of this controversial race and the so-called Mopar Mini-Nationals did not affect him, but the team had Lambeck's legal car here in SS/BA, possibly with a third, unidentified driver.

This is what transpired. By figuring the drivers would have to race flat out to win the huge program, the NHRA intended to use all the weekend's Super Stock class runs to reset all-new indexes. To create a 36-car field, the NHRA qualified only the class winner and the next-quickest car per class. So one by one, the Chrysler-associated racers in SS/B, BA, CA, and DA (nobody was in SS/D stick) quietly left the track on Friday and drove a couple of hours to a little track in Hamilton, Ohio. No other vehicle brands were racing in these classes that weekend. The Mopar racers then ran their own private class race there, three runs per competitor, with the agreement that only the two quickest cars from each class came up to the staging lanes for the real Indy class races on Saturday. These two then "staged" a single slow elimination round to get cars into each class's two positions without hurting the indexes.

"I didn't have anything to do with it that year," Dick told me later. "I was always in a meeting with Farmer Dismuke at NHRA, trying to get them to set up a deal for us to run heads-up though; no more of the handicap/index BS."

At any rate, the team's SS/BA Dart was not in that class pairing, and the car stayed on the trailer the rest of the weekend. With those indexes left exactly where they had been to start with when handicapped eliminations got underway, Hemi cars dominated the Super Stock field and the NHRA could do nothing about it. The following Tuesday morning, with many of the best names from both the racing fields and the Detroit manufacturers on hand, the NHRA sat down and the group hammered out the basic rules for a Pro Stock class for 1970. These were finalized in October.

Lambeck was in the SS/EA Hemi Super Bee at Indy, and Dick was in the Charger in B/MP and won class, but the A-Body Darts did little at the Big Go for 1969. A/MP was so crowded that some factory guys also had cars in B/Gas. At Indy, Dick also picked up his first Challenger from Chrysler, which was the basis for his new heads-up Pro Stocker for 1970. Soon after, Dodge also released a conversion parts package that made it possible to change a 1968 Hurst-built Dart into a 1970 model for the same reason. Still, the 1968-turned-1969 Modified Production Dart ironically led off the winning charge into 1970 for *Landy's Dodges*.

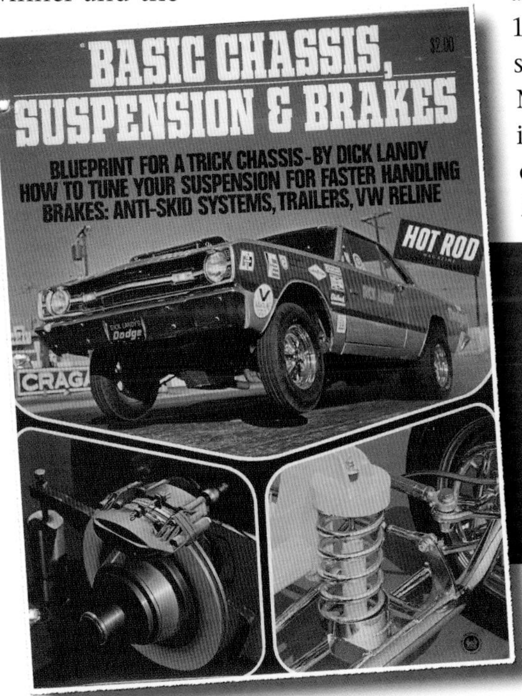

Many such volumes had Chevrolets on the cover, but the 1969 Dart was on the cover of this special suspension publication produced by* Hot Rod *magazine. (Photo ©TEN: The Enthusiast Network. All rights reserved.)

1970: Dart Program in Pro Stock and Modified Production

Dick knew he would be very busy in 1970. Indeed, in a group of terse, short letters Dick had to apologize to acquaintances at Chrysler and explain why a June trip to Detroit had not allowed him to meet with everyone. Time was very tight. First of all, the shop was doing most of the 16-plug cylinder head conversions for the factory that year; other work was mostly related to either the team race cars or the Chrysler business association. Second, the AHRA and NHRA had both greatly expanded their schedules for 1970, limiting the number of off weekends to the bare minimum. Finally, the clinic program was still going to dealerships, but it actually slowed a bit for 1970, both because its promotional aspects were changing and some in management felt its benefits had run their course.

Although the Challenger was now the most visible entry for the team in racing, one of the Darts, likely the automatic that Lambeck had been racing, was given a dramatic upgrade to 1970 Swinger specs. The new Swinger had replaced the GTS as the sport model that year, and the Dart was no longer available from the factory with a big-block. While the basic Dart substructure remained mostly unchanged, the sheet metal was massaged from the 1967–1969 design to a more slick appearance, and a number of teams did the conversion on 1968 Super Stocks.

In addition to redesigned front-end pieces, this swap required a portion of the rear quarter panels and the tail panel to be removed and replaced by welding in 1970 panels. Dodge made this easier with a set of conversion instructions and all the parts needed to make the swap. In a period interview, Dick noted that the benefit of the Dart might be additional overhang, but it does not appear to have been effective, and very few of the 1970 Swinger Darts remained in the Pro Stock ranks once the new Demons arrived in 1971.

Once again, Bob Lambeck was the primary driver of this car, as it stayed on the West Coast most of the season. In fact, to keep the car in the running for the season-long standings, Bob traveled with it across the Northwest's Division 6 that year, winning in places like Mission, British Columbia, to take home that division's Pro Stock crown for a seeded spot at the World Finals. He also drove the team's 1970 SS/EA Charger closer to home to put that *Landy's Dodge* via points into the top berth of Super Stock for Division 7.

With Pepsi onboard as a new associate sponsor and the Pomona Fairgrounds as a backdrop, Dick took home a big win at the NHRA Winternationals to start the new decade. (Photo Courtesy Landy Family Archives)

This is believed to be the former Landy/Lambeck automatic Dart, converted using panels supplied by Chrysler. It is seen here at Bakersfield in March 1970. (Photo Courtesy Landy Family Archives)

We are not sure who carried Pro Stock number 390 in NHRA competition at Bakersfield in 1970; we do know that the Dart required attention, likely a differential gear change here. (Photo Courtesy Landy Family Archives)

Pomona 1970: The Double-Up Deal

Home for Landy had always been Pomona, and the tenure of his sportsman-class gas-powered Darts that began with the win in SS/EA class in 1968 ended with a second-consecutive overall victory in what had just become Modified Eliminator. The muscle car era and factory participation had changed the face of drag racing by 1970, and the NHRA had just combined a number of former Competition and Street classes into Modified and moved the faster and hotter cars, including supercharged altereds, into a reformatted Competition Eliminator category.

The Dart was set up to run B/MP at this event; there were not a lot of rules revisions, and it is likely that Dick realized that the car could be weighed down to the very top of the B class rather than fight it out heads-up in A/MP with a bunch of other entries. It was a solid calculation, as he again was the class winner. Then he proceeded to march through Sunday's field to meet the same team he had raced for the Street crown the previous season, the J/Gasser of Stickel & Riffle, now with Rod Shop backing and Jim Thompson behind the wheel. At the green, Thompson was red, and Dick legged out a new B/MP record of 10.74 to return to the winner's circle at Pomona for the second time in as many years.

This Dart doesn't really show up again; the team built a clinic Challenger that ran in C/MP that year. A flagship team for Dodge running a past-year model did not help dealerships sell new cars. The 1968 440 Dart was raced at Pomona under Lambeck's tutelage, but he used the new Hemi Charger in EA for the rest of the season. As

The winner's circle at Pomona. This was the first of Dick's two national-event titles in 1970 and his final big one in sportsman racing. (Photo Courtesy Landy Family Archives)

The Return of Landy's Dart Circa 1993

Following verification of the automatic car by Dick Landy, owner Ed Vandersnick put the car back into period-correct paint. In 1993, Carlisle hosted its second Chrysler-only event, which honored the A-Body Hurst cars and featured one of the largest gatherings of them in a nonracing setting. A true highlight for many attendees was a trek to the little 1/8-mile South Mountain Dragway for a match race between Dick in this car and a 1968 Barracuda that was being match raced by Ronnie Sox at the time. With gold dust down and engines revved up, the duo accurately re-created the past for a couple of hours in a wonderfully historical facility.

Landy looks directly at me through the windshield of the automatic Dart in 1993, when it was first restored, 35 years after the cars had shown up to terrorize drag racing.

The ritual of laying down gold dust for traction was part of this event. Both Dick and Ronnie Sox broomed it into their respective lanes.

"Gee, Dick, can't I just find you a match?" Ronnie Sox and Dick Landy, 1993.

things changed for the Dodge program toward the end of 1970, Bob bought a Hemi Dart and went out on his own in Pro Stock. Contrary to later assumptions, Bob noted at the time that this car had not previously been associated with the Landy program, though the paint scheme he selected was quite similar. Throwing Darts from the Landy corner was far from over, though.

The door was open on purpose, to gauge traction and tire tracks. It was as if Dick had never quit driving.

In the Carlisle indoor display, Dick talks with Ed Vandersnick while Gean waits in the car. This picture was taken just before they left for the match race that afternoon.

Dick drives during Modified eliminations on Sunday at Pomona. He reset the class record to 10.74 in the final round. (Photo ©TEN: The Enthusiast Network. All rights reserved.)

Where Are They Now?

The two Dick Landy Hurst-built Darts were among the most storied of the Hemi race car collecting hobby, and both have survived to the present. As we know from Dick's personal notes, the automatic version became the 1970 Swinger Pro Stock. After its day in the sun with Lambeck, the car was sold and was later changed back into a Super Stock-legal 1968 Dart. After contacting Dick with the VIN and some additional data on the car's details found during disassembly for a collector restoration, owner Ed Vandersnick verified with him that this was indeed the real car. It was eventually restored to its as-raced 1968 trim with a DLI engine. Its first major public debut was at Chryslers at Carlisle in 1993, and Dick actually drove the car at the 1/8-mile South Mountain Dragway that weekend in an impromptu match race with Ronnie Sox. Since then, it has changed hands twice. It now resides in a private collection.

Where Are They Now? *CONTINUED*

The 4-speed car also ended up back in the Super Stock ranks and was raced for about a decade. It was purchased by a noted Mopar muscle car collector in the mid-1980s as a rolling chassis, with no lineage to its provenance. The owner removed a number of the original parts, including the Airheart brakes, believing them to be simple aftermarket upgrades.

It was not until Daryl Klassen of Canada purchased the car as a project that the possibility of its original Landy ownership came to light. After Dick verified the Dart as authentic, Klassen began to put the car back into as-built form, as he had a background of restoring them. However, aware of its collector value, he later traded it as a rolling chassis to Fred Engelhart, in part for another near-complete 1968 Hurst Dart. This car has now been restored to a 1968/1969 appearance, with 1968 body panels but some of the 1969 paint details. It is presently in the Todd Werner collection.

The SS/EA car remains unaccounted for, though it is rumored to still exist. All 1968 440-ci Darts featuring Mr. Norm provenance are rare and are in great demand by collectors, but Dick's name is reportedly not on the list of those owners submitted to the NHRA in early 1968. It is certainly possible that strings were pulled to have this car converted with a proper VIN and then shipped to California before the remainder of them were built. Regardless, this car's lineage remains shrouded as to its subsequent use once the team was done with it.

The 4-speed Dart as it sits today in Todd Werner's extensive collection.

The interior was quite sparse in the Darts, but Dick used a factory wood-grain steering wheel in the car.

The circa-1968 legal Super Stock engine in the Dart today. Dick used a more modified version in 1969.

1973: Dart Sports and World Championships

Although Detroit's muscle car era had succumbed to changing mores and tastes by the time the 1973 drag racing season began at the AHRA Winter Nationals in Arizona, the Pro Stock class was alive. Perhaps a plus for the purveyors of minicar/small-block combinations, it was again a frustrating time for Mopar racers. During the off-season, a rule that Chrysler wanted to see enacted was a minimum weight of 2,300 pounds for the minicars. Some critics noted that on the 6.5 weight break from small-blocks, this would force the mouse-motor combinations to go to about 350 ci, eliminating the higher-RPM advantages of the Chevy 302/327-ci configurations. For Chrysler, though, reducing weight on the Hemi E-Body and A-Body models was very expensive and difficult. Even at the 2,400 (later 2,300) minimum, the Chryslers were still locked in at 7.0 pounds per inch (approximately 340 ci), and there really was no small-block development to speak of yet.

For the new year, Dick teamed up with noted chassis builder Kent Fuller to go back to the A-Body, which was now a Duster-like fastback called the Dart Sport. Fuller entered the Pro Stock business with specific direction from Dick on its build design.

"We [eventually] built four of those cars," Dick noted in an interview in 2004. "One went to Irv Beringhaus, Larry Huff, myself, and a team named Miller & Son got the other one. I don't think they ever raced it; they tried to run it at an 1/8-mile track and ran it off the end and crashed it. The roll cages were strong, a little ahead of their time, so luckily no one got hurt."

According to an overall review in the June 1973 *Super Stock & Drag Illustrated* magazine that featured Dick's ride, the biggest change in the Pro Stock business was lightweight materials, including titanium fasteners and brake assemblies, with body panels so thin that polyurethane foam was sprayed on them from behind for support. Although a complete Hemi engine from some builders cost only about $5,000, just a set of Bob Mullins–ported D4-style heads cost almost $1,600. Of course, DLI was doing all this in-house. The Hemi bottom end came in four basic configurations: 366-ci, 396-ci, 405-ci, and 426-ci. There was no benefit to anything larger in Pro Stock, though fuel-engine assemblies to 480 ci or bigger were available. By now, the earliest Lencos were on the scene and quickly gaining favor.

For Dick in 1973, the choice going in was a 404-ci engine with a Moldex crank, DLI heads, a Crane roller cam with Isky valvetrain parts, a Weiend intake, and Holley 4500-series 6214 carbs. The car still had the blueprinted A833 4-speed and was backed by a 5.57 Dana rear. Most important were suspension changes that used Landy's own wheelie-bar/four-link design. In front, a reduction of shock travel kept the lightweight front wheel tight in the wheelwell even under launch; the car pulled the nose as easy as the 1965 Coronet had. Dick had a 366-ci Hemi combination as well and could get the car down to an amazing 2,562 pounds when needed.

It is not noted whether many aero changes were deliberately made on this car; knowing Dick's willingness to experiment, there were some obvious things that even Fuller had little to do with. By now, factory-associated

Moving from the Challenger to this new Dart Sport was part of the Landy team's 1973 efforts. Dick is seen here at Beeline Dragway in Arizona at the car's first big event. (Photo ©TEN: The Enthusiast Network. All rights reserved.)

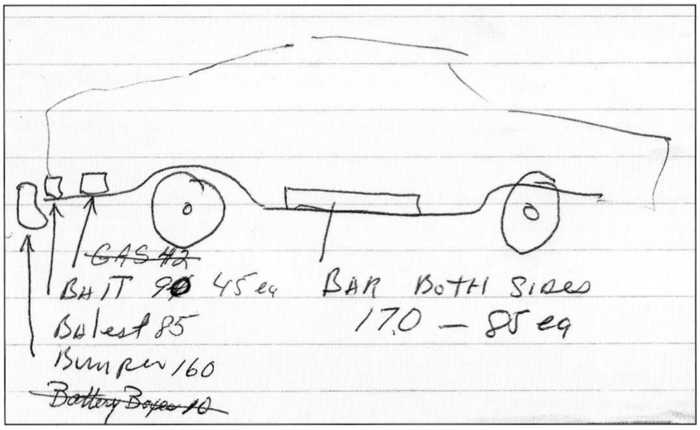

This sketch by Dick shows how the team hoped to put weight into the car they built for Irv Beringhaus. The frame-based ballast within the wheelbase made a big difference. (Photo Courtesy Landy Family Archives)

program cutbacks had left just Dick, Butch Leal, the Rod Shop, Sox & Martin, and the in-house *Mopar Missile* running under the auspices of Chrysler.

"The Landy/Fuller A-Bodies were basically all started at the same time, and my dad took the first one," recalls Robert Landy. "The jig and the bulk of the frames were done at Fuller's under my dad's direction.

"I was seven when I first toured with the team; I was the hot dog chaser. But I grew up in the shop, since I had motorcycles and stuff, and if we would do work around there on the evenings and weekends, we could make a little extra money. Grinding, lightening rocker arms, fiberglass work, anything he could explain to me how to do.

"We dropped the front ends of the Dart Sports. Since Fuller's shop was right down the street, the frames were built there, he hung the quarters and roof, and then we would work on them from that point. We pulled the nose down about an inch, so I helped mark up the fenders and did the trim work to fix that. We pinched the nose too. We needed to narrow the hood and get that just right; there were no templates for that. We pretty much eyeballed it. Later we got caught by the NHRA and were told to get the nose back up. I think we went about halfway and had to do another dropped nose."

Meanwhile, virtually all the competitive Chevy and Ford racers were in small-block equipment. Bill Jenkins did not follow up on his 1972 NHRA championship; that went to Wayne Gapp's 351-ci Pinto, which was the dominant combination for 1973. Butch Leal and Don Carlton each won an NHRA race, as well as a couple of runner-up finishes. Jenkins again won the Summernationals, where Dick had lost a rear wheel in the 1972 final, and the Pintos won everything else that season. Dick went three rounds at Pomona and then went match racing. He qualified number one at the March Meet but broke a differential

The United States Racing Team program continued into early 1973 but was hampered by internal politics and did not survive to the end of the season. This is the final program the group published. (Photo Courtesy Landy Family Archives)

Dick's 9.07 at the start of the season sent shock waves through the drag racing community; again Dick's car made the cover of* Drag News. *Again, a collector's item today. (Photo Courtesy Landy Family Archives)

Head-on, the Dart Sport's front-end design was recognizable. As in the past, wheel standing helped herald the latest Landy machine. (Photo ©TEN: The Enthusiast Network. All rights reserved.)

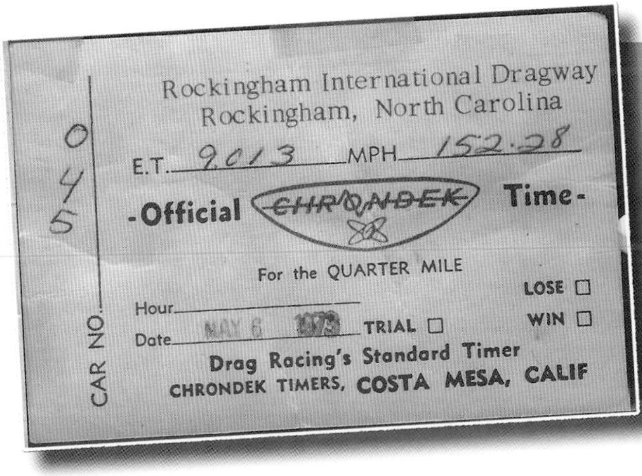

Rockingham International Dragway
Rockingham, North Carolina

E.T. 9.013 MPH 152.28

-Official CHRONDEK Time-

For the QUARTER MILE

Hour

Date MAY 6 1973 TRIAL ☐ LOSE ☐ WIN ☐

Drag Racing's Standard Timer
CHRONDEK TIMERS, COSTA MESA, CALIF

CAR NO. 045

In late spring, the car clocked this very solid 9.01 at IHRA's big national event in Rockingham, North Carolina, to take low-ET honors. (Photo Courtesy Landy Family Archives)

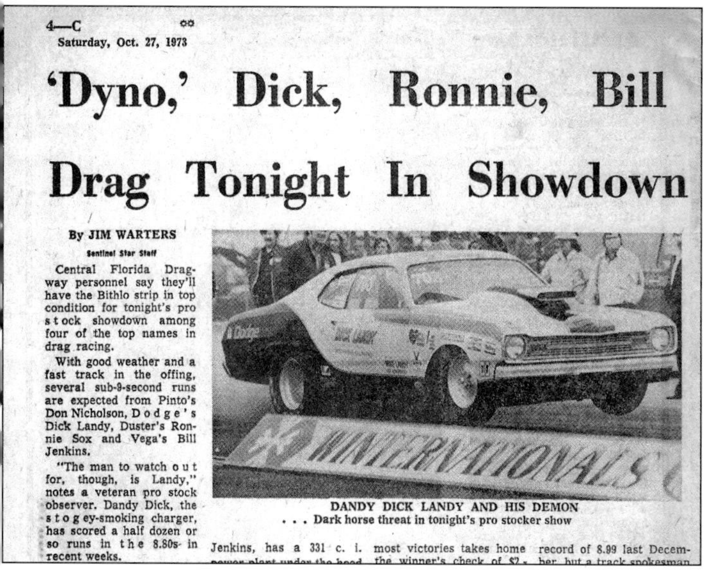

4—C
Saturday, Oct. 27, 1973

'Dyno,' Dick, Ronnie, Bill Drag Tonight In Showdown

By JIM WARTERS
Sentinel Star Staff

Central Florida Dragway personnel say they'll have the Bithlo strip in top condition for tonight's pro stock showdown among four of the top names in drag racing.

With good weather and a fast track in the offing, several sub-9-second runs are expected from Pinto's Don Nicholson, Dodge's Dick Landy, Duster's Ronnie Sox and Vega's Bill Jenkins.

"The man to watch out for, though, is Landy," notes a veteran pro stock observer. Dandy Dick, the stogey-smoking charger, has scored a half dozen or so runs in the 8.80s in recent weeks.

DANDY DICK LANDY AND HIS DEMON
. . . Dark horse threat in tonight's pro stocker show

Jenkins, has a 331 c. i. ... most victories takes home ... record of 8.99 last Decem-

Here is a headlining act: Dandy Dick, Clean Ronnie, Dyno Don, and Grump. Gean Landy saved many regional news clippings that showed Dick's cars. This one is from a paper in Florida. (Photo Courtesy Landy Family Archives)

in the first round. He went to an All-Pro Series final at OCIR the same month, and then he won the All-Pro Finals there over Butch in early April with a track record 9.17/149. He also qualified second, set low ET/top MPH, and posted a runner-up to Don Carlton in the *Missile* at the IHRA Pro-Am race in Rockingham, North Carolina. The new car was working very well.

However, on his way to the NHRA Springnationals in Columbus, the transporter was totaled in an accident on June 1. Through Chrysler, Dick was given the chance to drive Stu McDade's Dart, an ex–Don Carlton car, at this event. He missed the Ohio field by .009. The Dart Sport was repairable and went back East for the Summernationals a month later, but it may have had an interesting, albeit temporary, replacement in the meantime.

"The worst damage I know for any of the Challengers was actually the 1971 Sylmar earthquake," recalls Robert, "when one of the cars happened to be parked under the tire rack the night before. I was only 10 at the time, but I do remember seeing the car buried in Goodyears, Cragars, and wood with some miscellaneous parts thrown in for added ugliness! Trashed it; bodywork, paint, and ran it through. That car sat around and later got yanked from mothballs. It then had a Lenco stuffed in it to fill in during the wrinkled Dart era, probably during the truck wreck rebuild."

The rest of NHRA 1973 was nondescript for Dick, with some dramatic wheel stands but no cigars for actually winning. Conversely, on the AHRA circuit, Landy's Dart Sport was dominant. After going two rounds at Beeline Dragway's season opener, Landy fired his first shot at

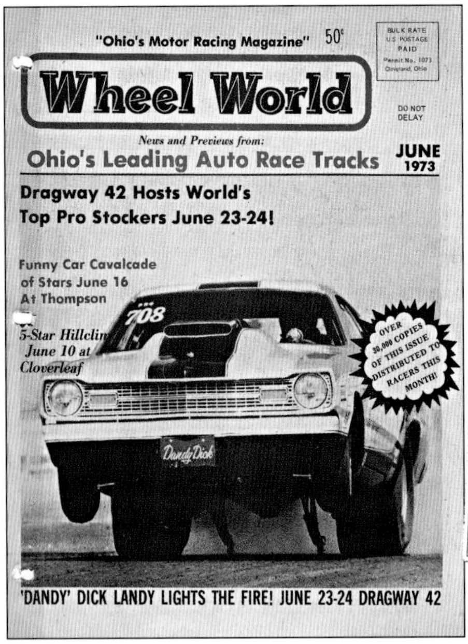
"Ohio's Motor Racing Magazine" 50¢

BULK RATE
U.S. POSTAGE
PAID

Wheel World

DO NOT
DELAY

News and Previews from:
Ohio's Leading Auto Race Tracks

JUNE
1973

Dragway 42 Hosts World's
Top Pro Stockers June 23-24!

Funny Car Cavalcade
of Stars June 16
At Thompson

5-Star Hillclimb
June 10 at
Cloverleaf

OVER 30,000 COPIES OF THIS ISSUE DISTRIBUTED TO RACERS THIS MONTH!

'DANDY' DICK LANDY LIGHTS THE FIRE! JUNE 23-24 DRAGWAY 42

The changes that resulted in minimal shock travel, leaving the wheel tucked up close to the car, helped many fans relish Pro Stock racing. This defunct local Midwestern newspaper was a free giveaway to promote regional racing. (Photo Courtesy Landy Family Archives)

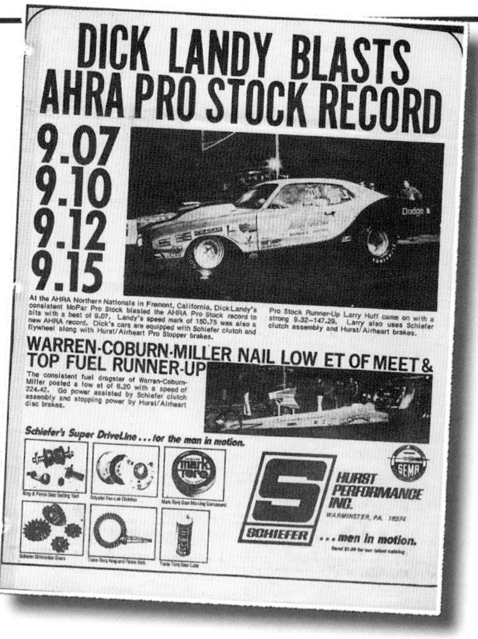
DICK LANDY BLASTS AHRA PRO STOCK RECORD

9.07
9.10
9.12
9.15

At the AHRA Northern Nationals in Fremont, California, Dick Landy's consistent MoPar Pro Stock blasted the AHRA Pro Stock record to bits with a best of 9.07. Landy's speed mark of 150.75 was also a new AHRA record. Dick's cars are equipped with Schiefer clutch and flywheel along with Hurst/Airheart Pro Stopper brakes.

Pro Stock Runner-Up Larry Huff came on with a strong 9.32–147.29. Larry also uses Schiefer clutch assembly and Hurst/Airheart brakes.

WARREN-COBURN-MILLER NAIL LOW ET OF MEET & TOP FUEL RUNNER-UP

The consistent fuel dragster of Warren-Coburn-Miller posted a low et of 6.20 with a speed of 224.42. Go power assisted by Schiefer clutch assembly and stopping power by Hurst/Airheart disc brakes.

Schiefer's Super DriveLine ... for the man in motion.

SCHIEFER
HURST PERFORMANCE INC.
WARMINSTER, PA. 18974
... men in motion.

Sponsors such as Schiffer Clutches noted the big numbers. This was one of many ads that ran after the Fremont race. (Photo Courtesy Landy Family Archives)

AMERICAN
AHRA

DRAG WORLD

OFFICIAL PUBLICATION OF AMERICAN HOT ROD ASSOCIATION

Vol. 10, No. 39 (COPYRIGHT AMERICAN HOT ROD ASSN., INC. 1971) Friday, October 5, 1973

The AHRA newspaper Drag World *heralded the fact that Dick would go into the final race of 1973 already crowned the champion. (Photo Courtesy Landy Family Archives)*

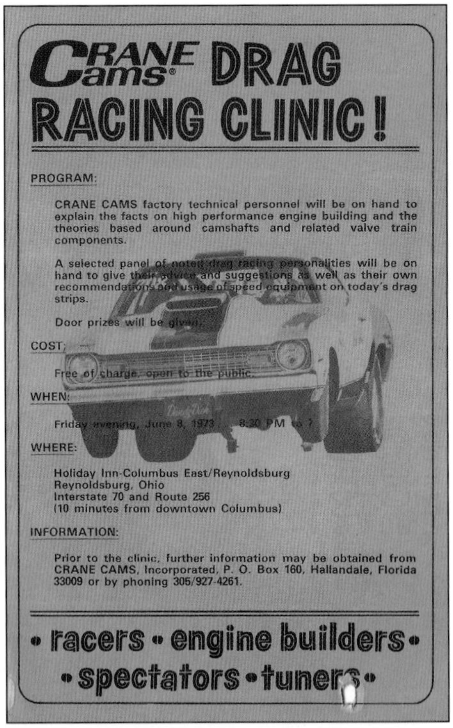
CRANE Cams® DRAG RACING CLINIC!

PROGRAM:

CRANE CAMS factory technical personnel will be on hand to explain the facts on high performance engine building and the theories based around camshafts and related valve train components.

A selected panel of noted drag racing personalities will be on hand to give their advice and suggestions as well as their own recommendations and usage of speed equipment on today's drag strips.

Door prizes will be given.

COST:

Free of charge, open to the public.

WHEN:

Friday evening, June 8, 1973 8:30 PM to ?

WHERE:

Holiday Inn-Columbus East/Reynoldsburg
Reynoldsburg, Ohio
Interstate 70 and Route 256
(10 minutes from downtown Columbus)

INFORMATION:

Prior to the clinic, further information may be obtained from CRANE CAMS, Incorporated, P. O. Box 160, Hallandale, Florida 33009 or by phoning 305/927-4261.

• racers • engine builders •
• spectators • tuners •

The dealership clinic era had ended, but Dick still did displays and seminars regarding performance. He also maintained sponsorships from companies such as Crane, which used his image in this promotional flyer. (Photo Courtesy Landy Family Archives)

Fremont's Northern Nationals. In fact, he and the new car obliterated the sanction's current Pro Stock records by running a best of 9.077 and never went less than 9.17. He won the race and took the MPH mark up to 150.75 before the weekend was over.

In the other lane was DLI customer Larry Huff in a Sox & Martin Challenger that Dick had done some work on. To show it was no fluke, Dick was low qualifier at the Bakersfield March Meet; won an OCIR open Pro Stock show in April, repeating the 9.17; and then won the NHRA WCS title at Sacramento with another 9.07 in qualifying and a 9.17 over Bill Bagshaw in the final.

He went out in round one at AHRA's summer event in Tulsa, but at the AHRA Spring Nationals near Denver, with his high-altitude tune-up, Dick qualified number one at 9.76 and then satisfyingly beat Jenkins in the final. At Dragway 42 in Ohio, he went to the final and Jenkins got him, but not the points lead. At the Gateway Nationals at St. Louis, Dick won the event over the Kimball Bros.' Vega. By the time the season was winding down again in Fremont, where Dick had lost the 1972 title to Don Nicholson, he had accumulated 5,200 points and had already won the championship. Larry Huff was second at a distant 3,700 and received a new car from the Landy/Fuller camp for the 1974 season.

Achieving a world championship is an amazing feat for any driver. For Dick, perhaps most satisfying was that this was based on a consistent season-long effort, not some lucky day at the NHRA World Finals. Indeed, the NHRA changed that for 1974. However, the rules for Pro Stock continued to make things frustrating for Chrysler racers, and unique solutions were part of 1974 and 1975.

"We don't talk about that much. People forget about the energy crisis and that whole mess. We did have factory support, but we raced as independents, so the federal government couldn't go to Dodge and say, 'Oh, you guys are using money to go racing.' We even had to take the word *Dodge* off the car to make sure there were no problems. That's why it doesn't show up in a lot of photos of the car."

Dick Landy summed up his position on the sport in that quote, which he gave me when his Dart Sport was restored. The mid-1970s was somewhat a trying time for America. Watergate, OPEC, and other crises dominated the headlines. The fact that Chrysler did not have a small car for Pro Stock was overshadowed by the reality that it did not have a small car for the street either. When the energy crunch hit, it suffered more than its competitors. It also suffered on the track, in NASCAR, and in drag racing, as displacements and weights came to favor smaller, lighter engine structures and cars. The Hemi stubbornly remained the bread and butter of Chrysler racing, though work was ongoing for a small-block cylinder head.

1974

For all of that, 1974 was not a total loss. In light of the rules, under factory edict, Dick did not run much NHRA or AHRA Pro Stock. The team built the SS/D Challenger that Dick ran at a number of major events. Due to AHRA rules changes, he ran both that car and the Pro Stocker at the Grand American at OCIR in April, resetting records in two classes in one day (E1 to 10.61 and A/G to 9.05).

But match racing was not over, and if rules could be agreed upon, *Landy's Dodge* remained a "have gun, will travel" competitor. Former teammate Ken Dondero had landed in Bill "Grumpy" Jenkins's car that year, and in June Dick took a two-out-of-three win right in the Grump's backyard, Maple Grove Raceway near Reading, Pennsylvania, with a 9.17 best.

Although summer was uneventful, September found a victory at the AHRA race at Firebird Raceway in Boise, Idaho, with a 9.37/148 best. Sonny Bryant had become a serious West Coast racer, but Dick trailered him there as well as at another open race at Orange County.

Beyond all that, Dick and Mike were busy with projects for other people. The most notable client was the late Larry Huff, a colorful character who ran a variety of business ventures, including Soapy Sales and Dyna-Gym. Huff was unrestricted by Detroit and did a great job with DLI power in the Landy/Fuller Duster he had bought for the new year to win the shop its second-consecutive world championship in 1974. Huff also fielded a serious Funny Car effort at this time, but he drove the Pro Stocker himself. The third car the team had built, for Irv Beringhaus, was sold in late 1973, and Beringhaus bought an ultralight Pinto for the new year to replace it; he was killed in a horrific high-speed accident at the season-opening AHRA race of 1974 shortly thereafter. It was a harbinger or sorts for Dick and 1975.

1975

Rule changes were not dramatic for 1975. The biggest issue in some cases was wheelbase, and several Ford racers went back to the circa-1970 Mustang body to take advantage of it. The AHRA had likewise followed suit on wheelbase changes after Huff's title, and IHRA rules were

Dick was one of a handful of Chrysler racers still competing when Indy 1975 rolled around. Note that Dodge had been removed as a sponsor by this time. (Ray Mann Photo, Courtesy quarter-milestones.com)

The 1973 car soon after it was done. Note the sponsor logos here; times had changed for Pro Stock and for Dick Landy. (Photo Courtesy Pit Slide Series, quartermilestones.com)

modified as well, though the little Colt was legal there. It was a long year.

After Dick qualified and went just one round at the first AHRA race in Arizona to open the 1975 season, he (as well as others) chose to take the exotic Pro cars down into Modified for the NHRA Winternationals. The Dart Sport won class handily and then went three rounds. As he had in 1974, Dick chose to run AHRA Modified as well when things got underway at OCIR. He reset the B/Gas record, won class, and then won the entire event. By this point the Dodge name had been replaced by paired Mopar/DLI logos on the rear quarter panels.

In May things picked up dramatically as the match races got underway. A minor rules adjustment following the NHRA Gatornationals did not affect the Mopars but put some other combinations in check. Meanwhile, DLI had found some power. On the West Coast Pro Stock Association circuit, Landy won back-to-back wins at Tucson and Albuquerque, setting track records at both tracks. Then it was to Fremont for a WCS NHRA event, again with a win and with an 8.90/154.37 best for low ET and top MPH. This was followed by a second WCS win in Seattle the next month, again with track-record numbers.

With those solid runs, the team towed all the way to Columbus, Ohio, for the NHRA Springnationals, only to lose in round one, ironically to Larry Huff. July brought the highlight and the darkest hour of Dick's 1970s A-Body racing. In Seattle for the Olympia All-Pro Nationals, Dick ran a match racing combination to clock an unreal 8.55/159 in round one, the fastest times any Hemi Pro Stocker had run to that date. He backed that up with an 8.63 single in the final to beat Bill Jenkins, who broke. Then disaster struck.

Racetrack operation in the 1970s was shoddy in a lot of cases. Dick left Seattle with a car that likely could have run with anything in the country and then raced Jenkins in Vancouver on a second trip into Canada that

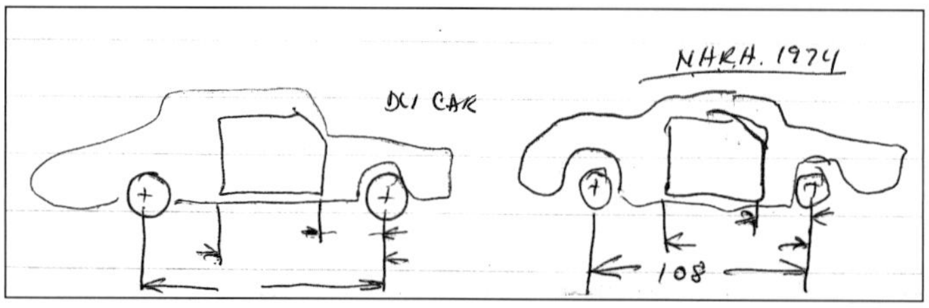

Some changes were needed for 1974. Dick sketched out the points of measurement that NHRA would be using for technical inspection.

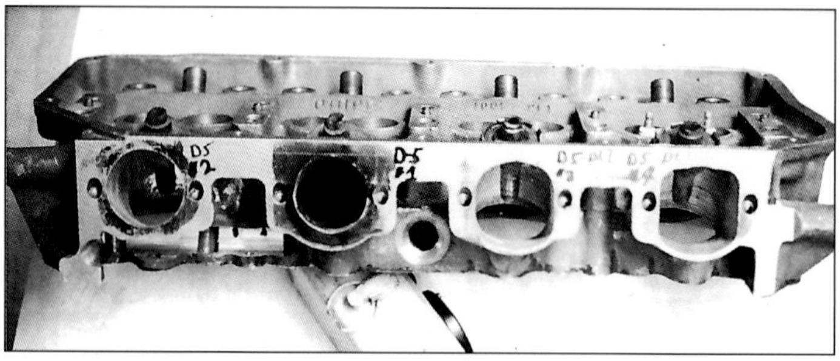

A port flow comparison on a D5 head. The port designs are (left to right) Westlake, Mullen rework, DLI design 1, and DLI design 2. (Photo Courtesy Landy Family Archives)

The car built for Larry Huff. It became the 1974 AHRA World Champion, as Dick was instructed by Chrysler not to compete in sanctioned Pro Stock to protest the rules. (Dan Williams Photo)

At the 1975 U.S. Nationals, photographer Dan Williams captured this image of Dick racing a 1971 Mustang, which some Ford teams used to take advantage of the rules on wheelbase length.

A D5 Pro Stock intake. Mike and Dick found, through testing, that a 9.7 runner length was optimal on this design. (Photo Courtesy Landy Family Archives)

The Dart Sport at the 1973 Winternationals. Weather hampered the running of the event, but the rules hampered the Mopar entries even more. (Photo ©TEN: The Enthusiast Network. All rights reserved.)

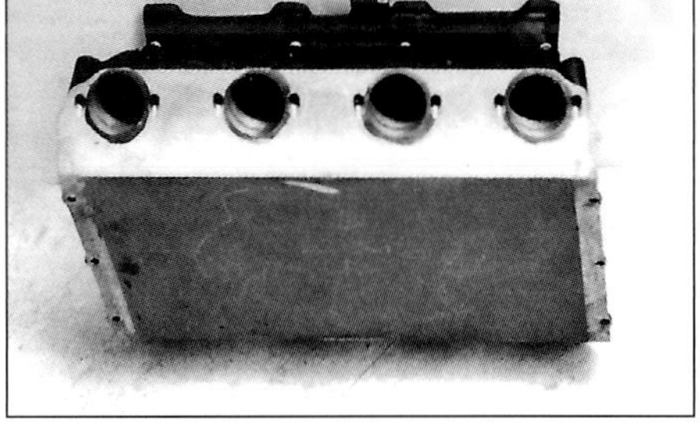

The port side of the D5 Pro/Stock intake as first designed. (Photo Courtesy Landy Family Archives)

The Portland guardrail following the accident. Note the missing upright that Dick broke on impact. (Photo Courtesy Landy Family Archives)

year, one that was broadcast on a local TV station. The duo left there to go to Portland, Oregon, for a booked-in race that featured several Pro Stock cars, including Dick and Jenkins, as well as TV Tommy Ivo against Shirley Muldowney match racing in Top Fuel.

Run in the evening, the final was set after the two nitro dragsters had just raced, and it was again down to Dandy Dick versus Da Grump. There had been some issues in the fuel race moments earlier, but the track operators had not checked the track surface for fluids, and Dick launched the Dart into the darkness. At half track, witnesses later reported, the car slid violently in oil, which in turn caused one front wheel on the stiff front suspension to come completely off the car.

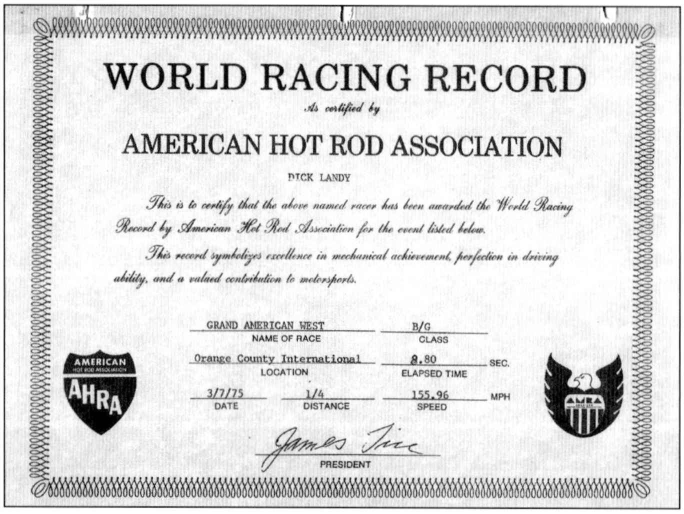

WORLD RACING RECORD

As certified by

AMERICAN HOT ROD ASSOCIATION

DICK LANDY

This is to certify that the above named racer has been awarded the World Racing Record by American Hot Rod Association for the event listed below.

This record symbolizes excellence in mechanical achievement, perfection in driving ability, and a valued contribution to motorsports.

GRAND AMERICAN WEST — NAME OF RACE
B/G — CLASS
Orange County International — LOCATION
8.80 SEC. — ELAPSED TIME
3/7/75 — DATE
1/4 — DISTANCE
155.96 MPH — SPEED

James Tice — PRESIDENT

During the boycott era, Dick sometimes ran in B/Gas. He set an AHRA record at OCIR at 8.80/155 in March 1975. (Photo Courtesy Landy Family Archives)

Moreover, during a guardrail repair prior to the event, one of the wooden uprights had been installed *inside* the Armco rail at trackside. This post was what Dick Landy hit at speed that night. It instantly pushed the front suspension directly into the driver's area, breaking multiple bones in Dick's foot and ankle. The car then pole-vaulted from that impact back onto the track and landed on its roof, skidding and grinding down the track at more than 100 mph. Indeed, the car still stopped the timers at 9.29.

This accident was a little more serious than the truck flip two years earlier. Indeed, Dick's foot damage was severe, though written reports at the time described it as "simply a broken ankle." Dick often thought about safety and considered the risks when he strapped into the car, but this had been irresponsibility by the operators. Lawyers became involved and litigation ensued. It was not a happy ending for anyone, but Dick Landy did get justice before it was all over several years later.

"My dad was not a 'sue happy' person, reluctant to participate in such things from any side, but not cleaning the track and that post sticking out was gross negligence," Robert Landy notes now. "Believe me, he paid dearly for the rest of his life with effectively a club foot and the associated suffering. In reality it was the track operators, their crew, and ultimately the sanctioning body that were responsible for that. My father sued them and won, on what points exactly and for how much I don't know."

On the mend and taking care of business with the boats and customers at the shop, Dick likely did some testing on the car prior to Labor Day. Now rebuilt for the third time, the Dart showed up for the U.S. Nationals, and Dandy Dick Landy was there as its pilot. By October he was driving regularly again. In one weekend of West Coast Pro Stock Association events, he went to two final rounds, both against the Vega of new Division 7 champ Lee Hunter. This resulted in a runner-up at Irwindale and a win at Fremont. He won the NorCal Nationals at Fremont soon afterward, again beating Hunter.

November found Ontario Motor Speedway opening for Saturday-night races, and Dick finished his 1975

With its streamlined grille and fresh appearance, the former Larry Huff car was riding high at Pomona. (Photo ©TEN: The Enthusiast Network. All rights reserved.)

efforts with a victory over Butch Leal, who was driving Roy Hill's Duster that night.

However, the rules situation for NHRA racing became no better. Indeed there were no less than 20 possible Pro Stock combinations during the 1975 season. That year, the Ford Cleveland was hammered with a 7.15-pound-per-inch weight break for vehicles featuring a 105-inch or greater wheelbase and an even tougher 7.30 break for under-105-inch wheelbase cars, effectively putting the Cleveland Fords out of competition. The Hemi stayed at 7.0 pounds per inch but received a 40-pound overall weight break. Conversely, the big-block Camaros received a huge 80 pounds off, and they in time took the dominant position in the category, although Wally Booth won the championship in an AMC in 1976.

David Carl Peters created this evening-light portrait of the Dart hooked up at Bakersfield, site of so much of Dick Landy's noted history. (Photo ©David Carl Peters. All rights reserved.)

1976–1977

In early 1976, Dick posted top speed at Tucson, now site of the AHRA opener, at 153.58, qualified third, and went two rounds. He was also at Phoenix and Pomona, both now NHRA-sanctioned. He won two events in March, at Ontario and Sacramento, but Pro Stock's rewards were fleeting, and outside of match racing and an occasional foray into the field when the tour was nearby, Dick had become tired of all of it. The first Dart Sport met its final demise in a weird late-season on-track accident.

"Yeah, the third time was a loser for that car," says Robert. "This happened not too long after the wreck in

The Huff car with its original paint. (Photo Courtesy Landy Family Archives)

The "For Sale" ad for the ex-Huff car from late 1978. (Photo Courtesy Landy Family Archives)

Portland, but it flattened a slick and went into the guardrail hard. My dad walked away from that, but the car was done. I was not there, but I know the car took a hard left into the guardrail about mid-track. I do remember seeing photos of the floppy tire track, and it might have been a testing accident, not at an actual race."

Dick got in touch with Larry Huff, who was also changing course for 1977, and bought the car Larry had run so well.

"I had built that car for Larry Huff at the same time I had built my own, and he sold it back to me," Dick recalled later. "As soon as we got it, we took all the stuff we had learned on the first one and changed the car over. We put a whole new rear suspension under it. I drove the car for a few more years. It was the final car I toured with as a driver."

The year 1977 found Dick once again leading the points race in the West Coast Pro Stock Association, and he was reported in *Drag News* to have totaled 2,695, with Sonny Bryant at a distant second with 1,707. Dick ran as fast as 8.78 in April of that year. By this time, things had changed substantially for all Chrysler racers due to the business environment, and the continued NHRA factoring of the Pro Stock class created additional frustrations.

Repainted in Dick's traditional colors, the ex-Huff car featured backing from dealer Norm King Dodge in Glendora. However, Dick Landy's career as a driver was effectively over not long after the purchase of this car. It was raced primarily in West Coast match races and then retired. The final Dart Sport left the Landy stables in late 1979, when Dick turned his attention to the new Omni/Charger designs and began serious development work on a small-block program in-house at DLI. He would no longer be driving, however; those chores were given first to Mark and Brad Yuill, and later old friend Ken Dondero took over.

An uncredited image from the Boise, Idaho, Firebird Raceway shows Dick smiling in the winner's circle. (Photo Courtesy Landy Family Archives)

The Final (and Little) Landy's Dodges

The little Omni that arrived in 1980. It made use of the small-block engine package that Chrysler was developing. (Photo Courtesy Landy Family Archives)

Following about a year's hiatus from racing, Dick Landy came back to competition, but not as a driver. Development on the W2 cylinder head for the Chrysler LA-series small-block had shown much promise, and the new imported minicar marketed as the Dodge Omni (later Charger) offered a suitable platform for the powerplant. Moreover, new NHRA rules adjustments gave the little wedge room to run (and even the Hemi cars received a little break that year).

Dick turned to veteran car builder Don Hardy for this latest vehicle, and he and Mike began designing the new engine. Very little of this powerplant was used as built; the cylinder heads had serious changes to their port layout, a Crane rollerized valvetrain allowed high-RPM shift points, and DLI was fairly quiet about what it was building into the package. The car ran 8.60s in testing with Brad Yuill as the driver; by early 1980, despite some additional adjustments by the NHRA, the car was down into the 8.50s. Also, in June 1980, Dondero came back into the fold to drive for Landy once again.

"That car came alive with Ken Dondero at the wheel," laughed Robert, who worked on the crew during this era. "He did exactly what my dad told him to do. . . . 'Scream the !X$%# out of it. You let me worry about the motor!'"

"The Chevrolet guys began making sheet-metal intakes, and when we went to small-blocks, we began our first custom-made manifolds," says Mike Landy today. However, no amount of work could overcome issues with the rules. The engine work was expensive and time-consuming, and the rewards were to find out that the sanctioning body was going to change things again. In August 1981, a story published in *Hot Rod* called "Dandy Dick Tells All" showed how extensive the reworking had been, as Dick also noted that he was done racing as well.

"The NHRA came at him with prohibitive weight breaks almost as soon as the Omni started running well, perhaps even while teams were still in the last of the Darts," says Robert in retrospect. "All said and done, the sanctioning body won that butting of heads by basically forcing my dad to quit. He did not want to. I remember my dad literally throwing his hands up in very great despair and saying, 'I can't win this way!' after getting refactored again. That is when he ran the *Hot Rod* article. He had so much money, time, and effort wrapped up in the development of that super-trick and barely realized car. No one really knows! I do recall the Omni was retired as the quickest and fastest small-block Mopar P/S ever."

The car had run a best of 8.42 at more than 161 mph at the time of the article. Ironically, in October 1981, the NHRA also decided it was done with factoring politics as well and went to a simple 500-ci/2,350-pound weight for all models for 1982.

Ken Dondero later drove the car to some impressive low-8-second performances. (Photo Courtesy Landy Family Archives)

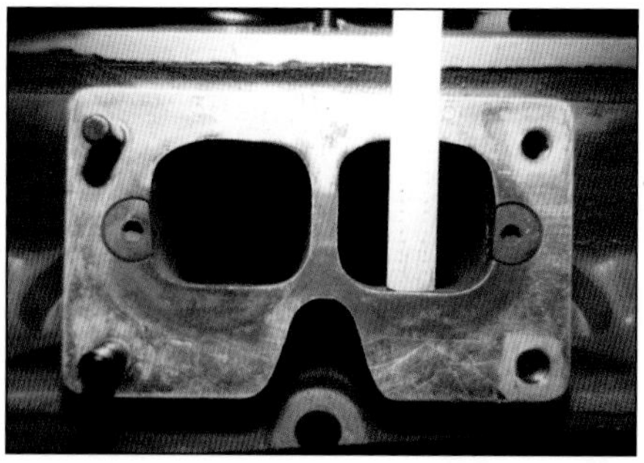

Work done on the W2 package. The plate was attached to the head and then ported open for better airflow. (Photo Courtesy Landy Family Archives)

The W2 combustion chamber shows the reshaping of the valve pockets. The inline design left little room for an additional exhaust valve size. (Photo Courtesy Landy Family Archives)

A DLI piston in the W2 head. Deep machining for valve reliefs was needed, and small gas ports can be seen at the upper edge. (Photo Courtesy Landy Family Archives)

Dick created a complete sponsorship proposal for 1983 for Unocal 76, but when there were no takers, the team was disbanded. DLI subsequently focused on work for other racers. (Photo Courtesy Landy Family Archives)

Where Is It Now?

The final remaining Dart Sport, once owned by Larry Huff and the final A-Body raced by Dick Landy, was basically sold as a rolling chassis and had a short life in the defunct West Coast Pro Gas series under the tutelage of Dave Giese. Giese bought the car for $11,000 and chose not to modify it heavily, installing a wedge engine and then simply parking it in the garage after only a couple of race seasons.

With some assistance from Dick himself, supercar locator Dean Klein of Minnesota was able to buy the car in 2002. He turned to Landy as well as restorer Erik Lindberg to bring it back to mid-1970s specifications. After the period-correct parts were located, Dick and Mike built a DLI restoration engine for the project, using a standard 426 bottom end and a Lenco combination. Most important was that many of the period pieces were still with the car thanks to its brief use and some extras located through Don Grotheer. When Klein decided to thin out his collection several years after completing the project, the car was sold. It is presently with noted race car collector Marco DeCesaris.

The Kent Fuller-built 1973-era Dick Landy and Miller & Son cars were both noted as totaled. Neither the ex-Irv Beringhaus Dart nor the small-block Hardy Omni have been located as of this date.

The detail of Landy's Pro Stock interiors impressed many. They even featured faux wood grain like that used in the 1973 factory model.

The restored Landy/Fuller car that Dick bought from Larry Huff after his own car was damaged beyond repair in testing.

Dick Landy built this 426-ci engine for the Dart's restoration, using parts and pieces that were correct to the time it was built.

Hemi Mopars in Pro Stock were in the twilight of the era when Dick finished his driving career in this car in 1978.

CHAPTER 4

E-BODY ENERGIZERS 1970–1972

The first version of the Dodge Challenger was, frankly, a bottle rocket. Introduced in 1970 as the final all-new major release to emerge during the muscle car era from Detroit, it lasted a short four-and-a-half model years before all Chrysler E-Body production was discontinued in mid-1974. For Dick Landy, the new Challenger was more than just a sporty car. It marked the culmination of his dealership clinics, gave him his most visible national event crown, and placed him into the highest echelons of Pro Stock, a class that had taken the sport by storm when it had showed up for the first time at the 1970 Winternationals.

He ran the E-Bodies in the professional divisions of the NHRA, AHRA, and IHRA until 1973. He returned to the 1970 body design one final time in 1974 as a Super Stock racer when Chrysler chose to boycott the Pro Stock class as a result of the ongoing rules changes.

The E-Body models proved to be iconic stylings. In fact, Dodge gave the design new life in the 21st Century through a popular retro-styled version, and original Hemi-powered convertible examples of this car and the sister 'Cuda by Plymouth are the most highly desired collector muscle cars today. In keeping with VP Bob McCurry's philosophy of "more car for the same price," the Challenger was marketed as a competitor to the Mercury Cougar and was actually not much smaller than the B-Body models that preceded it. As a result, in some ways it unfortunately did not satisfy either the smaller pony car or the midsize muscle car market. It also arrived at the same moment insurance hikes began to affect performance vehicle purchases, which did not aid the situation.

Nonetheless, available with a plethora of options that first year, the Challenger R/T was an exciting addition to the Dodge Scat Pack, and Dick had examples with both the Hemi and the Six Pack engine. He had one that he later drove on the street. For drag racing in 1970, the Challenger fiberglass shell proved to be popular in Pro Stock as well as on Funny Cars. Alas, this year also spelled

The Dodge Challenger became one of Dick Landy's most important vehicles in professional racing. The 1970 car is seen here in action, during the first year of Pro Stock. (Photo ©TEN: The Enthusiast Network. All rights reserved.)

The 1970 press kit portrait of Dick Landy during his first year of Pro Stock. (Photo Courtesy Landy Family Archives)

The 1970 press envelope for the Dodge Scat Pack Performance & Safety Clinic shows its new logo. (Photo Courtesy Landy Family Archives)

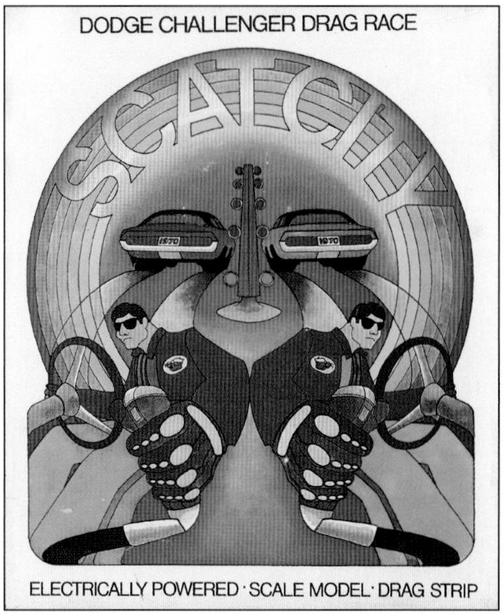

The cover of the new Challenger dragstrip giveaway set, which was available by raffle drawing at clinics and also from the Scat Pack Club. Surviving kits like this one are now very rare and expensive. (Photo Courtesy Landy Family Archives)

(DEALERSHIP)
presents
Dodge Scat City Performance Clinic
featuring
Dick Landy
(DATE) (TIME)

Meet one of the nation's top drag drivers, Dick Landy, and his Dodge super stocks.

The Dodge Scat City Performance Clinic includes an exciting racing film, a session of performance and safety tips, plus a chance to see the Landy super stock setup. While you're at the clinic, be sure to sign up for a chance to win a 1970 Challenger and other valuable prizes. If you're serious about performance, talk to a pro—Dick Landy—with the Dodge Scat City Performance Clinic.

DODGE SCAT PACK PERFORMANCE AND SAFETY CLINIC

LANDY'S DODGE

Ad No. D70-9

Ad No. D70-9
4 cols. x 150 lines = 600 lines—B&W
Advertisement prepared by
Batten, Barton, Durstine & Osborn, Inc.
to appear in
Newspapers—1970
P.O. D9-398

A newspaper advertisement showing the Challenger. Areas were left open for dealerships to note their personal information. (Photo Courtesy Landy Family Archives)

The year 1972 was Dick's final one in a Pro Stock Challenger. Note the parts on the doors of the transporter. (Photo Courtesy Landy Family Archives)

The staging lanes were full of Pro Stockers at the Popular Hot Rodding race in Michigan in 1970. Dick is seen alongside the Dick "Barney" Oldfield-driven Motown Missile of Ted Spehar. (Photo Courtesy Pitlideseries, quartermilestones.com)

the end of the in-dealership clinic display program. In 1971, before Chrysler annulled sponsoring the program entirely, most of the clinics were held at the racetrack using special display equipment. Part of this change came from Landy's own racing schedule, the result of the expanded NHRA, AHRA, and match race schedules. They involved a huge time commitment even with air travel, and scheduling was fairly hectic. On top of this, Dick managed the race shop and multicar teams.

Although the race-bred engine remained part of Pro Stock for some years, the production Street Hemi disappeared from the model line after 1971, at the same time the factory commitment to the clinic displays formally concluded. Although 1972 brought new excitement and acclaim to the Pro Stockers, dark clouds arose at the end of 1971 for the Hemi as a competitive racing engine when the sanctioning bodies sought to give other makes equality. As the 1972 season wound down, additional rules changes gave an advantage to longer-wheelbase models, and the era of the competitive E-Body Pro Stocker came to its end. Thanks to Dick's solid showings, well-publicized development work, and event wins, the Challenger would always be most associated with Landy's Pro Stock efforts.

The E-Body returned to the Landy fold during the boycott era with another Super Stocker. When Dick was invited to go up the hill at Goodwood in England, he reacquired this same vehicle, which uniquely served as the final car that he built and raced himself. Powered by a Hemi featuring the best DLI tricks, this machine was a fitting end to his career.

Even the Ford guys were mesmerized by the Challenger's unique developments. This crowd gathered at the 1970 Gatornationals. (Photo Courtesy Landy Family Archives)

1970: Dawn of Professional Stockers

Following the 1969 U.S. Nationals, the NHRA announced that it would be following AHRA's lead for a professionally oriented heads-up doorslammer division to be named Pro Stock. Many Super Stock teams quickly turned their attention to preparing new equipment for this division. NHRA rules were finalized just as the season ended at the World Finals at Dallas, with the following basic requirements for the new class: 7 pounds per cubic inch, minimum weight of 2,700 pounds, matched vehicle/engine by manufacturer, 2 x 4–barrel (or 4 x 2–barrel) carbs maximum, minor fiberglass part replacement, and stock-type interior.

For the Landy team, the process of creating a Challenger for this class likely began at the 1969 Nationals as well, which was also where Charlie Allen debuted the first Funny Car skinned in the new body. Seen in the pits that year with the plethora of Landy race entries was a Challenger R/T that the factory had just delivered to Dick. This was possibly the donor used for trim and components, as Chrysler's body-in-white program had gotten underway; several teams used production line performance car parts to prepare them. The body-in-white was an acid-dipped body shell that could be used as the carcass from which to build a race car, and again AeroChem on Batavia Street in Orange, California, did the job for the factory.

Although the race car was assembled in the team shop, the roll bar was fabricated at Exhibition Engineering. The class in its formative stages involved little more than A/MP-type equipment with minor changes. The interior needed to remain close to stock in appearance, and Gean Landy recalls finding materials that could be used as lightweight replacement backing for factory upholstery. The crew fabricated a new dash panel that housed mechanical gauges from longtime source Stewart Warner, and a set of 1968 Super Stock seats was in the car at first.

To prevent radical unseen changes, Pro Stock entries were mandated to a 55/45 front-to-rear weight distribution, an amount that still allowed some minor redistribution for balance. To make the front suspension as light as possible, the crew mounted 1967 Dart hubs and spindles to the front, with 1967 upper ball joints welded to the Challenger's control arms. Again working with longtime sponsor Hurst, the crew mounted race-designed Hurst Airheart front discs to this arrangement. The team chose to run a similar Hurst Airheart disc assembly on the differential housing; that adaptation was completed with help from Ronnie Scrima of Exhibition Engineering.

The frame consisted of 2 x 3 .050 square-tube subframe connectors, with additional .060 side plating on the rear frame rails. Because this was integral to the rear subframe, this change was likely necessitated by the weaker condition of this all-important component after its time in the chemical milling process. Of course, the change put more weight toward the rear of the car as well.

Dick goes up against Bill "Grumpy" Jenkins at the first NHRA Pro Stock race, at the 1970 Winternationals semifinals. Alas, it was the Grump's day, but Landy's Dodge was an NHRA race winner later that year. (Photo ©TEN: The Enthusiast Network. All rights reserved.)

The racing rear suspension included a well-braced pinion snubber and a pair of recurved Super Stock rear springs, which were moved inboard for tire clearance via 1/2-inch offset hangers. The front mount position brackets for the springs were equipped with multiple-point adjustment brackets, and a secondary lateral tube ran between and through the two rear frame rails just above the rear universal joint to brace the pinion snubber.

The exterior exhibited the always sanitary Landy condition. For example, the glass inner headlights and the parking lights were replaced with spun-aluminum disc covers. One additional safety point involved holding down the unlatched hood using a pair of nylon straps that went from the hood to the splash pan; this setup was on the car very early and may have been the result of flexing during the initial testing of the car. Two pins were

Dick Day of Motor Trend *magazine examines the new Challenger R/T with Dick Landy (on crutches following a motorcycling accident) at the 1969 NHRA Nationals. It is not known what engine was delivered with this car. (Photo Courtesy Landy Family Archives)*

Note the somewhat stock appearance of the trunk area with its factory mat. A Super Stock battery and high-volume electric fuel pumps are also visible here. (Photo ©TEN: The Enthusiast Network. All rights reserved.)

fitted at the rear of the hood as well, and Pro Stock Challengers in particular were noted for buckling their thin hoods at speed, resulting in "flutter" that could crack the fiberglass. The scoop at this point was a simple Six Pack model. The front fenders were also fiberglass.

The driveline was straightforward and identical to what had been in the Dart, a B&M-blueprinted slick-shift A833 New Process 4-speed backed by a 4.88-ring Dana 60 rear. Cragar wheels on all four corners were the crowning

Longtime friends at Exhibition Engineering helped build the new Pro Stocker, including adapting Hurst Airheart brakes to the rear axle assembly. (Photo ©TEN: The Enthusiast Network. All rights reserved.)

Dick attended to a never-ending list of details, including making and receiving various calls on the shop phone. (Photo ©TEN: The Enthusiast Network. All rights reserved.)

The heavy undercar bracing for the pinion snubber beneath the Challenger. This layout prevented the floor of the car from being stressed by hard launches. (Photo ©TEN: The Enthusiast Network. All rights reserved.)

A modified Landy 16-plug head being assembled for Hot Rod *magazine's first big story of the project. Tubes used to properly position the plug in place without stripping have been press-fitted to the second, or B, position. (Photo ©TEN: The Enthusiast Network. All rights reserved.)*

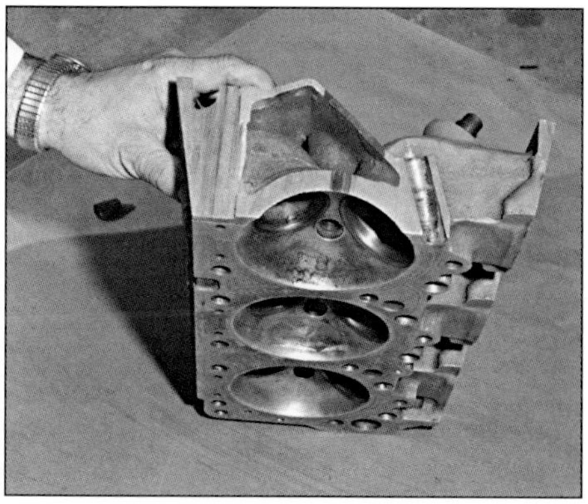

This cross-sectional view of the head shows where the new plug was positioned. Dick used 1965 A990-type Super Stock heads for this initial work, so racers had to bring their own versions. There is no written verification of how many sets were actually created, but many factory Pro Stock teams had them by midseason. (Photo ©TEN: The Enthusiast Network. All rights reserved.)

touch, with 5 x 15 models in front and 9 x 15 rear units. Goodyear was Dick's tire supplier for most of his career, and the tires were 8.25 up front and wide 12.25 slicks out back. Legendary SoCal paint man Nelson Carter of Imperial Customs was called on to prep the body and lay down the multicolored stripes once the car was done. Dick later figured it had cost $13,000 to build and equip the first car.

Sweet 16

Tom Hoover noted in *HEMI: A History of Chrysler's Iconic V8 in Competition* that the company had gone to BRM in England for advice on putting a second spark plug on the 426 design; this had happened in 1969. Dick Landy recalled later that seeing this during a visit to Detroit was the catalyst to putting it to work on the new Pro Stock engine. Truth be told, this work was likely not completely independent of factory oversight, but it is firmly believed that no one had this combination on a race car before he did.

John Dianna covered some of this development in an extensive analysis of the 1970 Landy Challenger in the May 1970 issue of *Hot Rod*. Dick had taken a set of aluminum heads and had them machined to accept a second plug directly opposite the original location. On gas, the Hemi had a tendency to foul plugs at lower RPM levels. The second plug never proved to be a huge purveyor of more horsepower, but the setup did help clean up lower RPM–level combustion considerably.

Dave Rockwell noted that the Ramchargers fuel team had done the first 10 sets of heads, but DLI had the job of doing another 100 castings (50 sets) for the factory. In Landy's case, it is thought that these were all 1965-era A990 aluminum castings or identical re-creations. The new plug location was positioned straight into the head and tapped for threads. Next, a section of tubing was spot-welded above this location for supporting the plug tube inserted through the valvecover, which also had to be modified for the second location.

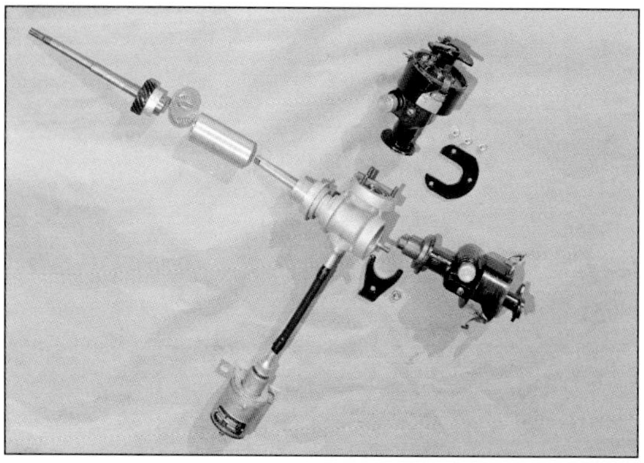

As first created, the distributor was a very complicated piece of equipment. A 90-degree offset allowed the advance to be set for each distributor, and a single timing event sparked both sets of plugs. The biggest challenge was eliminating spark scatter at higher RPM levels. (Photo ©TEN: The Enthusiast Network. All rights reserved.)

This image of the engine shows how the valvecovers were modified. Note the twin coils on the opposite fender. (Photo Courtesy Landy Family Archives)

"Those first heads had premachined billet 'B' plug bosses and tubes inserted into specially machined heads," says Robert Landy today. "This was done using a press-fit bottom and then a heli-arc welded piece at the top to the back side of each aluminum head. I am quite certain DLI didn't do iron conversions. We had boxes of the tube-like aluminum billet plug bosses for years and years."

Memorabilia dealer Mike Goyda turned up this very rare recording with an image of the Challenger on its cover. It was possibly marketed as a Scat Pack Club promotional item. (Photo Courtesy Mike Goyda)

Part of the initial difficulty was getting two distributors to work in perfect sync, and a lot of time was spent making adaptions for this. Timing events were critical at the RPM levels this 13.0:1 engine would be spinning. Eventually, a Hilborn fuel pump drive was modified to accept the Chrysler oil pump drive that normally spun the keyed distributor. A set of thrust washers and spacers positioned the unit to the oil pump. Now two very short shaft distributors could be mounted to the unit, one at an offset of 90 degrees. One was machined to go into the standard oil pump slot and the other into the Hilborn's hex drive (with the additional mechanical tach drive coming off the same area 180 degrees from that), and additional machine work was needed to make it all work.

Next, with the two Prestolite boxes and coils wired in parallel, the primary distributor generated the initial spark demand, and both it and the second distributor were fired by this single event. It is not certain if all of this was done by Landy's crew or if it was a combination of efforts by them and Chrysler Engineering. At any rate, this extensive level of conversion was not like some of Landy's superfast new-model changeovers seen in certain years past, and track testing in the winter of 1970 appears to have been done quietly. The unit generated immediate attention and scrutiny when Dick arrived at Pomona for the first Pro Stock race.

As initially built, the rest of the engine was fairly straightforward according to *Hot Rod*. Dick used the lighter

Dick posted another semifinal finish to Jenkins at the first-ever Gatornationals in February. (Photo Courtesy Landy Family Archives)

A hard launch behind the starting line showed the bite was there at Bakersfield. Dick took home the win in the abbreviated field at the 1970 March Meet to get his first personal Pro Stock crown and Dodge's first title for the Challenger in Pro Stock. Bob Lambeck can be seen in the background. (Photo Courtesy Landy Family Archives)

The new Pro Stock Championship in Colorado found Dick again taking a victory in Pro Stock. The team was the dominant West Coast force in 1970.

pre-1970 blocks, blueprinted with a .020 overbore, 13.0:1 pistons, factory rods, and a.606-lift Chrysler Engineering–developed cam. A new intake manifold, low in profile, which author Bob McClurg noted in a period article was being developed with help from Edelbrock, was atop this. At this point the power potential from an open plenum region beneath the carbs had not yet been fully recognized. Although Dick's pre-Pomona filing paperwork noted that the engine would be using Race Hemi–type 3116 Holley carbs, he showed up with a pair of the just-released NASCAR-type 4500 Dominators on the intake instead.

Springing Out of 1970

Dick came into the NHRA season as one of the best-prepared Pro Stock competitors in the nation; the car had been built from scratch using the latest technology, and even with the experimental engine parts, it was capable of the sort of power that he had come to be known for. His most serious competitors were the usual hitters: Ronnie Sox for Plymouth, Bill "Grumpy" Jenkins for Chevrolet, and "Dyno Don" Nicholson for Ford. There were others, but these were the guys who knew how to win better than most. With 16 spots open for that first program at the 1970 Winternationals, a large field of racers was on hand to shoot for glory.

Landy qualified fourth at 10.11, behind Sox, Jenkins, and Wally Booth, and went to the semifinals before he clocked a red-eye against Jenkins, who went on to win. Of course, his day was not done, as he put the B/MP Dart into the winner's circle within the next hour. A couple of weeks later, Dick and the racers made their first trek to Gainesville, where the results were almost identical. He qualified fourth at 9.96 and went to the semifinals only to see Jenkins win again. To top it off, the NHRA told him as soon as the race was over that the exotic ignition system was being banned, as it was not an internal modification. It is unfair today to hazard a guess as to who pushed for this "letter of the law" change, but it required pressure from Chrysler to get it back into use again.

And that event seems to have ended Dick's bad luck for the spring of 1970. Soon after, the short tow to the Patch for the Bakersfield March Meet on March 14 found him winning another one of the funny triangular trophies after he beat Bill Bagshaw's Dart in the final. Then it was a string of solid finishes, including a win on March 27 over local racer Bob Jenkins at the Northern Nationals at Sears Point and a victory at the Seattle National Open soon afterward. So despite missing the series' first event at Fremont, Dick won the Division 7 NHRA 1970 Winter Circuit Gold Cup Pro Stock title with a total of $1,626 in earnings.

Back in SoCal the following month, he won a fourth straight race on April 17, this time at OCIR, with a 10.00 low ET/137.40 top MPH single in the final when his competitor's Maverick steering broke. In early May he went

Dick easily made the first 32-car program, which occurred at the Springnationals in Dallas. He is seen here in round one of eliminations on Sunday, June 14. (Photo Courtesy Jon Steele Archive, quartermilestones.com)

to the "Dirty D" (Detroit Dragway) for a six-car headliner event. Dick Landy was declared the victor when he won three of four matches; Sox won two of four, Dyno won three of three and then broke, and Jenkins was two of four. Landy's only loss came from dropping a driveshaft in round one, and he beat Dyno in the final with a great event low ET of 9.85/138.

Two weeks later was another big deal, the Colorado Pro Stock Championships at Continental Divide Raceway in Castle Rock. Landy was featured on the cover of the program and dominated the 16-car show, winning over Bill Bagshaw and clocking a 10.77 for a new high-altitude Pro Stock track record.

Back to the Big Ones

In June, the big-show tour got underway again. At Bristol's AHRA Spring Nationals the weekend after Memorial Day, Dick showed that his hard development work was paying off when he took the pole at 10.13 over a large field of competitors and then went all the way to the final round only to fall to Sox on a very close hole-shot, 10.23 to Dick's 10.21. Sox, who was now having a stellar season, took Dick out a week later in round three at the NHRA version of the event in Dallas, Texas, which featured a 32-car program.

Dick had not had a lot of luck at the Super Stock Nationals at York US 30 Dragway in late May, but the NHRA scheduled its new Summernationals event at this same Pennsylvania track in mid-July. Landy, ever cognizant of front-end weight, showed up with a set of experimental 3 x 15 Cragar front wheels that looked like shiny discs. This was the first set of the new Super Trick wheels released. On Sunday afternoon, the wheels and the car ended up in the winner's circle after four rounds of racing, running 10.0 times. In the final, Herb McCandless, now full-time with Sox & Martin, left a little early to red-light, and Dick used a slowing 10.38 to win. Other parts changes for this stellar showing included the newest Hooker headers with 2¼-inch pipe, also heralded in post-event advertising.

That the first Summernationals ended up being Dick's only victory in NHRA Pro Stock never crossed anybody's

Dick faced off against Ronnie Sox in round two. Sox was not to be denied, and before the day ended, he took home the first of his very dominating 1970–1971 Pro Stock race titles. (Photo Courtesy Jon Steele Archive, quartermilestones.com)

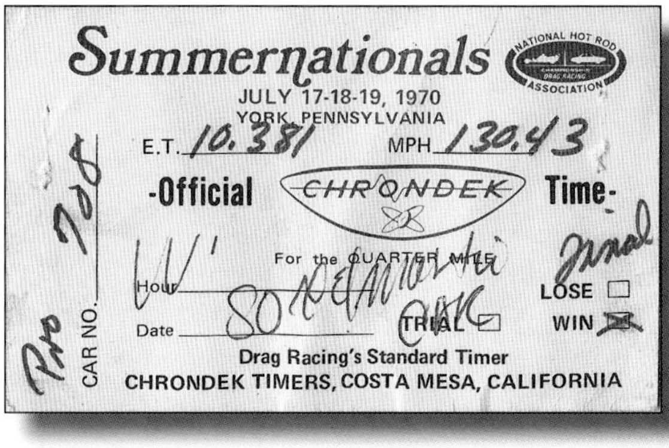
NATIONAL HOT ROD ASSOCIATION

Summernationals

JULY 17-18-19, 1970

YORK, PENNSYLVANIA

E.T. 10.381 MPH 130.43

-Official CHRONDEK Time-

For the QUARTER MILE

LOSE ☐

WIN

CAR NO.

Date

TRIAL

Drag Racing's Standard Timer

CHRONDEK TIMERS, COSTA MESA, CALIFORNIA

The handwritten time slip from Dick's 1970 win at the NHRA Summernationals. This was the highlight of his career in professional-class drag racing outside of the 1973 AHRA World Championship.

mind at this point. The car was running consistently well, but Pro Stock development never stopped. The top qualified car at York was the new *Motown Missile* Dodge, which not only had dual-plug heads but had a Clutch-Flite similar to the one Lambeck had used in the A/MP Dart at Pomona, along with other tricks. In fact, when Dick had beaten driver Richard "Barney" Oldfield during this event, *Super Stock* magazine had called it the upset of the meet. Still, cutting-edge factory development for all Chrysler racers was often thanks to the *Missile*, and this type of support helped frustrate all other makes until the NHRA changed the rules to favor less-competitive combinations. In the end, these were indeed the best of times.

At Indy, Dick fell in Pro Stock to Melvin Yow in a 1968 Dart on a holeshot, and later, with a 10.17 best, Dick ended up as first alternate at the World Finals in Dallas, which featured a 16-car program with the division-seeded cars. Because Bob Lambeck was already seeded into Super Stock with the SS/EA Charger, he was not driving the Pro Stock Dart here, shutting out the team in Pro Stock entirely. Two rounds of action at the new Supernationals at the just-opened Ontario Motor Speedway ended the national event tour, but that weekend was highlighted with a lengthy television program on Dick Landy and Pro Stock racing. By then, the 1970 car had been updated with a 1971 grille and trim, but it was showing its year of use.

The match race trail out West had proven to be better than national event efforts. Just before Indy, Dick drove both cars on one weekend, chasing points for Dallas: He went to Seattle to qualify the Dart and then flew to Salt Lake City late that night to qualify the Challenger at Bonneville Raceway the next morning. An early afternoon flight back to Seattle netted a Saturday-night round-one loss, but he returned to Utah on Sunday to win the Division 6 WCS event. Bob Lambeck also put the SS/EA Charger into the winner's circle here for a double Landy victory.

Then, on October 2, Dick won the final Division 7 race at OCIR. He went to Fremont on October 9 to race the Drag-On Lady, Shirley Shahan, and her AMX. This event witnessed the Landy Pro Stocker, which had often used rosin, now doing smoky burnouts.

The year ended with the formal announcement that due to budget cuts, Dodge was choosing to end the clinic programs. The funds were not completely eliminated, as Dodge continued some support of specific race teams, but Dick seriously reformulated his clinic programs for 1971. In the October 16 issue of *National Dragster,* Dick announced new plans for 1971: There would now be a formal DLI engine business, and the clinics would take place at racetracks. Besides, after 210 days on the road that year, he was ready to make some changes.

The Other 1970 Challenger

In addition to the Super Stock Charger and Darts, the team had a second Challenger that was primarily for clinic work in 1970. This factory-built V-code 440 Six Pack Challenger was raced on very rare occasions. Classed into C/MP, the car appears to have been a fairly standard model, almost identical to the Pro Stock machine in appearance. There is no record of it using a Hemi on the days it raced. It would be safe to assume that the focus on racing Pro Stock professionally placed all other vehicle programs that Dick might have

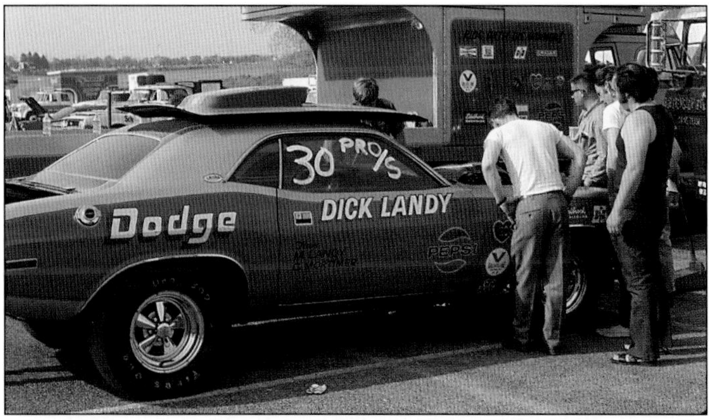

In the pits at York for the Super Stock Magazine Nationals, moved to May in 1970. The transporter, with its unique design for parts and tire storage, was used by several Chrysler teams that year. Plymouth driver Don Grotheer's example can be seen (barely) in the background. (Photo Courtesy Pit Slide Series Archive, quartermilestones.com)

participated in personally into the background. This car seems to have made only a handful of appearances during the season, and Dick likely determined that making the car truly competitive would not be worth the time away from more pressing matters.

That noted, the Six Pack engine package again helped keep Landy in the forefront of the media, as he was featured doing a buildup on one of them in *Popular Hot Rodding*. However, both Robert and Mike Landy agree that the Six Packs were always for street cars, not for racing.

"Dad never raced a Six Pack; if he did, it was maybe once or so," Robert recalled. "Later, we worked on other people's projects, but he always used to say he never raced one. Honestly, he disliked them; his line was, 'Take every carburetor problem you've ever had, multiply it by three, and you've got a Six Pack!'"

When changes in Chrysler's marketing strategies at the end of 1970 concluded the dealership clinic era, the emergence of Dick Landy Industries as a stand-alone business enterprise, coupled to racing hard, was now front and center for the legendary drag racer.

The C/MP Challenger was the fourth car based out of the Landy shops by mid-1970. The others that year were the NHRA Pro Stock Challenger and Dart and the SS/EA Charger. (Photo ©TEN: The Enthusiast Network. All rights reserved.)

Steve Savage was on hand when Dick won Pro Stock at York. The new Super Trick Cragar wheels can be seen here. (Photo Courtesy Steve Savage)

Dick at the winner's circle at York, with the winner bracketed by Miss Golden Shifter Linda Vaughn (left) and her protégé Nikki Phillips (right), as well as the crew wearing Hurst hats. (Photo Courtesy Landy Family Archives)

DRAG NEWS
& EQUIPMENT REPORT
JULY 25 1970 VOLUME 16, NUMBER 2 25¢

ROBINSON, SNOW AND LANDY SCORE AT YORK

YORK, PA. - JULY 19 -- Dick Landy won Pro Stock honors at the NHRA Summernationals over Herb McCandless in the final who foul[illegible] Fuel was nabbed by Pete Robinson, while Funny Car went to Gene Snow. Larry Brown notched Top Gas honors.

Getting the cover of Drag News *was always a big deal. The fact that Dick's Challenger was chosen over Pete Robinson (Top Fuel) and Gene Snow (Funny Car) when he won the first NHRA Summernationals in July shows how popular Pro Stock had become. This paper is in demand on the collector's market today. (Photo Courtesy Landy Family Archives)*

Dick gets off the line at the World Finals in Dallas, which the IHRA took over in late 1971. The Challenger was unable to qualify for the tight 16-car program here. (Photo ©TEN: The Enthusiast Network. All rights reserved.)

1971: On the Road Again

Dick Landy Industries was already open at 19743 Bahama Street in Northridge by 1971, and this was the home of the company for the remainder of its existence. For the new season, its business focus was both the construction of engines and, to an extent, car prep, while Chrysler also continued to call on the Landy operation for piecemeal work, including cylinder head prep. During the year, Dick put together a possible performance book/catalog to supersede the previous clinic booklet, but it appears that he used the 1970 edition again as a giveaway until supplies were exhausted.

The shop had already built a fairly well-noted Super Stocker for Lee Cameron and the PDQ Dodge guys; there could now be other vehicles built under contract. Although not as prolific in race car construction as Sox & Martin had become, DLI was a premier operation even in shop-heavy Southern California, and work came in fairly quickly. For the team itself, the first order of action was to build a new race car for 1971. At the same time, another change was obtaining a new truck for 1971, which was converted to display the clinic parts.

Although the season started out with the old Challenger running the winter races, Dick and Mike already had a new car underway. This again featured some heretofore unseen changes, including the use of rack-and-pinion steering. Dick had some experience with off-road equipment and understood the benefits of this kind of steering. Dick took the factory steering pieces from a Cricket (a little import Plymouth received from English manufacturer Hillman), and adapted them to the Hemi K-frame with some notching and welding. In addition to better toe-in characteristics, the rack design allowed for changes to header layout and piping. These changes were noted in a Pro Stock section published in *Hot Rod* magazine.

Construction of the acid-dipped body structure followed suit from the 1970 car, but there were some changes to the cage design. To aid rigidity, a second set of frame tubes, set in parallel above the frame rails, was added on both sides. In some ways, this was more similar to the way Funny Car frames were being created at the time. *Hot Rod* showed these changes in a one-page feature that ran in the June 1971 issue, but other suspension mods were notably absent. Pro Stock was ultracompetitive even at this juncture, and nobody else knew exactly how the latest recipes worked.

Nonetheless, Terry Cook used Dick's new car later that year for another Pro Stock analysis in the October 1971 issue of *Car Craft*. He indicated the pieces done by

This dramatic launch, at the 1971 AHRA Winter Nationals, was captured by a photographer at Petersen Publishing. Big wheel stands like this prevented Dick from winning any of the early races that year. (Photo ©TEN: The Enthusiast Network. All rights reserved.)

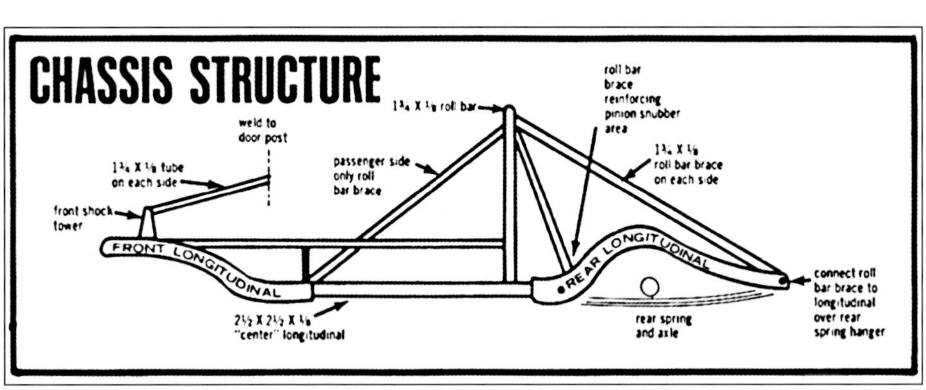

The chassis structure for the 1971 car featured dual frame rails, which Funny Cars then employed, with a well-supported roof roll bar. Although superseded by the more stable "tent" concept, with forward bars connected to the front suspension, this design was state-of-the-art for that era. (Photo ©TEN: The Enthusiast Network. All rights reserved.)

A sketch of a self-published version of the clinic book that might have been produced had sponsor support been available. It would have been more of a guide to modifications and parts usage than the catalog put out by Sox & Martin. (Photo Courtesy Landy Family Archives)

The cover of the clinic program for 1971. These giveaways were the last ones produced by Dodge for the effort. (Photo Courtesy Landy Family Archives)

When the new car was put together, the various support sections had to be carefully fitted to the interior. The stacked dual-rail frame is visible here. (Photo ©TEN: The Enthusiast Network. All rights reserved.)

This Cricket rack-and-pinion layout was perhaps the first design to be adopted on a Pro Stocker and was certainly the first to be put on any Hemi-powered vehicle. (Photo ©TEN: The Enthusiast Network. All rights reserved.)

The shop was cleaned up for this photo of the 1971 car being prepped. Richard Landy recalled that he was given the job of cleaning and later painting the floor when the magazine guys were coming. (Photo ©TEN: The Enthusiast Network. All rights reserved.)

The first John Bauman-designed ramp scoop, as seen on the Landy entry. It was photographed at Irwindale at the April WCS race, which Dick won. The scoop was the result of changes in intake design requiring more hood clearance. It was first used at this event. (Photo ©TEN: The Enthusiast Network. All rights reserved.)

Competitors faced the challenge of different Christmas tree starting-line lights. Here at Beeline Dragway near Phoenix, the track had a simply yellow, green, and red layout. (Photo ©TEN: The Enthusiast Network. All rights reserved.)

AeroChem and their associated costs, noted that Landy had a titanium K-frame and used 2.25-inch square channel connectors going straight back to tie the car together, and pointed out that the cage had additional angled bracing from the top of the roll bar to lateral braces in the area of the K-member. A 2-inch rearward movement of radiator frame and chrome-moly shock supports finished it. Even by 1971, building a competitive Pro Stocker could be summed up in one word: *expensive.*

Areas coming under investigation in engine construction were intake design and the plenum. The plenum is the open area directly beneath the carburetors, and it was becoming more obvious in tunnel ram applications that if the spacing was opened wider between the carb base and individual runner area, the engine's fuel demands could be better met, as RPM levels had increased. However, these parts could go only one way, up.

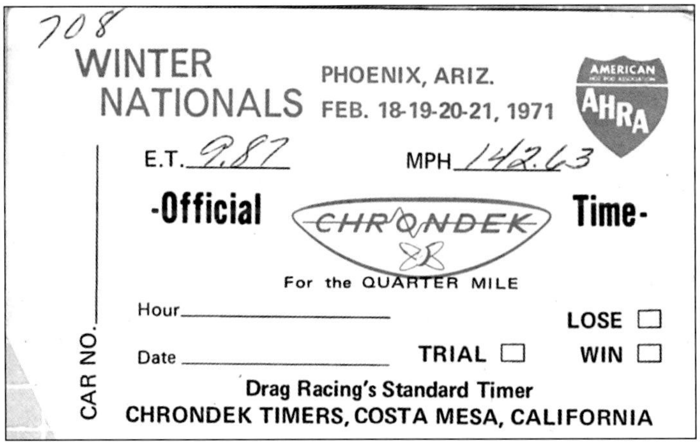

708
WINTER NATIONALS
PHOENIX, ARIZ. FEB. 18-19-20-21, 1971
AMERICAN AHRA
E.T. 9.87 MPH 142.63
-Official Time-
CHRONDEK
For the QUARTER MILE
Hour
Date
TRIAL
LOSE
WIN
CAR NO.
Drag Racing's Standard Timer
CHRONDEK TIMERS, COSTA MESA, CALIFORNIA

This 9.87 at a healthy 142.63 at the season-opening AHRA Winter Nationals was the result of big wheel stands. (Photo Courtesy Landy Family Archives)

To that end, the era of the Six Pack and T/A-model scoop was over. Dick had already developed a more open version, which the team called the "one-and-a-half scoop," that was slightly taller than the OEM version. The newest factory version was now based on new boundary-level air experiments (air traveling across the hood surface) by John Bauman of Chrysler Engineering and featured an upswept ramp leading to the front opening atop a hood blister large enough to cover the engine and the twin-distributor outfit. As a result of all of this, elapsed times in early 1971 began to fall quickly, with Ronnie Sox going into the 9.50 range.

Planning for a two-car 1971 effort, crew member Gale Mortimer was scheduled to drive the original 1970 Pro Stock car as a backup car after Bob Lambeck left at the end of 1970. When he instead went to work at the Sox & Martin operation, the opportunity was given to Ken Dondero, another West Coast driver, whose prior efforts had been in the gas and modified divisions. Once the new car was done, by late spring, Dondero was put in the updated 1970 model that Landy formerly drove. Dick continued with solid support from Chrysler, as well as from his many associate parts sponsors. Rather than selling new cars, these companies became the focus for the clinics.

Thunder (and Clouds) in 1971

Dramatic changes in the new-car marketplace made 1971 the final year of the A102 Street Hemi, and although nobody knew so at the start of the year, the Pro Stock Hemi was in its twilight as well. World champ Ronnie Sox continued exactly where he had left off in 1970, eventually taking home six event titles in NHRA competition and losing just two rounds of racing in that organization's eight events. "Dyno Don" Nicholson won the Summernationals and scored Ford's only NHRA victory in the first two years of Pro Stock after Sox had a tire failure there. The feared Plymouth also faltered slightly and lost to the Rod Shop Dodge of Mike Fons at the 1971 World Finals; that same afternoon, Fons took the event title to become the final NHRA Hemi-powered Pro Stock world champion. The season-long story in the AHRA Pro Super Stock series and the new IHRA sanction found the

As this 9.712/144.00 at Gainesville in March showed, times continued to fall. Intake manufacturer Weiend advertised this number, but Sox won again. Dick fell to Ron Hutter on a round-one hole shot. (Photo Courtesy Landy Family Archives)

Bristol, baby! Dick was at the new IHRA Spring Nationals with the raised-top Six Pack scoop he had recently designed. After beating John Livingston's Demon, he fell to Don Carlton, new driver of Motown Missile*, in round two. (Photo ©TEN: The Enthusiast Network. All rights reserved.)*

Although successful in West Coast matches, the Landy team endured continued NHRA frustration at Indy in 1971. Dick had trouble making the top half of the field and fell to Bobby Yowell in round one. Here, Ken Dondero in the 1970 car is out on Lee Smith's Crazy 'Cuda *in qualifying. Bo Laws beat him on a round-two hole-shot. (Photo ©TEN: The Enthusiast Network. All rights reserved.)*

During qualifying for Indy, things are always tough. (Photo ©TEN: The Enthusiast Network. All rights reserved.)

It looks as if the engine is going away here. The use of specialized parts set on their ragged edges was expensive, especially at the Big Go, where dozens of guys tried to get in. (Photo ©TEN: The Enthusiast Network. All rights reserved.)

Gold dust, the dance floor rosin that doubled as a great traction agent, was broomed down when allowed. The driver had to "burn through" it hard several times to make it sticky. (Photo Courtesy Landy Family Archives)

Hemi dominant as well. There were a lot of unhappy Chevrolet racers and fans, and by the end of the season, radical change was in the air.

During the first 1971 events, Lions and Phoenix for the AHRA and Pomona for the NHRA, the old car pulled some big wheel stands, which cost round wins. By June at Dallas for the NHRA Springnationals, Ken Dondero was in the old car and even out-qualified Dick's new Challenger by a small margin, but both entries were out by round three.

At the relocated Summernationals in Englishtown, New Jersey, Dick looked very solid, going to the semifinals, but the car was still not hitting the numbers like some of the other Mopars. That spring, the factory announced the first true head redesign since the 1965 A990 with the port-redesigned aluminum D4 model. Sox had clocked a huge 9.53/143 at Gainesville using the heads, and Don Carlton ran an even faster 9.50 at Englishtown. These aluminum heads were reportedly being used by Chrysler for "fuel and supercharged" racing because the cost of a set of original 1965 heads had skyrocketed.

By the World Finals at Amarillo, both Landy cars had done well enough in the western WCS series to be seeded into the final program, and both cars advanced on round-one singles as a result. However, victory was not to be, and the team ended the NHRA tour with no victories for 1971 (as did everyone else except Don Nicholson in New Jersey and Mike Fons here) due to the Sox & Martin effort.

However, the Pro Stock rules announced at the NHRA World Finals showed what would happen in 1972. The most radical change was a drop from a 100-to a 94-inch minimum wheelbase, which frankly spelled the end of the American supercar as a dominant force. At 93 inches, the Cricket missed the cut (as did the Dodge Colt); the Vega and Pinto did not. Hemi, SOHC, and canted-valve engines were now raced at a 7.5-pounds-per-inch basis, while wedges were at a 7.0 rating. This was later adjusted to reduce the weight break on canted-valve models as well to create three distinctions, thereby saving the Chevy big-block and giving an inherent advantage to the Ford Cleveland design created during Ford's tenure in Trans-Am racing.

Still, there were bright spots for Landy in the racing process, most of them on the rich California match racing trail. The Challenger was the low qualifier at Bakersfield with a 9.90. At the Fremont WCS Northern Nationals on April 4, Dick scored his first win of 1971, beating Bill Bagshaw with a 9.69 to a quicker 9.66, with both cars using the new hood scoop for plenum tunnel-ram clearance. He then won the Division 7 WCS points opener at Irwindale, beating Jim Clark's new *Hemi Express* Demon for that title. Clark was on the receiving end of Ken Dondero over Memorial Day Weekend again going to a final only to see a Landy entry in front of him.

Dick lost the rear wheel studs under the strain. This same problem cost him a shot at victory the following year at Englishtown. (Photo Courtesy Landy Family Archives)

The two Landy Challengers then met in the final at the Bonneville Raceway WCS race in Utah. Dick won Saturday's open show title over Butch Leal's new Duster and then came back Sunday to win the WCS crown over teammate Dondero for a $2,200 weekend. The local newspaper stated that Landy had constructed special high-altitude changes to the car. On August 8, again in the thin air of Continental Divide Raceway in Colorado, Dick beat an eight-car field, taking the final over Irv Beringhaus's 'Cuda.

For all the Chrysler guys, 1972 was a year of huge and unknown changes, as well as the finale of Dick in an E-Body model for Pro Stock.

Amarillo, Texas, was the site of the NHRA World Finals in 1971, and both Dick and Ken Dondero were seeded in from the Western Conference due to their stellar effort in Western Conference action. (Photo ©TEN: The Enthusiast Network. All rights reserved.)

Unfortunately, even with first-round singles at Amarillo, neither car was able to advance. This late-season image shows the newest scoop design with an extra box blister, which may have been an ongoing development of paired, gear-driven, dual-plug distributors (which replaced the 90-degree offset versions). (Photo ©TEN: The Enthusiast Network. All rights reserved.)

The team raced back home at Ontario Motor Speedway for the Supernationals, where the field was short. Ken Dondero (shown) finished his Landy driving duties in round one. Dick went to the third round before coming up against Ronnie Sox, who won his final NHRA career title here that same afternoon. (Photo ©TEN: The Enthusiast Network. All rights reserved.)

The rules changes mentioned previously were actually first initiated by the AHRA in mid-1971 to reformat the way Pro Stock was structured. The media had been fairly relentless in noting how the factory Chryslers were so dominant (namely Sox, teammate Herb McCandless, and the Don Carlton–driven *Motown Missile*), though never minding that Bill Jenkins had been under the aegis of Chevrolet R&D since the 1960s. Regardless, in 1971 when it was announced that a shorter wheelbase and new minimum vehicle weights were coming, racers such as Dick stayed with the tried-and-true Hemi and took their chances on running what they already knew.

Then came Pomona and the first *Grumpy's Toy* Vega, using a tubular chassis and a high-winding 331-ci Chevy, showed that business as usual was over. Indeed, Jenkins dominated the 1972 season much the way Sox had conquered 1971 and often had the field covered by a tenth or more of a second in a car that weighed less than 2,200 pounds. It took some months for the rest to catch up, but Ray Allen of 1970 Chevelle notoriety won the 1972 NHRA Nationals in a Vega as well, and by the fall of 1972, minicar conversions were happening everywhere.

The 1972 Landy Challenger was also unique. This was actually the 1971 model with new body parts and tricks. At this point, Dick continued with his ongoing development of horsepower; one change had been the creation of a new dual-distributor layout that used two heads on a gear-driven base driven by the conventional drive location. This eliminated some of the issues of spark scatter.

Meanwhile, factory work on *Motown Missile,* with a soon-to-be debuted crank-trigger ignition event system, was yielding some solid results, and once the first MSD (multi-spark discharge) boxes arrived, any need for twin distributors in gas applications was over. Cylinder head flow work and more aggressive camshaft development never changed.

Mike Landy notes that any time you radically modified cam specs, you also had to redo the intake plenum size requirements. DLI had a set of various-height open-plenum spacers that could be inserted in groups below the intake top to do this work.

Meanwhile, future race car construction moved toward the "skin and frame" model that Jenkins was proving worked so well. This was considered the first really serious departure from stock in Pro Stock, but other ongoing developments during the year gave way to better rear suspensions with bar-style four-links, dry-sump oiling systems with kick-out pans for lower engine position, and better valvetrain science for increased RPM levels. Perhaps the biggest change came when the factory revised some of the D4 head port science, finding some big power and flow gains at .700 valve lift. Mike and

Times were changing; it is 1972, and Dick is again racing a one-car program. Here at the Lions season opener, the fresh Challenger displays new paint, a chrome snorkel extension, Bauman's final ramp scoop layout, and 1972 grille styling. The track closed forever at the end of the season. (Photo ©TEN: The Enthusiast Network. All rights reserved.)

Richard Landy both remember that the shop machined and built a large number of cylinder heads during this era under contract to the factory.

As a result, the Mopars were faster by year's end, but so were the penciled rules changes from headquarters. For 1972, there was not a huge number of rule changes after the racing started. Everyone chased Jenkins most of the season, but by fall, the Ford Cleveland development was taking center stage, with Don Nicholson beating Dick for the AHRA series title at the World Finals in Fremont. There was even talk of banning all out-of-production engines (Hemi, SOHC, and so on) for the 1973 season, but that possibility was rescinded. Without a viable Mopar small-block, expensive work turned to figuring out how to effectively destroke the Hemi engine to 366 ci using some of the NASCAR technology being developed.

Racing and More Racing

Although the early races were uneventful for Dick, changes to the car were solid; one adaptation was the chrome snorkel nose that now extended from the hood scoop opening. This had first shown up on the *Missile*, and Dick had it on his car when he won a West Coast Pro Stock Association meet over Butch Leal at Sacramento in April. However, the real issue for many racers in 1972 was breakage, caused by drastic

Bakersfield had been the sight of a number of Landy wins and records, but even with grip, it was not to be in 1972; the Dusters of Butch Leal and Bob Lambeck raced for the money. (Photo ©TEN: The Enthusiast Network. All rights reserved.)

Dick prepares to climb into the car at Bakersfield. The era of the muscle car was ending on both the street and in drag racing, as new minicars' including Pintos and Vegas, took center stage in Pro Stock. (Photo Courtesy Landy Family Archives)

The 1972 program cover for the new USRT circuit. Dick appears in the center star. This was a successful effort that season, packing venues everywhere, even on weeknights. (Photo Courtesy Landy Family Archives)

A Shift in Colors

Again applied by Nelson Carter, the paint for 1972 was different, due to an MPC model kit that Richard Landy had built. Now a teenager, Richard spent his summers working in the shop, and after a toy company released a kit of the Landy team entry, he got creative.

"They had brought out this kit of my dad's car in 1971," he recalls. "I built one, and I messed around with the paint when it was done. I came up with this new look, and my dad liked it so much we used it on the car for that next year. MPC also made a model of the 1972 car with the new paint job."

The paint scheme was red, white, and blue, featuring dramatically curved lines. The lower area was blue, with an upswept white side area that encompassed the door, then narrowing once again on the top of the deck lid. Red went over the front fenders and through the side window openings and came together imaginarily in the rear window area as a wide, centered rear stripe. A centered blue stripe led up to the scoop opening and over the roof to end in a centered point above the back window. With wide white areas between this stripe and the red areas, pinstripes along the white-area edges finished the patriotic look.

After two solid seasons, sponsor Pepsi had moved on to other horizons, and the Landy team was again relying primarily on automotive aftermarket firms for racing support, with minor help from Dodge, so the Pepsi logo was no longer on the car. Although politics reared its head at mid-season with a number of event boycotts, the 1972 Landy Challenger was a real head-turner.

Original kits of the 1972 car, kept by Dick Landy. Sponsorship from kit builders such as MPC was prevalent on many competitors, and unbuilt examples like these are rare collector's items today. (Photo Courtesy Landy Family Archives)

The USRT driver portraits were shot on the steps of the Capitol in Washington, D.C. In his team blazer, Landy fit the part of the modern professional driver. (Photo Courtesy Landy Family Archives)

lightening changes undertaken to remove weight from the bigger cars.

With power and balance, Dick went to the semifinals at the NHRA Springnationals in Columbus, but his biggest day in NHRA racing that year was at the Summernationals at Englishtown. With 32 cars on hand, he beat Roy Hill and Arlen Vanke to meet with Ronnie Sox in round three. In a turnabout from the past two seasons, he outran Sox 9.63 to 9.65 and beat Don Grotheer, a fourth Mopar racer, to go to the finals. A coin flip gave him lane choice, and he picked the left-hand side to face the Grump. Jenkins took off while Dick went about 12 inches, and then all five wheel studs sheared clean off on one slick. This and the aforementioned AHRA World Finals race versus Nicholson (which was also lost as the result of parts breaking) were his two national event finals of the 1972 season.

The 1972 season was not, however, a total loss for Mopar racers, and Pro Stock remained very popular. The best drivers in the nation joined together and started the United States Racing Team (USRT), under the leadership of promoter Al Carpenter. There were 16 full members, including Landy, Sox, Jenkins, and Nicholson, and the idea was to bring a full-tilt professional show into a facility with guaranteed money and appearances. There were four cars per brand: Chevy, Ford, Plymouth, and Dodge; Wally Booth stayed in the Chevy group after he went with AMC that season. Most of these shows were Wednesday-evening affairs held within a couple of days of a national event that had already brought racers into the region. After a single qualifying shot, the cars were divided into groups A to C, based on elapsed time, with four cars in each group (one from each manufacturer) and four alternates. Each group then raced a semifinal and a final to crown three winners per event, and points were awarded.

"Once we got involved in the United States Racing Team program, things went pretty well," Dick recalled later. "It was a moneymaking deal, and we bought a motor home and had someone doing all our prerace PR for us. A few of the guys in that group got upset because they thought they should get a guarantee as big as Grumpy got; they dropped out, but they weren't Bill Jenkins. The purse was set up to pay the bigger-name racers a bigger guarantee. Some of them, though, turned it into a real problem; they tried to rally the troops and make it into politics or something like that. They weren't dealing with reality; that was a really good circuit.

"That was made up of the 16 best Pro Stock racers in the country, and we [the Mopars] still had to add 100 pounds there to keep them happy."

Debuting in Phenix City, Alabama, to a crowd of 8,000, the USRT was a huge success. The group raced mostly in the East and Midwest that year. At the first race, Dick won the B-class crown when Don Grotheer's Plymouth pulled a big wheel stand, and then he did well enough that he helped win the series Manufacturers Cup title for Dodge. That team was formidable: Dick, Don Carlton, 1971 world

The Fancy Truck

Among the paperwork that survives in the Landy files are the original drawings for the 1971 clinic truck. With Chrysler announcing that it would be reducing its support for the new year, this was a major change in focus for the program, as the clinics would now be held primarily at racing facilities. Dick Landy had hoped to continue being a conduit of information to his loyal fans regarding performance changes that could be made to their own vehicles. To facilitate this, the parts were semipermanently mounted to the side doors of the truck's enclosed bed (the first fully enclosed trailer that the Landy operation used). These doors could be simply swung open and locked in place, and Dick could then explain the displayed pieces.

However, the times had changed. Having clinics at the racetrack while noisy, distracting work was being done on nearby cars was not easy, so the truck clinics were often held early in the day, which hurt attendance. Moreover, the dealership environment had been mostly indoors, and films and so on could be easily shown there. Not so with the truck clinics. They were never very big, except on occasions when Dick could display the rig and car at a shopping mall, as was sometimes organized by Al Carpenter during the USRT era in 1972.

Although Dick actively recruited possible sponsors to continue the programs for 1973, the days of large displays had ended. The truck was offered for sale as part of the package when the 1972 Challenger was sold. Its whereabouts today remains unknown.

This is one of the original drawings for the 1971 clinic truck.

The doors on the truck could be swung open and locked in place for Dick to provide further details. (Photo Courtesy Tommy Erwin/USC Archives)

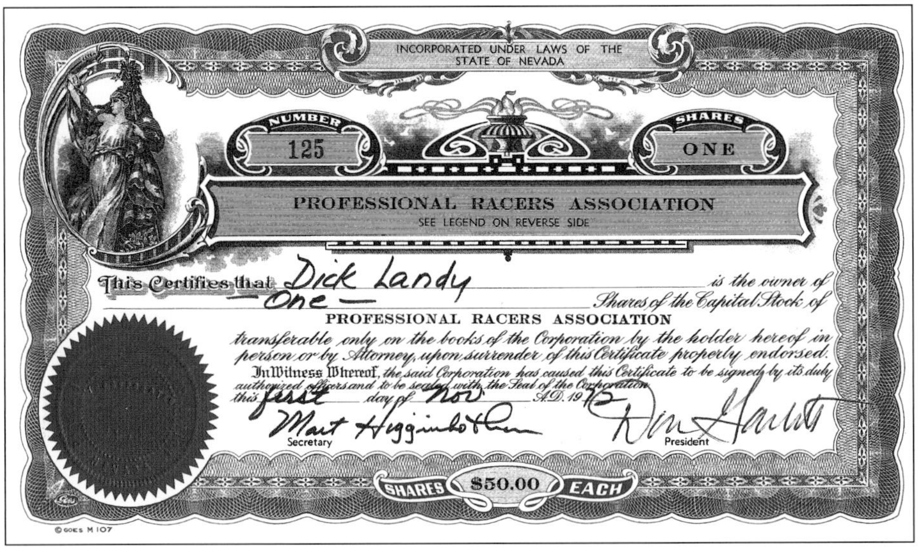

INCORPORATED UNDER LAWS OF THE STATE OF NEVADA

NUMBER 125 | SHARES ONE

PROFESSIONAL RACERS ASSOCIATION

SEE LEGEND ON REVERSE SIDE

This Certifies that Dick Landy is the owner of One Shares of the Capital Stock of PROFESSIONAL RACERS ASSOCIATION transferable only on the books of the Corporation by the holder hereof in person or by Attorney upon surrender of this Certificate properly endorsed.

In Witness Whereof, the said Corporation has caused this Certificate to be signed by its duly authorized officers and to be sealed with the Seal of the Corporation this first day of Nov A.D. 1972

Mart Higginbotham, Secretary — Don Garlits, President

SHARES $50.00 EACH

Dick was vested in the new Pro Racers Association, buying two shares in the enterprise following the Tulsa event. Filled out for Dick Landy, note that the certificate is signed by Don Garlits and funny driver Marty Higgenbotham. (Photo Courtesy Landy Family Archives)

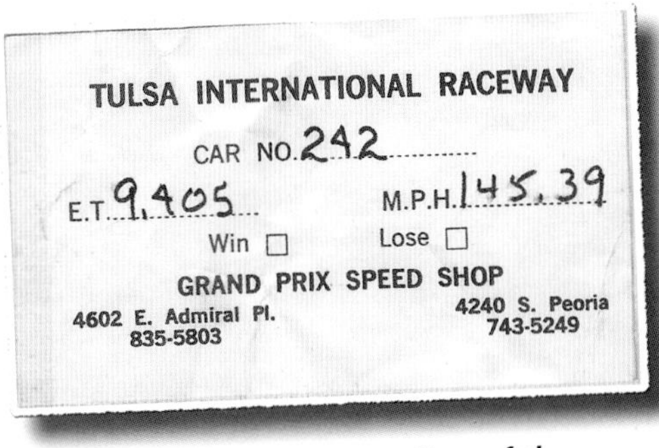

TULSA INTERNATIONAL RACEWAY

CAR NO. 242

E.T. 9.405 M.P.H. 145.39

Win ☐ Lose ☐

GRAND PRIX SPEED SHOP

4602 E. Admiral Pl. 835-5803

4240 S. Peoria 743-5249

One of the fastest time slips of the early season was this 9.40, recorded at a Tulsa match race in July. The car was not this quick again until the cooler months and final races of the season. (Photo Courtesy Landy Family Archives)

champ Mike Fons, and Herb McCandless, who cleaned up with five consecutive USRT wins after his new Sox & Martin Demon showed up in June. Sox was named driver of the year, and this was the one place where Bill Jenkins did not have the rules in his favor that season.

The first NHRA Pro Stock boycott by Chrysler was unofficially at Sanair, Canada, but the biggest one of 1972 was for the Big Go at Indy. Don Garlits, assisted by AHRA's Jim Tice and sponsored by the Navy, agreed to hold a big-money race against the NHRA Nationals at Tulsa International Raceway over the same Labor Day Weekend. In Dick's files was his paid-for membership share in the new Professional Racers Association (PRA) that Garlits had started. All the big Mopar names showed up, but Dick was not in the final. Rather it was McCandless who faced Jenkins for $25,000 on Sunday evening, and the Vega went to the pay window yet again.

"In spite of the implemented weight breaks, that 1972 car was a runnin' machine!" says Robert. "My dad broke a lot of parts that year but gave the little cars fits. In Tulsa, Grump and he were goin' back and forth for Low during the first couple days of qualifying; I was there. We blew up the motor, then put in the spare and blew that up too. So my dad airfreighted some heads and parts in, thrashed it together in the pits, and he went out, and I think it dropped a valve in that one. We took everything we had and built a Frankenstein from the destruction! We were pitted between Sox and McCandless; at one point they came over looking at different sides of the car and then went around by the back and started arguing about what dad was running. 'He's got D4s... No, that's their D6. . . No, D4!' Actually, they were both right! That thing had whatever was left and that's it!"

In match race trim, the car ran as quick as 9.40/145 based on surviving time slips; this was also at Tulsa in a booked-in race during midsummer. Dick won another big race at Epping, New Hampshire, with steady 9.60s; he had actually beaten an off-pace Jenkins there in May. The aforementioned engineering changes showed better dividends that fall. After the loss to Nicholson, Dick was on his game at Orange County for the Pro-Stock Showdown on November 15. The Challenger ran flawlessly at legal weight, going 9.31 and 147 for low ET and beating Bruce Walker in the Barry Setzer Vega for the money.

Robert Landy recalls that the team broke a lot of equipment trying to make the tough field at Tulsa, which had a huge $25,000 purse for Pro Stock. The Challenger is seen here on another pass in front of the track's unique round tower. (Photo ©TEN: The Enthusiast Network. All rights reserved.)

Nonetheless, the era of the E-Body for serious Pro Stock had ended. Longer (and potentially narrower) cars, including McCandless's Demon and Butch Leal's Duster, were now the plan according to Chrysler. Dick began laying the ground work for 1973 to once again return to the A-Body platform, where he concluded his Pro Stock driving career. The Challenger and display truck were both put up for sale, and the change was a successful transition back to championship form.

Collector Jeff Husk located this original "For Sale" ad in a racing periodical from October 1972. Dick was making some big changes for the new season.

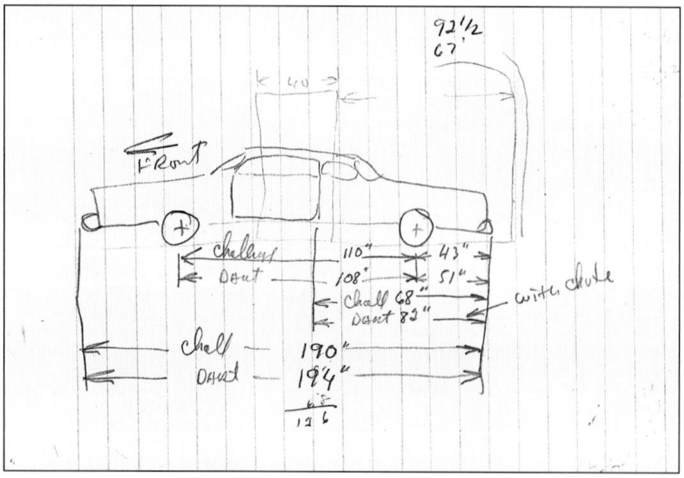

This sketch by Dick shows a primary reason for changing to the A-Body for 1973. The overhang from centerline-to-rear-bumper went from 68 to 82 inches, allowing for better weight transfer. (Photo Courtesy Landy Family Archives)

Where Are They Now?

There were really only two Pro Stock Challengers during the three-year period. As noted, after Lambeck left and the Swinger Dart was sold, the team built a new 1971 car and the 1970 car was campaigned by Ken Dondero with trim upgrades. I have been told that this car is presently in a private collection awaiting restoration to its 1970 appearance; I have not been able to verify that, however.

For 1972, the 1971 race car was given new trim and paint; the chassis was not radically changed. The focus was on further (and more expensive) lightweight components and building on the RPM gains that had come from ongoing DLI Hemi development. As noted, the fancy show truck and 1972 car were put up for sale together.

Restoration director/collector Dean Klein chased a number of leads and managed to find both cars in bracket race trim. The 1971–1972 car was subsequently restored to its 1971 status by Erik Lindberg. This car is now part of Todd Werner's collection in Florida. Meanwhile, the third car, the rarely seen non-Pro Stock C/MP 1970 clinic Challenger, has not been accounted for. An actual V-code serial number model, it is being actively looked for by restoration hobbyists.

The interior is very clean; note the sparse number of gauges to monitor engine functions, with a large hooded tach centered above the steering wheel. The unmistakable frame design is evident as well.

The restored 1971 Challenger was completed by Erik Lindberg. Note the scoop design and the use of an air block-off plate behind the grille.

The engine in the car today is an early version of Landy's 426-ci Pro Stock powerplant, with independent intake runners, no plenum beneath the carbs (stock 4500 Dominators with intact air horns), and a 90-degree offset to the distributors.

The stunning restored 1971 car is part of the collection maintained by Todd Werner in Florida.

The Last Challenger: From Super Stock to Goodwood

For 1974, changes in NHRA's wheelbase, cylinder head, and displacement rules basically spelled the end of the Hemi in Pro Stock. Although a driver occasionally broke through to a final round, the thrill of victory was short-lived and frustrating, as any sign of life seemingly caused additional rules adjustments. This was more than simply inconvenience; Sox & Martin, which had been shut out of the winner's circle since the end of 1971 in NHRA racing, closed its doors for good. Still under factory direction, a number of prominent drivers moved back into Super Stock, where recently liberalized rules had made competitive changes to Hemi cars effective.

So Ronnie Sox was back in a 1968 Barracuda, Butch Leal returned quite successfully to a 1965 Hemi Belvedere, and Dick showed up with a 1970 SS/D Hemi Challenger sporting the T/A scoop option. This was legal based on paperwork filed with the NHRA in 1970. Also, the 1970 NHRA minimum weight of 3,633 for the Challenger was less than 1971's 3,656 minimum. It has been rumored that this car came from a local used-car lot. At any rate, once the car was prepped for competition by DLI, Dick wasted no time taking a class title at the 1974 Gatornationals and resetting the SS/D record to 10.55 at the SportsNationals in Bowling Green, Kentucky. Unfortunately, as it was a sportsman entry, it received no major magazine exposure, but the Super Stocker featured many ideas that Dick came to be known for in the higher class.

Never a big fan of handicap racing, Dick put the car up for sale toward the end of the year, refocusing on the heads-up Pro Stock Dart Sport package for 1975. The Challenger was raced quite sparingly during the next 25 years, and then Dick himself raced it once more at one event, in England.

"There was only one owner of the Super Stock Challenger between the time Dick sold it and I had it," Bernie Mangnitz told me. Bernie had found the car in 2001. "Actually, Dick had called me and told me, 'Hey, there is a car for sale and I am pretty sure it is my old one.' At that time, we were already making plans to go to the Goodwood Festival of Speed with Dick and Gean. We were going to take the 1968 Dart that Ed Vandersnick had restored, which I also owned by that time.

The SS/D "boycott" 1970 Hemi Challenger R/T races Butch Leal in a 1965 California Flash Belvedere, during the era of the boycotts in 1974. Dick kept this car less than a year. (Photo ©TEN: The Enthusiast Network. All rights reserved.)

The Super Stock car today. The grille has been blocked off for the sake of aerodynamics.

"Anyhow, the woman who had the car for sale had all the paperwork from Dick, so once we were put in touch, I went there and looked at it in a big warehouse. While I was there, I called Dick, who told me to verify some little details, and sure enough, it was that car.

"The car had been most recently raced with a 440 Six Pack and automatic, and Dick told me, 'Instead of taking the Dart to England, how about you send that car out here, and we will restore it here at the shop like it was when I raced it?'

"So we did that together; he put a rebuilt Hemi back in it, and the 4-speed transmission. He used some of the old pictures he had and did everything to bring it back to what it looked like in 1974. This process started in February 2001, and in July that same year, we put it into a Lufthansa jet and flew overseas. He drove it at the festival, and we all had a good time. He was very proud of it.

"When we got back, we decided he should keep the car for a little while longer and show it around California. He then got invited to the SEMA [Specialty Equipment Market Association] show and was honored there. They displayed the car up on a big pedestal in Las Vegas, and it was also on display at the NHRA museum for a time."

Although purists may cringe, the Challenger as it appears today has some modern upgrades, all done by Dick himself for the Goodwood effort. The rat roaster–type intake is heavily massaged and topped by the correct Super Stock A102 Street Hemi Carter carbs, and ignition components are all modern. The car sports an updated cage with additional bars, but this was not simply for artistic license.

"To run at Goodwood, the car needed to be updated for safety, so it should be noted that some of that is more up

Dick with the Challenger Super Stocker after it was restored at DLI in early 2001. It was the last car he drove in a public venue. (Photo Courtesy Bernie Mangnitz)

Dick and Gean Landy enjoyed an international audience when the restored Challenger was shipped to England for the Goodwood Festival of Speed. Dick is in the car in the pre-staging area.

Bernie Mangnitz and Dick Landy at the Goodwood Festival of Speed, along with other notable U.S. race cars. (Photo Courtesy Bernie Mangnitz)

Dick Landy was responsible for restoring the boycott car. This was the final E-Body he raced in competition and the final car he drove at speed, during the exhibitions at Goodwood.

Built for endurance during its run at Goodwood, this Hemi features a combination of new and old technologies. Dick assembled it at DLI, and it is a lasting tribute to his legacy.

This is how it ended: Dandy Dick and the 426 Hemi. Gean has the helmet Dick wore that last time. Todd Werner has the one he used in the 1970s.

to date than what it was originally," said Bernie. "Dick did change some stuff so it would be able to do that. But he restored it entirely, the only such car he ever did himself, which makes it very special. At the time, I had a big collection of Hemi race cars myself (Landy, Sox, and some others), but later I began doing Corvette stuff, so I let some of those cars go."

The recipient of that change in focus was collector Todd Werner, who added it to his collection and can now lay claim to having four documented Dick Landy race cars, the Hemi Magnum wagon Dick used at the DLI business until he died, and many one-off and rare mementoes from Dick's business office. The 1970 Challenger was the last race car that Dick Landy drove in a public venue; that he and DLI also restored it is ample enough reason to leave it exactly as it appears to this day.

The large tach in the 1970-built, 1974-raced car is now augmented by a shift light. The rest of the interior is classic Landy style with nice attention to detail.

The last Challenger seen from behind. This view shows how Richard Landy's paint scheme, developed in 1971, worked over the roof and onto the deck lid.

The Challenger among its brethren at Werner's spacious garage. Following Dick's death, Todd bought a majority of the memorabilia and clothing from the DLI office from Gean for his collection.

Ken Dondero: Journeyman Driver 1939–2014

During two eras of *Landy's Dodges*, the Challenger period and the minicar finale, Dick chose a peer from among the many excellent Southern California competitors to drive team cars. Ken Dondero ran with the team for only two seasons, 1971 and 1982, but proved to be an excellent choice. A partial reason for his seemingly brief Landy efforts was his in-demand gifted shifting skill, leading Dondero to work for the likes of Don Nicholson and Bill Jenkins as well before his career ended.

Born in Massachusetts in 1939, Dondero moved to California in 1960, just as the performance era really picked up steam. He spent his youth practicing power shifts on tractors and street cars but landed a visible ride in the B/Gas Anglia of Bob Panella, which he drove to acclaim in the late 1960s. He later became the final 4-speed winner in the fading B/Gas Supercharged division. It was Landy who put him into a Pro Stocker in 1971. He qualified for the World Finals with it on points accumulated primarily in West Coast action, but that car was parked in 1972.

Therefore, Ken accepted an offer from Nicholson and did very well with a new Pinto in 1972, but his main claim to fame was driving the second touring *Grumpy's Toy* entry on the AHRA and match race circuits while owner Bill Jenkins focused primary on his NHRA effort in the second half of the 1970s. That resulted in back-to-back season crowns for the Tulare resident.

In 1982, he came on to replace Brad Yuill in the Landy Omni/Charger effort, netting some solid performances but never taking an event win. Then he drove for Bob Panella once again when Panella Trucking went Pro Stock racing. A driving career behind him, he later opened Ken's Auto in Tulare, which he operated for 30 years. Ken died following a brief illness in 2014; he was 74 years old.

CHAPTER 5

DLI: BEHIND THE SCENES AND BEYOND

In the mid-1950s Dick Landy was one of tens of thousands of young men yielding to the siren call of horsepower. Of that group, perhaps 10 percent continued beyond the passing fad stage and committed to the passion. Of those diehards, an elite few, less than 1/10 percent, climbed to the possible pinnacle of fame and, yes, even fortune. For Dandy Dick, it was his understanding of image coupled with hard work that led to success. The professionalism that appeared in the Andy Andrews Ford era ended up making the Landy name synonymous with Dodge and drag racing in general by the Pro Stock era.

Dick noted in a number of interviews the amount of effort his calling had taken. He even understood the jealousy that his upper-management connections in Chrysler could generate, but the company got its money's worth. Part of this was the reality that Dick Landy was not caught in any illusions of grandeur. The hustle was on, whether it was finding one more horsepower, making unplanned sponsor appearances, missing important family events, or simply biting his tongue when need be. His work was not as scientifically oriented as some of the gentlemen in Chrysler Engineering would have agreed to, and coupled with Landy's healthy sponsorship, even their animosity sometimes simmered under the surface. Nonetheless, when practical development was needed, especially under deadline, a phone call or telegram came from Detroit with questions or requests. Dick Landy proved to be more than up to every one of those challenges; indeed, he relished the effort it took.

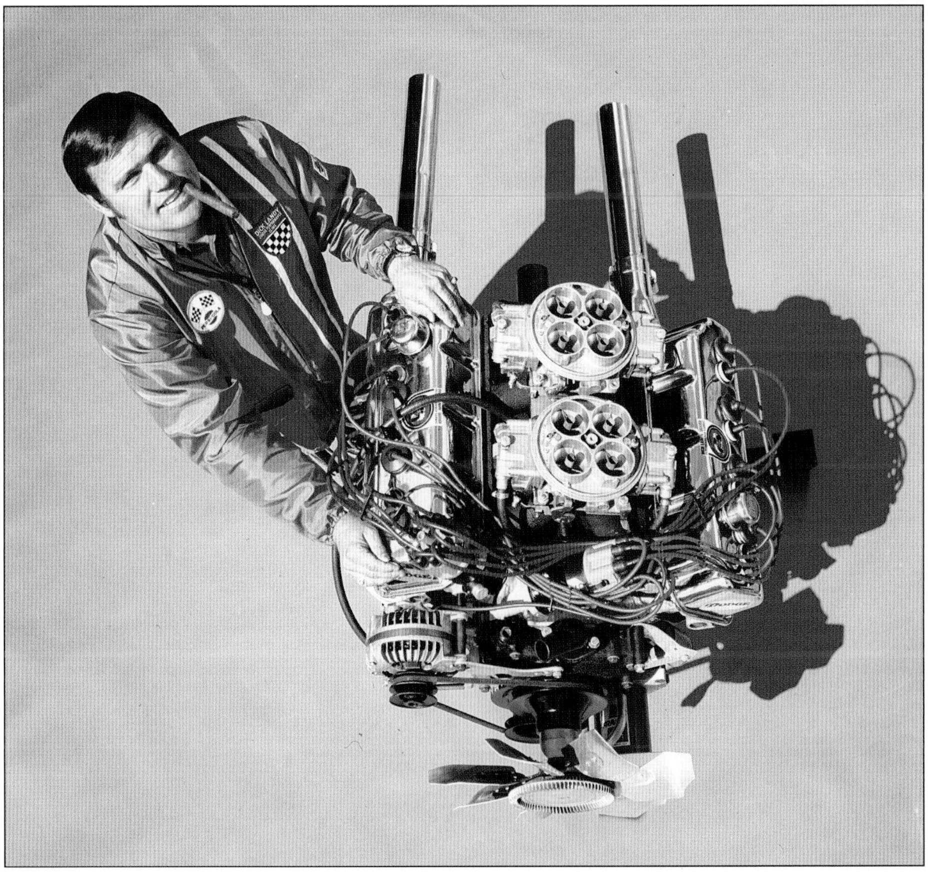

Dick Landy shows off the latest in Pro Stock horsepower in 1971. DLI was an ongoing force in development the entire time the 426 Hemi engine was used in Pro Stock competition. The business eventually marketed parts that specifically addressed OEM design shortcomings for extreme RPM environments. (Photo ©TEN: The Enthusiast Network. All rights reserved.)

In the preceding chapters, I covered some of the race vehicle development in depth, but what became Dick Landy Industries in 1970 actually had started with young Landy's foray into race boats with Brendella Boats in the late 1950s. He could well have made his fortune there, but the pavement and hot American muscle beckoned. When he opened the Automotive Research dyno shop in 1962, he had the only 400-hp dynamometer in Southern California, and he worked it. Hard. Customers included Butch Leal and Bill "Maverick" Golden. Golden was the catalyst for Landy moving to the Dodge brand for 1964 when he recommended Dick to Bob Cahill for the newest Dodge in late 1963.

Landy never looked back. He made sure those Sunday-night telegrams and phone calls were made to Detroit, proved to be frugal with company resources, did what he was asked, and won the top factory calling when Dodge chose to focus on Super Stock in 1967. As I have shown, beyond that, PR proved to be Dick's strong suit. He hired Jerry Gross, Mike Dobrin, Stan Adams, and others to get the word out about his racing and sponsors. He rarely, if ever, turned down requests made by magazines for technical help and photos, and he became a familiar face in advertising as well.

The final shop location was at 19743 Bahama Street in Northridge. Not large by today's standards, the 10,000 square feet offered enough space for machine equipment, work benches, assembly "clean rooms," storage, offices, and eventually a state-of-the-art engine dyno room. It was here that Landy's operation began doing services for outside customers needing engines or blueprinted parts.

During the 1970s, the Landy name returned to the water as DLI-powered entries, including *Hot Damn Hondo,* that Irv Brendell's son Mike drove to big speeds and world records, in part due to Landy's ongoing higher-RPM engineering work on the Hemi engine. Soon after, DLI also packaged the first commercial 440-ci wedge performance engine kits for marine use.

In drag racing, after winning the 1973 AHRA World Championship, Dick and DLI tuned Larry Huff to that crown in 1974, in a race car the shop had prepped for him. Meanwhile, as design work continued for the drag racing effort, Dick began using his deep connections in the performance industry to design, create, and market needed replacement parts such as Hemi roller rockers and offset wedge rocker assemblies. He performed large amounts of development work for longtime friend B&M as it moved beyond the transmission business.

Mostly unknown outside the Mopar subculture was DLI's notable efforts in Volkswagen and aftermarket superchargers, prepackaged electronic fuel injection as early as 1985, off-roading efforts with both a little Colt and 4 x 4 trucks, and Boss 429 Pro Stock engines after the 500-ci NHRA era started.

Race cars abound at the second AR location at 7670 Woodman in Van Nuys, during the era when Mike was in the army. (Photo ©TEN: The Enthusiast Network. All rights reserved.)

Dick with the early 400-hp Clayton dyno at the Magnolia Boulevard Automotive Research shop in Sherman Oaks. (Photo Courtesy Landy Family Archives)

Working at the Shop

Of course, Dick Landy Industries was a family business. After his army work finished in 1969, Mike's full-time job through the turn of the century was working at DLI. Dick's sons, Richard and Robert, both worked in the machine shop and could proficiently do most of the things needed to assemble high-quality racing engines. Richard moved on to his own career, but Robert stayed at DLI through the ensuing years.

"I would help swap the engines out even when I was 12 years old," he recalled. "In the summertime, Richard and I rode with the trucks and did the tour. I remembered hearing all the stories. I was immersed in it, even when I was young. For instance, my dad had prewar Cadillac 16-plug distributors to test with, and later we experimented with some Accel stuff. When we cleaned off shelves in the shop, we tossed huge amounts of those old parts out. Hemi exhaust manifolds, intakes, Cragar wheels; we scrapped a lot of stuff long before it became collectible; we just needed the space.

"A lot of our work shifted to the street machines out of necessity, and then in the 1980s we were back doing Pro Stock engines for other guys. At one point we maintained seven engines for Roy Hill, a couple for the NHRA, a couple for the IHRA, and backups. We did engines for Reid Whisnant and the Bassett car of Jim Meyer and later Gary Hansen. You would not believe how busy we were and how much we airfreighted out of that shop.

"By then I had become the shop manager, Mike was the general manager, and my dad ran the whole thing. I think if my dad had continued driving, he would have done even better. When I look back at those years, it was a lot of work, but it was a lot of fun."

Some of the work the shop took on required finesse. One such job came in during the mid-1970s, when Chrysler had cast the first replacement D6 heads, as DLI had a long commitment with the company for subcontracting jobs.

"We did get the deal to do the D6 Chrysler heads," says Mike Landy. "Those were close in design to the 1965 heads, and some of them were not good castings. We still assembled them under contract here at the shop and had to mark the

A mailing envelope showing various products from companies supporting the new DLI clinics held at racetracks and speed shops. (Photo Courtesy Landy Family Archives)

Robert Landy recalls that when it was time to clean up the shop, the items going to scrap were pretty interesting. Here is one of the full shelves in the second shop. (Photo ©TEN: The Enthusiast Network. All rights reserved.)

bad ones as rejects. Now the D5 was completely different; it wasn't like any other Street Hemi head. It was a Pro Stock head; they were good."

"I pounded in thousands of seats and thousands of guides into those aluminum heads by hand with big heavy gloves and big hammers; when you got done with doing that, your ears would be ringing for weeks," says Richard Landy about the project. "Uncle Mike had a procedure to put them in the oven and would get them up to about 400 degrees. The temperature had to be perfect or the ones you did already would pop back out when you hit the head again, and then we would have to remeasure all of the seats and machine them. That was a lot of work back then."

Richard also recalled some of the parts testing that was done when he was younger and often had to be the gofer. "There were these test days we did for Goodyear, who sponsored us; I think some of it was done near the tire plant. They would have all of these slicks stacked up. They had to be moved and put on the car. I got pretty good at figuring out how to bounce that tire; instead of rolling it, you could get it bouncing it like a basketball!

"On those days, we would make two or three runs on each set of slicks and figure out an average for them and mount another set on the rims. There were no cordless guns back then, only speed handles for the rim-lock screws. And all the spark plugs were changed after every run, 16 of them.

The front of DLI on Bahama Street in Northridge during its heyday. The Challenger shown was a shop build from the mid-1970s. (Photo Courtesy Landy Family Archives)

One of the boats DLI provided power for was Hot Damn Hondo, *driven by Mike Brendell, son of Dick's former boat business associate Irv Brendell. (Photo Courtesy Landy Family Archives)*

watch the fuel cars run. There were so many cars, we could take a little break to do that.

"When my dad raced, I was always in the bleach box. Even as a kid, I could fit right in with the crew."

"When we got Pepsi as a sponsor, we got a half truckload of Pepsi at the shop. I think I was 13 or so. We drank so much of it, I cannot drink Pepsi to this day."

Richard also recalled at length touring done with the racing teams as well as the shop work. "The trips were not too bad; they were like military drills, and you came back a little better and bigger. I invited a couple of my friends from high school to come along; none of them ever went twice though! [laughter] It was hauling water and gas, cleaning and waxing the cars, changing clutches and rear ends. You would be changing the stuff on your back, with the car up on little ramps and a blanket on your chest because everything was still so hot. Pull the 4-speed, keep it resting on your chest while the other crew member would change the clutch out, then stab the trans back in again. You would pull the bolts out, swap parts, and do it as fast as you could to get back in the staging lanes.

"I know Sox and Grumpy were guys we raced regularly. Dad got serious when the car was going rounds. Not that he wasn't otherwise, but things would tense up. Especially with the Super Stock and factory deal; we had to be the good guys with the white hats, and everything had to be perfect. So when you won, the big reward was tearing the motor down. 'Awww, Dad, glad you won but . . .'

"And he is off getting his picture taken, and we were taking the engine apart. Sometimes I had to drop the head in the ice chest to cool it off and make sure it would cc legally. I thought I was pretty sneaky.

"Indy was always the big deal. The track was big, and the whole town was about racing. I remember the slipper clutches in the dragsters and Funny Cars. Those things were exploding and cutting the cars up. You would hear it blow and look up and see the clutch discs flying through the air. We would always run to the fences to

The Shop Back Home and More

"I remember changing parts from steel to aluminum. We would fabricate that stuff in the shop," Richard Landy continues. "From a young age, I learned how to TIG-weld and make little things. I would ask him, 'Why are we making all this stuff up when you have to put the lead ballast back into it anyway?' He told me it gave him the option of putting the weight back where he wanted it. Before some match races, he might put 150 pounds in it, and I had to pull that off without anyone knowing it. You could figure out how fast the other guy was going and adjust for it.

"I learned how to paint gray. We often repainted the shop floor when a magazine was coming. One time as a kid, I had to sandblast 25 sets of Hemi cylinder heads one day; they would give me a mask and 50 pounds of sand and off I went. My brother and I would grind all the excess weight and small pieces away from the bare blocks with a grinder. It was like this old 8-inch 2-hp handheld unit, and it could not overheat.

In the dyno room at DLI with a Boss Ford engine during the 1980s. (Photo Courtesy Landy Family Archives)

The 1970 Challenger R/T that Dick kept as his personal muscle car. It was powered by a 440/4-speed combination and is reported to now be in a private collection. (Photo Courtesy Landy Family Archives)

"When I first saw it, my dad said to me, 'I dare you to pick this grinder up.' I did.

"The next thing I know, I have a set of goggles and I'm working with it."

Robert agrees. "Yeah, you know, I wouldn't trade those days for anything. Actually, you couldn't do it like that today anyhow; they would lock your parents up for violating child labor laws."

Clinics and Personal Cars

"We had all of the giveaways; we would go through sponsor T-shirts, hats, little things like that," says Richard. "Most of those were raffled for filling out a contact card that same night. You could be contacted through your card, and at the end of the year, Dodge would give away an entire car to one of the clinic attendees using them.

"My mom would get some pretty cool cars to drive sometimes from Dodge. My dad actually enjoyed the twin-turbo Stealth he got later. In fact, when the shop closed up, he still had two or three Mitsubishi engines for that. We had the Colt that he ran as an off-road car; he always liked driving off-road events for fun, that and motorcycles. The Colt had this little turbo'ed-up 4-cylinder. I built the front-to-back skid plates for it that covered the full length of the car. We could take that thing out in the chaparral and drive right all over the vegetation like skipping a rock because of it. It eventually went to Hawaii."

Speaking of personal cars, Dick had a number of street machines. One of the most visible was a silver 1970 Challenger R/T with a T/A-style hood and a 440-ci engine that he had built under the hood. This car became familiar to thousands of magazine readers as the muscle car restoration hobby took off in the 1980s. Dick's final muscle machine was a Dodge Magnum wagon with a gen-three Hemi engine. Though forays into other brands came with the shop, Dick Landy remained loyal to Chrysler products to the end.

There was a 1972 Dodge Demon around the shop that both Richard and Robert used in high school as well. "For 1972, my father took delivery of a new stripped model Demon for building into a race car, a complete car," says Robert. "That was the closest thing he could get to a body-in-white: 198-inch six, three on the tree, and in white paint! As I recall, Dad's words were, 'The higher ups of Dodge Division wanted [me] to remain in the big car.' Therefore, we yanked the plug on the little one.

"The car sat for a couple of years and eventually became my brother Richard's first car. He extensively modified the body, suspension, and driveline like a 'baby NASCAR' ride but left a 225-inch 6-cylinder in it. Later, I owned it for an even longer period of time and switched it over to a mild-built 360-headed 318. We still tease each other about who's Demon it was. [laughs] I later sold the car to Steve Atwell; he bought it sight unseen because of the titling and had it shipped across the country. I heard he put a Hemi in it and gave it to his son."

Inside the garage area of the shop. Visible are the Dart Sport between races and the little Colt with some body panel wear following an off-road jaunt. (Photo Courtesy Landy Family Archives)

CHAPTER 6

ON THE ROAD: THE TRUCKS AND TRAILERS OF THE DICK LANDY RACING TEAM

It is sometimes said that getting there is half the fun. For Dick, Mike, Richard, and Robert Landy, plus the team's crew members and drivers, including Bob Lambeck, Jim Wetton, Gale Mortimer, Greg Renkenberger, Willie Honsberger, Robert "Leroy" Kure, and others, that effort included thousands of miles in the transporters and the literal grind of vehicle maintenance in hotel parking lots or poor weather. For many who remember the time, drag racing travel was a combination of good times spiced by kidney-busting byways, sunsets turning into deep midnight, roadside repairs, and the resolve to finish the job in time for the next scheduled date. Dick Landy's connections at Dodge allowed him to have some then-modern support equipment. Gean Landy's files contain the following images of some of this equipment.

Seen at Bakersfield in 1965, the first crew cab may have been a loaner since the big Dodge station wagon shows up later in the season.

The supercharged funny Dart on its tagalong trailer, at the end of 1966 in Phoenix, Arizona. The team still had the Monaco wagon for support that year.

Two clinic cars, a ramp bed, and a two-wheel tagalong, with driver Jim Wetton in early 1967. This truck was the team's new D700 crew-cab, which used a 413-ci wedge, 5-speed manual transmission, and 2-speed rear gear for highway use.

The team rigs at Indy in 1969, with the 1967 D700 and the brand-new T-truck. The truck was based on the same basic D700 chassis/driveline but was customized specifically for racing teams, with ramp and storage capacities. This was perhaps the T-truck's first road tour after delivery.

In the pits with friends at Pomona in 1970. Note the new Sox & Martin T-truck and the big roof-mounted A/C units. The Landy team's 1967 D700 is shown as well.

New 1970 sponsors such as Pepsi had colorful designs and logos on the toolbox area. With Dick's Challenger on the T-truck that year, the 1967 D700 was used for touring by Bob Lambeck , though the Pro Stock Swinger stayed mainly on the West Coast.

Big 1971 changes in the clinics resulted in the team's first enclosed-box rig. This press kit photo shows the just-finished mobile clinic truck, with its doors designed for viewing the latest parts. This too was based on a custom Dodge D-series cab and chassis.

In 1974, the new Oleynik-boxed Dodge D800 custom box truck replaced the truck wrecked in 1973. Dick used this support vehicle until he quit driving.

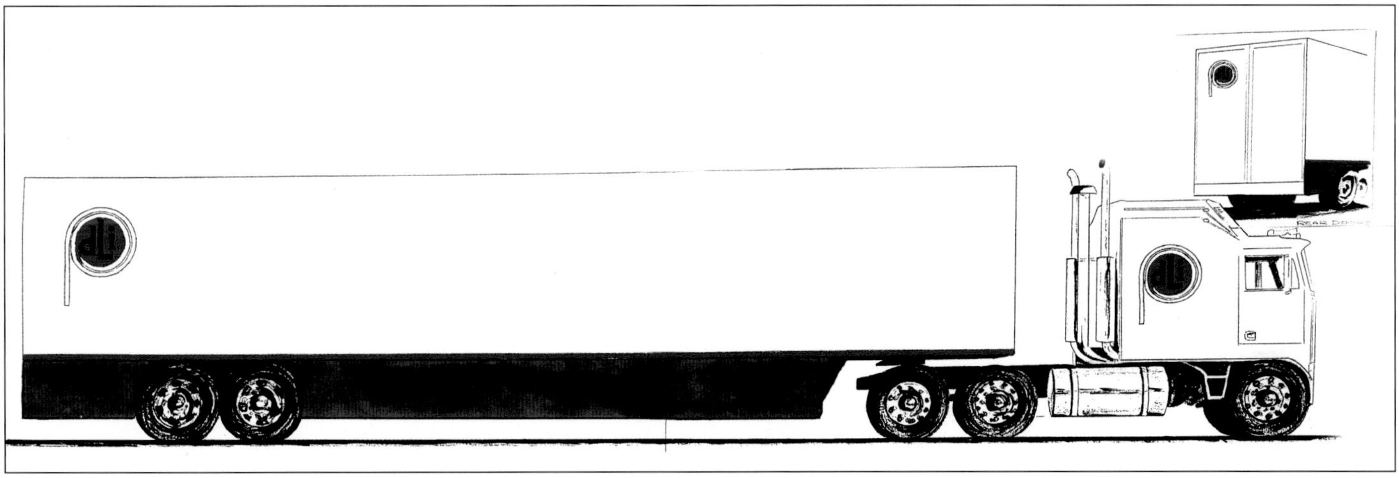

Had Dick Landy continued campaigning Pro Stock in 1983, he would have used this new 18-wheeler as a support vehicle.

And Then There Was One

Tom Yeager of California knew what he was looking at, but it was not what had been sold by Dick Landy as a race transporter/support vehicle back in the day. Landy's team had received a 1968 D700 conversion truck, probably in the early summer of 1969. This was unique in that it featured a T-shaped area built behind the crew cab and an extended bed to carry a race car, plus towing capacity for a tagalong. The 1969 image of it in this chapter is the earliest one I've found. It was taken in a motel parking lot during the 1969 U.S. Nationals trip. This truck was notably shown on the cover of the final Dodge clinic program that Dick Landy distributed as well.

When found, the truck had been heavily modified, including the T having been topped off. Yeager began a multiyear process of restoring it to the way it had looked when the Landy team had used it in 1970. Tom bought other Dodges to obtain correct donor pieces for the project and specific NOS parts from around the world via the Internet. A 413 is back in the old frame, and care is being taken to save as much of the original vehicle as possible. Thanks to Tom's significant other, Elana Scherr, I had a chance to bring Danette and Richard Landy to the shop to see it. No other Landy transporters have been documented to date; this one will be a keeper once it is finished.

Remnants of history on the Tom Yeager truck.

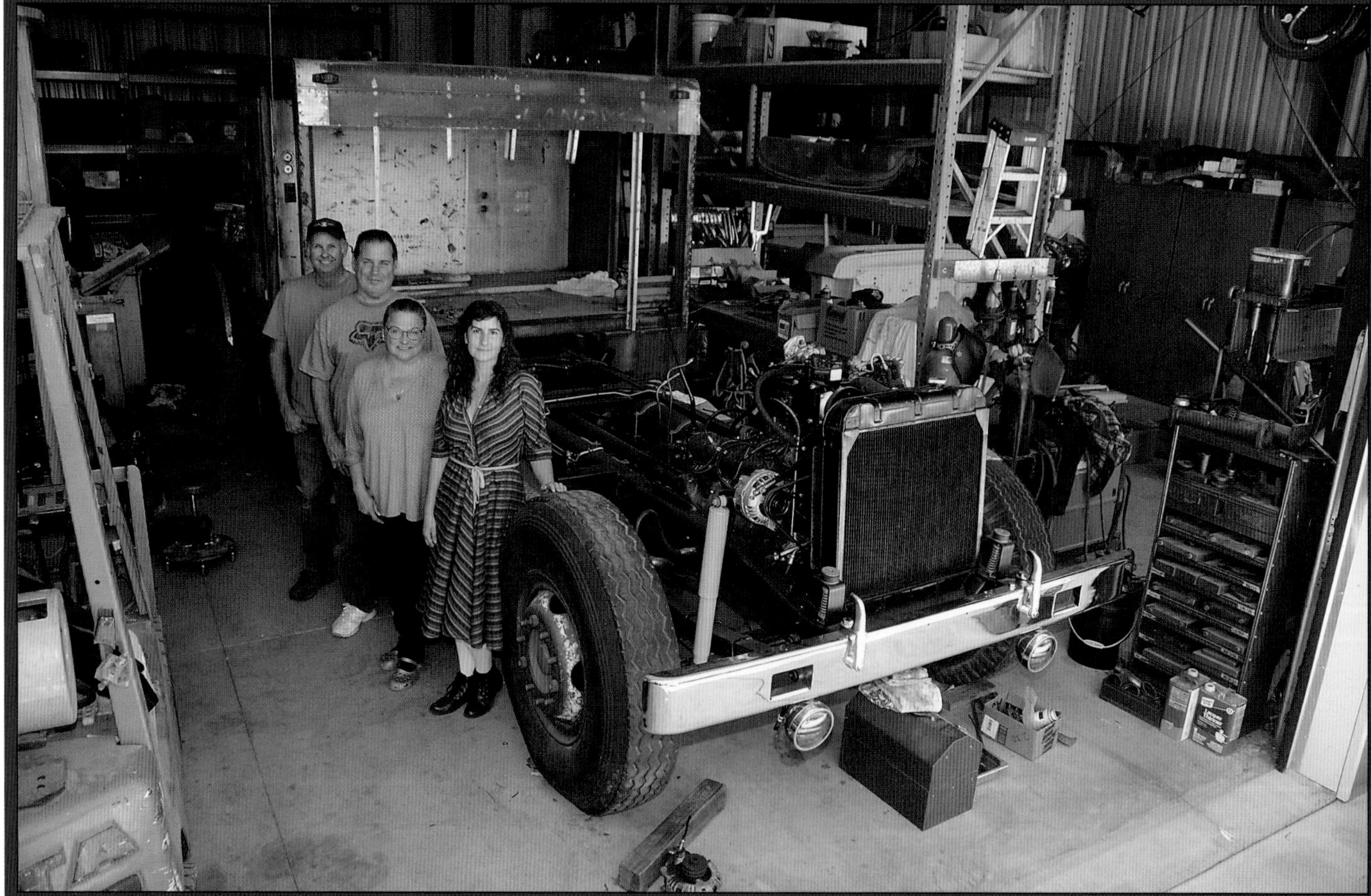

From front to back, Elana Scherr, Danette Landy, Richard Landy, and Tom Yeager stand with the ongoing restoration of the T-truck in Yeager's shop bay in 2015.

CHAPTER 7

THE LEGACY OF DICK LANDY

The long stretches of old Route 66 across the Mohave Desert have not changed much in the 50 years since Dick Landy took his first big trip East with that first 1964 Hemi Dodge. David Hakim and I were in a brand-new Dodge Challenger Scat Pack, powered by a 392-ci Hemi engine and on our way to see the Landy family for this project. In looking at Dick's life, it was fitting to not simply fly out West. Our quick four-day run from Detroit to Tennessee to the San Fernando Valley was more like the way things used to be.

After my tenure as editor of *Mopar Muscle* ended, I still ran into Landy on many occasions. I documented the 1973 Dart Sport as a freelancer, created a big story on the clinic program for Carlisle Events, and knew Dick was always available to talk on the phone when I had questions. In 2006 he and Gean came to Minnesota for a big car show that Fred Engelhart was doing in the town of Elkton. It was like a homecoming; the Landys, Butch Leal, Arlen Vanke, Buddy Martin, and many others had arrived as well, all to be part of what was then the largest gathering of Hemi race cars in the 21st Century. By then, Dick was not in good health, but he made time for everyone, and we all hoped for his quick recovery. To our dismay, he passed away the following year, on January 11, from complications that led to kidney failure. Dick Landy was 69 years old.

Geoff Stunkard, Robert Landy, and David Hakim, over the hill to the Patch in Bakersfield for the 2015 March Meet.

Would it be a stretch to consider that our 2015 Challenger, as it ate away the hundreds of miles toward the Golden State, was a descendant of Landy's effort? Consider the impact Dick Landy had on Dodge as a performance brand back in the day. It was about the "Good Guys in White Hats," a big trademark smile, and beating those Brand X guys. It came with the roar of a Hemi, and wheels-up action, and clean, colorful paint. Although there were other capable Dodge drivers in the sport, Dick Landy always looked the part of a winner and represented the company in a way that made it a winner as well. No one, including Dick, would have guessed that in 2015, Chrysler would be building Challengers that appeared and performed even better than what had been available in his heyday.

As for drag racing, Dick once told me that he wished he had kept going. In some ways, like his peers (Don Nicholson, for instance), he found that the big-money/big-attitude effort that characterized the quarter-mile following the 1970s was not what the sport had once been. He certainly could have adapted, but he instead focused his energies on the continued success of DLI and did not push toward the fiscal insanity into which drag racing has since evolved. The Hemi had paved a pathway for many here, and Landy (indeed, all Chrysler racers) paid a dear price for its success once the high sheriffs had determined to make racing "fair" at its expense.

In the ensuing decades, Dick's accomplishments were recognized by many. He was an honoree at the NHRA Hot Rod Reunion, inducted into the International Drag Racing Hall of Fame, posthumously part of the first Mopar Hall of Fame, and invited to take a race car up the course in Goodwood, England. DLI engines set records at Bonneville and on water, as well as pavement, and Dick even provided power for one of

Trophies from Dick's career are a treasured part of Gean Landy's memories.

Mike (left) and Richard Landy (right).

the most notorious street machines ever put on film, the 145-mph Brock Yates/Hal Needham Trans-Con Medivac ambulance driven in the final cross-country Cannonball Run and later seen in the movie of the same name.

Hakim and I ended up putting more than 8,000 on the Challenger during our trip. Once we arrived, we went with the Landys to the March Meet in Bakersfield and had a Sunday barbecue brunch with Mike Landy. We went through boxes of paperwork and looked at hundreds of slides and photos. We witnessed a lot more than simply a racing icon; we saw a father, a friend, and a much-missed family member. I was humbled to find that he had preserved even brief correspondence written by me in years past.

Once it was time to leave, we blew back across America in that Dodge to view Todd Werner's Landy car and memorabilia collection in Clearwater, Florida, and to go to the NHRA Gatornationals. For two journalists in the age of jet lag, it was a once-in-a-lifetime trip. Whether we could have handled things all summer the way Dick, Richard, and Robert Landy and the crews did all those many years ago is still up in the air; at least we can admit we tried to find a little of it.

Danette (Landy) Satenstein.

Many of the legends of drag racing are now gone. What remains of Dick Landy are memories and mementoes, recorded accolades of victory, and visual cues in books and magazines. We will not again see the likes of "Dandy Dick" Landy again. He was a personality formed in an era when Detroit breathed fire and performance was "the in thing." I think he would be okay with that, too. . . .

Robert Landy.

Gean Landy puts clinic patches on jackets for David Hakim's two sons.

CLINIC PROGRAM 1967–1974

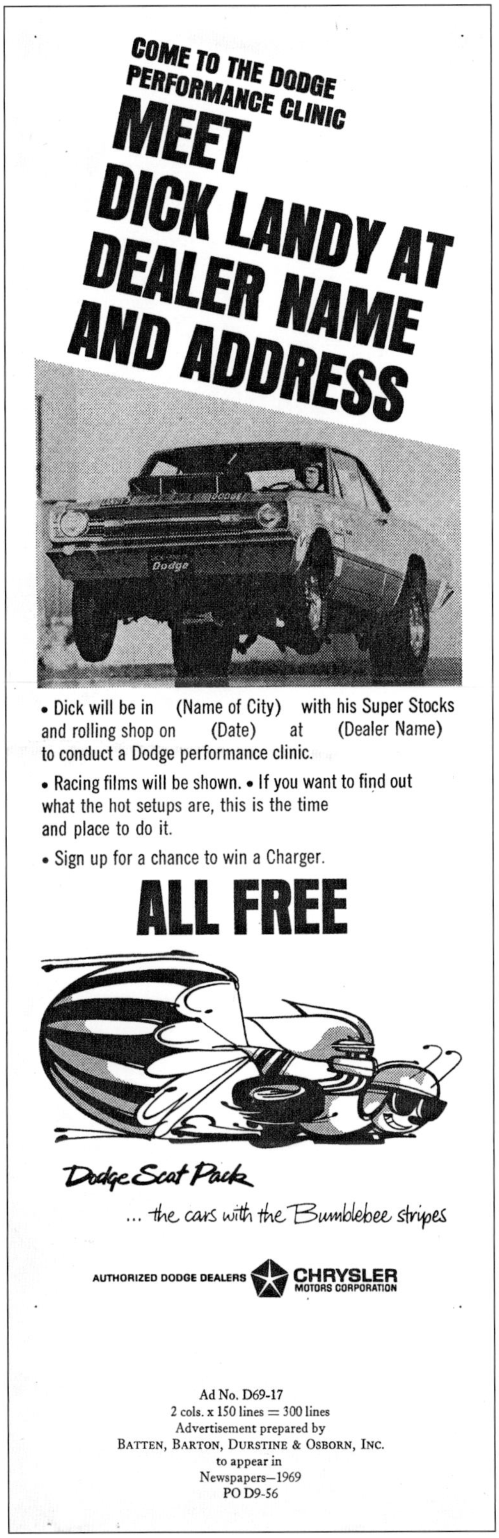

The clinic program was initiated in early 1967, perhaps sometime after Dick won his class title at the 1967 Winternationals. Plymouth had already begun its program with Sox & Martin, and Dick went to Daytona Beach to witness the first one. Following its huge success, Dodge quickly geared up to put Dick Landy into his own series of performance clinics. Starting in the middle of 1968, clinic attendance figures were also recorded. Following are the known clinic dates and locations from the Landy files.

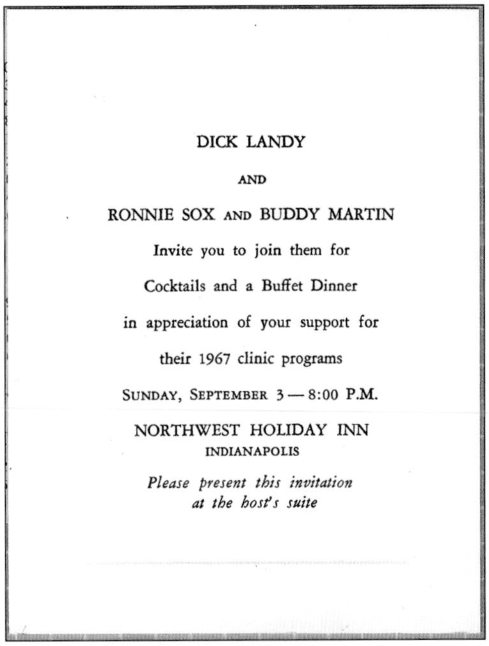
DICK LANDY

AND

RONNIE SOX AND BUDDY MARTIN

Invite you to join them for

Cocktails and a Buffet Dinner

in appreciation of your support for

their 1967 clinic programs

SUNDAY, SEPTEMBER 3 — 8:00 P.M.

NORTHWEST HOLIDAY INN

INDIANAPOLIS

Please present this invitation at the host's suite

An invitation to a joint Landy/Sox & Martin cocktail party at the U.S. Nationals from 1967, the first year of the clinic programs.

1967 Clinic Program

Daytona 500, with Sox & Martin
Scottsdale, AZ
Phoenix, AZ
Community College, San Diego, CA
Iverson Motor Co., Santa Maria, CA
Empire Dodge, San Bernardino, CA
Crockett Bros., Fresno, CA
Korum Motors, Puyallup, WA
Spokane, WA
Frank Antone, Portland, OR
Teague Motor Co., Salem, OR
Seattle, WA
Wichita, KS
Atlanta, GA
Goode Motors, Bristol, TN
Detroit, MI
Dodge City, Rockford, IL
Minnesota Dragways,
Coon Rapids, MN
D. L. Stetler & Sons, York, PA
Sid Broughton Dodge,
Wilmington, DE
Indianapolis, IN
Omaha, NE
Ferris Miles Dodge, Redwood
City, CA
San Jose, CA
Saddleback Dodge, Santa Ana, CA
Studio Dodge,
North Hollywood, CA

Dick probably got to sleep in his own bed after attending the Empire Dodge Performance Clinic on April 6, 1967.

The half-page newspaper insertion sent out in publicity kits for the 1969 clinic program, with space for adding the dealer name, address, and clinic dates.

One of the team's 1967 Super Stock Coronets in the showroom of Frank Antone's Dodge in Portland, Oregon.

Dick (center) educates the masses about underhood components in 1967.

A rare stop in the north at Minnesota Dragways, 1967.

The new 1968 Charger sporting a Landy clinic decal during its first appearance in Nebraska in late 1967.

Dick Landy himself probably took some of the slides in this book with his personal 35-mm camera; shown here in 1967.

A stock Charger resides on the back of the Landy hauler in front of Sid Broughton Dodge in Wilmington, Delaware, in 1967

Newspaper clippings from 1967 had appeared very similar when announcing the Dodge Performance Clinics.

The final clinic of the year at North Hollywood Dodge in 1967, featuring Linda Vaughn. (Photo Courtesy Landy Family Archives)

Dick, engaged in conversation, looks the part of a professional driver in 1967.

Riding herd on the transporters as the team gets ready to head out in 1970. Note the tagalong for the SS/EA Charger behind the Dart.

Meeting fans in 1968 in the pits at the racetrack was as important as the clinics to Dodge's racing superstar.

Mike and Dick Landy hang out with race fans in the pits. Notice the abundance of lighting and megaphones in the background.

Fans gather in the early evening as a Landy Performance Clinic begins in a dealership showroom in 1967. Two 1967 Coronet roofs can be seen as well.

Wherever Dick went, you were sure to find a cigar protruding from his mouth.

1968 Clinic Program

Date	Location	Attendance
1/2	Delano Dodge, Delano, CA	
1/3	Studio Dodge, North Hollywood, CA	
1/18	March Air Force Base, CA	
1/19	Moss Motors, Riverside, CA	
1/20–21	Motor Trend 500, Riverside, CA	
2/15–16	Hollywood Dodge, Los Angeles	
3/5–10	Motorama Auto Show, Anaheim, CA	
3/14–15	Carl Burger Dodge, San Diego, CA	
3/17	Riverside Raceway press review	
3/26–27	Bill Breck Dodge, Tucson AZ	
3/29–30	Dana Bros. Motor, Tempe, AZ	
4/2–3	Las Vegas Dodge, Las Vegas, NV	
4/4–5	Earl Ike Dodge, Inglewood, CA	
4/8	Glenn E. Thomas, Long Beach, CA	
4/10	Inland Center Dodge, San Bernardino, CA	
4/11–12	LaHabra Dodge, LaHabra, CA	
4/13	Snavely & Langford, Compton, CA	
4/16	Crocket Bros., Fresno, CA	
4/17	Frontier Dodge, Modesto, CA	
4/18	Braleys Jack Nelson Dodge, Stockton, CA	
4/19	Pioneer Dodge, San Jose, CA	
4/23	Hillsdale Dodge, San Mateo, CA	
4/24	Diener Motors, Roseville, CA	
4/25	John Drew's Arden Dodge, Sacramento, CA	
4/26	Swift Dodge, Sacramento, CA	
5/6	Hartwig Motors, Iowa City, IA	
5/7	McCredil Dodge, Keokuk, IA	
5/9	Madison Motors, Madison, WI	
5/10–11	Dodge City Sales, Rockford, IL	
5/13	Dan Miller Motors, Zion, IL	
5/14	Arlington Park Dodge, Palatine, IL	
5/15	Oak Park Dodge, Forest Park, IL	
5/17–18	Northwest Dodge, Detroit, MI	
5/20–21	Crestwood Dodge, Garden City, MI	
5/22–23	Town & Country Dodge, Farmington, MI	
5/29	Paul Willison Dodge, Toronto, ON	
5/30	West End Chrysler-Dodge, Toronto, ON	
5/31	NHRA Canadian Nationals, Toronto, ON	
6/1-9	AHRA Spring Nationals, Bristol, TN	
6/10-16	NHRA Springnationals, Englishtown, NJ	
7/2	County Dodge Sales, New Haven, CT	250
7/3	Hampden Dodge, Springfield, MA	350
7/5	Natick Dodge, Natick, MA	400
7/6	Bock Dodge, Norwood, MA	—
7/8	D. E. Stetler & Sons, York, PA	500
7/9	Lutz & Bitterman, Robesonia, PA	450
7/10	Nagle Motor, Inc., Pottstown, PA	500
7/11	Martin Glauser Dodge, Vineland, NJ	500
7/12	Sid Broughton Dodge, Wilmington DE	350
7/22	Suburban Dodge, Metuchen, NJ	—
7/23	Newark Dodge, Newark, NJ	450
7/25	DeMicco Motors, Kingston, NY	400
7/26	Miller Motors, Binghamton, NY	600
7/29	Bob Banning Dodge, Hyattsville, MD	350
7/30	Herb Gordon Dodge, Fairfax, VA	400
7/31	Tidewater Dodge, Norfolk, VA	1,000
8/1	Royal Dodge, Fayetteville, NC	1,200
8/13	Arroco Motors, NY	450
8/14	Cy Green Motors, Manhasset, NY	275
8/15	Ebbets Field Dodge, Brooklyn, NY	100
9/4	Kilborn Motors, Decatur, IL	400
9/5	Vandeveer, Evansville, IN	700
9/6	Sisk Motors, Hopkinsville, KY	300
9/7	Parker Dodge, Paducah, KY	400
9/9–10	Rixman Dodge, St. Louis, MO	300
9/11	Florissant Dodge, St. Louis, MO	350
9/12–13	King Dodge, St. Louis, MO	260
10/7	Huntsville Dodge, Huntsville, AL	600
10/8	Lenox Dodge, Atlanta, GA	300
10/9	Massey Dodge, Jacksonville, FL	700
10/10	Southside Dodge, Jacksonville, FL	400
10/11	Winter Park Dodge, Winter Park, FL	450
10/14	Cape Dodge, Merritt Island, FL	450
10/15	Biscayne Dodge, Miami, FL	500
10/16	Brooks-Massey Dodge, Tampa, FL	225

Whether it was in staging, in the pits, or at a Performance Clinic, there were always eyes looking at Landy and his Dodges.

The 1970 organization booklet for the new Scat Pack Club promotion. Dick was the charter member

The top of a sheet of letterhead used in the first of the Scat Pack-era clinic press releases, 1968.

Date	Location	Attendance
10/17	Mobile Dodge, Mobile, AL	700
10/21	Cumberland Motor, Nashville, TN	350
10/22	Chuck Hutton Dodge, Memphis, TN	400
10/23	Bevis Dodge, Little Rock, AR	600
10/28	Dependable Dodge, Austin, TX	300
10/29	Freeway Dodge, Fort Worth, TX	900
10/31	Hutton Donaldson, Shreveport, LA	550
11/5	Spencer Dodge, Wichita, KS	650
11/6	New Dodge City, Tulsa, OK	600

1969 Clinic Program

Date	Location	Attendance
2/24	Dave Schenk Dodge, Whittier, CA	520
2/25	Carl Burger Dodge, San Diego, CA	650
2/26	Valley Dodge, Van Nuys, CA	—
3/3	Downey Dodge, Downey, CA	350
3/3	Pomona Dodge, Pomona, CA	920
3/5–6	Saddleback Dodge, Santa Ana, CA	670
4/14	Glass City Dodge, Toledo, OH	930
4/15	Ed Carpenter Sales, Wayne, MI	515
4/16	Crestwood Dodge, Garden City, MI	730
4/17	Muskegon Dodge, Muskegon, MI	1,240
4/22	North Motors, Springfield, OH	1,220
4/23	Queensgate Dodge, Cincinnati, OH	1,470
4/24	Falls City Dodge Louisville, KY	780
4/25	Eastside Dodge, Indianapolis, IN	650
4/30	Plainfield Dodge, Plainfield, NJ	1,330
5/1	Rockville Centre Dodge, Rockville Centre, NY	1,110
5/2	D'Elia Motors, Greenwich, CT	700
5/6	Ken Goeway Dodge, Troy, NY	840
5/7	Culver Dodge, Rochester, NY	1,580
5/8	Kenton Dodge, Kenmore, NY	790
5/12	Village Dodge, Painesville, OH	2,290
5/13	Garrett Dodge, Akron, OH	800
5/14	Kempthorn Motors, Canton, OH	1,310
5/15	Northland Dodge, Columbus, OH	900
5/19	Hillcrest Dodge, Rochester, MN	950
5/20–21	White Bear Dodge, White Bear Lake, MN	3,100
5/22	Town's Edge Dodge, St. Paul, MN	500
5/23	LeFevre Motor Co., Brookings, SD	1,350
5/27	Harold Medow Dodge, South Bend, IN	800
5/28	River Oaks Dodge, Peoria, IL	1,240
6/16	Freeway Dodge, Fort Worth, TX	790
6/17	North Star Dodge, San Antonia, TX	680
7/22	George Stewart Motor, Washington, PA	850
7/23	Vern Staley Dodge, Pittsburgh, PA	1,320
7/27	Sam Brown Dodge, Salem, OH	650
7/28	Churches Motors, Manchester, CT	800
7/29	Elmwood Dodge, Providence, RI	1,650
7/30	Dag Motors, Putnam, CT	510
8/5	Lehigh Valley Dodge, Allentown, PA	750
8/6	Martin Glauser Dodge, Vineland, NJ	725
8/7	D. E. Stetler & Sons, York, PA	600
8/12	Blackwell Motor Co., Danville, VA	1,390
8/13	Beach Bros. Motors, Salem, VA	1,210
8/19	Lou Brock Dodge, East St. Louis, IL	850
8/20	Vandeveer Inc., Evansville, IN	950
8/21	Vigo Dodge, Terre Haute, IN	720
9/8	Massey Dodge, Jacksonville, FL	800
9/9	Southside Dodge, Jacksonville, FL	475

Date	Location	Attendance
9/11	City Dodge, Decatur, GA	1,360
9/12	Lenox Dodge Atlanta, GA	1,160
9/15	Royal Dodge, Fayetteville, N C	1,560
9/18	Independence Dodge, Independence, MO	1,725
9/19	Husker Dodge, Omaha, NE	900
9/24	Bill Breck Dodge, Colorado Springs, CO	840
9/25	Dodge City, Denver, CO	1,000
10/6	Dishman Dodge, Spokane, WA	910
10/7	Lewiston Dodge, Lewiston, ID	750
10/9	King Dodge, Portland, OR	470
10/14	K C Dodge, San Francisco, CA	780
10/15	Jerry Smith Dodge, Sunnyvale, CA	1,100
10/16	Sandy Crochet Dodge, Fresno, CA	920

A large window-hung poster shows the 1968 Charger and announces the dates and locations of upcoming clinics.

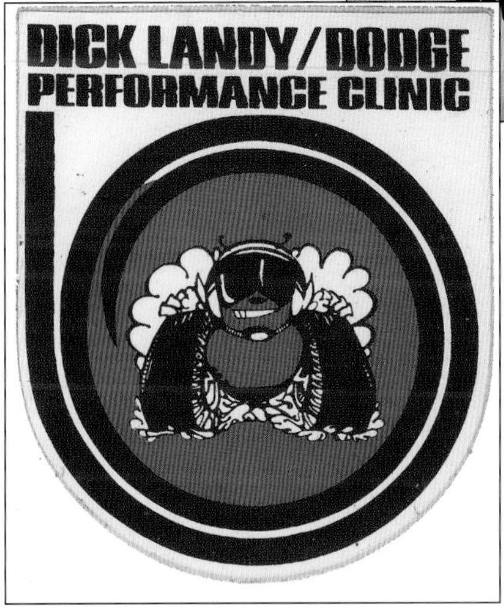

A Dick Landy Performance Clinic decal would be a great addition to any Landy collection. (Photo Courtesy Landy Family Archives)

D. E. Stetler & Sons featured two Landy's Dodges on its showroom floor in 1967.

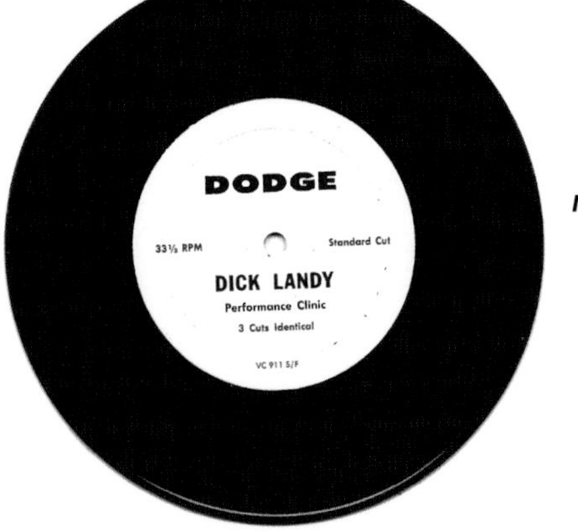

A 33⅓-speed record with three radio commercials for upcoming clinic programs was included in the dealer press package in 1970.

A Scat Pack adhesive decal issued in 1969 by D'Elia, a dealership that hosted a clinic program.

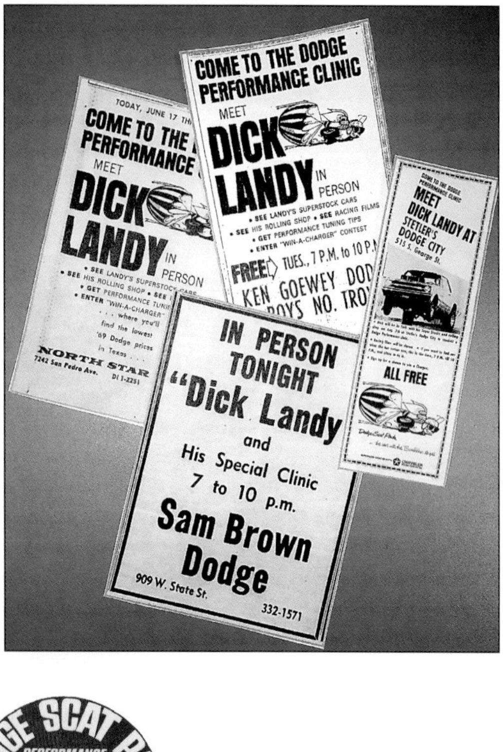

As Dick Landy and the Dodge Performance Clinics gained popularity, dealerships took it upon themselves to create specific advertising campaigns geared toward their event.

DICK LANDY DODGE PERFORMANCE CLINIC HEADQUARTERS
P.O. BOX 551 NORTHRIDGE, CALIFORNIA 91324

The top of the press kit's stationery.

1969 Special Event Displays

Location	*Attendance*
Fort Bragg personnel and hospital	15,540
Chicago Auto Show	600,000
NHRA/AHRA national events (9)	610,000
Match Races (42); average 4,800 per race	201,600

1970 Clinic Program

Date	*Location*	*Attendance*
3/11	Palo Alto Dodge, Palo Alto, CA	450
3/12	Concord Dodge, Concord, CA	425
3/13	Stan Motors, Fairfield, CA	660
3/19	Lynwood Dodge, Lynwood, WA	1,160
3/20	Bellevue Dodge, Bellevue, WA	670
3/31	Weggy Motors, Pasadena, CA	725
4/1	Ingram Motors, Oxnard, CA	525
4/2	Iverson Motor Co., Santa Maria, CA	770
4/7	Covina Dodge, Covina, CA	1,070
4/8	Reseda Dodge, Reseda, CA	660
4/9	Wil'Mar Dodge, Los Angeles, CA	150
4/28	Motor City Dodge, Pontiac, MI	375
5/1	Muskegon Dodge, Muskegon, MI	775
5/5	Burgunder Motors, Bridgeville, PA	1,125
5/6	D. E. Stetler & Sons, York, PA	550
5/7	D. E. Stetler & Sons, York, PA	475
5/12	Pueblo Dodge, Pueblo, CO	1,300
5/13	Dodge City, Denver, CO	588
5/14	Cheyenne Dodge, Cheyenne, WY	1,160
5/19	Independence Dodge, Independence, MO	680
5/20	Raytown Dodge, Raytown, MO	380
5/21	Fairway Dodge, Ellisville, MO	1,060
5/25	Western Dodge, Marion, IN	1,340
5/26	Tri -County Dodge, Cincinnati, OH	1,270
5/27	John Gibson Dodge, Athens, OH	500
6/3	Terry Motors, Rogersville, TN	760
6/4	Callaghan Dodge, Bristol, TN	840
6/15	Freeway Dodge, Fort Worth, TX	560
7/10	Clearview Dodge, Metairie, LA	1,700
7/21	Beach Bros. Motors, Salem, VA	750
7/22	Blackwell Motor Co., Danville, VA	680
7/23	Town & Country, Woodbridge, VA	970
7/28	Elmwood Dodge, Providence, RI	860
7/29	Brockton Dodge, Brockton, MA	2,200

The envelope for the final year of dealership clinics (1970), sent out by Landy's advance team to dealerships and racetracks.

Date	Location	Attendance
7/30	Pioneer Dodge, Danvers, MA	1,010
8/3	Fort Wayne Dodge, Fort Wayne, IN	825
8/4	Hunter Dodge, Madison Heights, MI	260
8/5	Crestwood Dodge, Garden City, MI	475
8/13	Music City Dodge, Nashville, TN	680
8/14	Chuck Hutton Dodge, Memphis, TN	225
8/20	Rockville Centre Dodge, Rockville Centre, NY	1,020
8/24	D'Elia Motors, Greenwich, CT	870
8/25	Plainfield Dodge, North Plainfield, NJ	1,440
10/27	Hedgecoke Dodge, Amarillo, TX	(unknown)

APPENDIX B

RACE SCHEDULE 1969-1971

For 1970, the team also recorded race attendance by driver and vehicle. Unfortunately, no records were located for 1972, and the 1967 listing was compiled using national and regional news clippings that Gean Landy had preserved in her scrapbook. This book is the only exhaustive reference of the Landy team tours and schedules for the era. Look closely to see if "Dandy Dick" Landy and his Dodge performance clinics came to your neighborhood.

1969 Big Race Events; Landy and/or Lambeck Drivers*

AHRA Winter Nationals, Phoenix, AZ
NHRA Winternationals, Pomona, CA
Smokers meet, Bakersfield, CA
Hot Rod magazine meet, Riverside, CA
Memorial Day SS meet, Union Grove, WI
AHRA Spring Nationals, Bristol, TN
NHRA Springnationals, Dallas, TX
July 4 SS meet, Union Grove, WI
Cars Magazine Race, Cecil County, MD
Super Stock Magazine meet, York, PA
AHRA Summer Nationals, Long Island, NY
NHRA Nationals, Indianapolis, IN
NHRA World Finals, Dallas, TX
** Not including match race dates*

1970 Pro/Stock Challenger Schedule; Dick Landy Driver

2/8	OCIR, Irvine, CA
2/22	Irwindale Raceway, CA
3/14–15	Sears Point Raceway, CA
3/21–22	Seattle Raceway, WA
4/4	OCIR, Irvine, CA
4/12	KCIR, Kansas City, MO
4/26	NYNS, Long Island, NY
5/3	Detroit Dragway, MI
5/16	Bonneville Raceway, UT
5/17	Continental Divide Raceway, CA
5/23–24	Detroit Dragway, MI
6/27	KCIR, Kansas City, MO
7/4	Green Valley Raceway, TX
7/11	Houston Raceway, TN
7/25	Memphis, TN
7/26	Spokane, WA
8/15	Memphis, TN
8/12–22	Seattle, WA
8/22–23	Bonneville Raceway, Salt Lake City, UT
9/3	Amarillo, TX
9/19–20	OCIR, Irvine, CA
9/26	Fremont Raceway, CA

1970 Pro/Stock Dart Schedule; Bob Lambeck Driver

2/8	OCIR, Irvine, CA
2/22	Irwindale Raceway, CA
3/14–15	Sears Point Raceway, CA
3/21–22	Seattle Raceway, WA
4/4	OCIR, Irvine CA
5/9–10	Firebird International Raceway, Boise ID
5/23	Irwindale Raceway, CA
6/26–27	Fremont Raceway, CA
7/25–26	Spokane, WA
8/22–23	Bonneville Raceway, Salt Lake City, UT
8/23	Seattle International Raceway, WA
9/19–20	OCIR, Irvine, CA

1970 HEMI Charger R/T Super Stock Schedule; Bob Lambeck Driver

2/8	OCIR, Irvine, CA
2/22	Irwindale Raceway, CA
3/14–15	Sears Point Raceway, CA
3/21–22	Seattle Raceway, WA
4/4	OCIR, Irvine, CA
5/23	Irwindale Raceway, CA
6/27–28	Fremont Raceway, CA
7/25–26	Firebird International, Boise, ID
8/8–9	Bakersfield Raceway, CA
8/22–23	Bonneville Raceway, Salt Lake, UT
9/19–20	OCIR, Irvine, CA

1970 C/MP Challenger Schedule; Bill Schrewsberry, Bill Cooper and Other Drivers

4/12	KCIR, Kansas City, MO
4/26	NYNS, Long Island, NY
5/3	Detroit Dragway, MI
5/16	Bonneville Raceway, Salt Lake City, UT

5/17	Continental Divide Raceway, CA
5/23–24	Detroit Dragway, MI
6/27	KCIR, Kansas City, MO
7/4	Green Valley Raceway, TX
7/11	Houston Raceway, TN
7/25	Memphis, TN
7/26	Spokane, WA
8/15	Memphis, TN
9/3	Amarillo, TX

1971 Race Schedule; Dick Landy, Ken Dondero and MP Drivers

1/8–10	AHRA Lions opener, Long Beach, CA
1/16–17	Irwindale, CA
1/19–20	Goodyear/Dodge commercial
1/23–24	Fremont, CA
2/2–4	New vehicle demonstrations
2/4–7	NHRA Winternationals, Pomona, CA
2/8–12	Chrysler test, press kit photo
2/13–14	Las Vegas National Open
2/13–14	OCIR Pro/Stock Championship, Irvine, CA
2/19–21	AHRA Winter Nationals, Phoenix, AZ
3/5-7	March Meet, Bakersfield, CA
3/13–14	AHRA, Fremont, CA
3/16–17	Chrysler test, Florida Dodge Dealers
3/19–21	NHRA Gatornationals, Gainesville, FL
3/27–28	Hot Wheels 2 race, Seattle, WA
4/4–6	Hot Wheels 3 race, Fremont, CA
4/15–18	IHRA, Rockingham, NC
4/22	Jerry's Speed Shop, Charleston, IL
4/23	Flechbeche Speed Shop, Decatur, IL
4/24	Coles Co. Dragway, Charleston, IL
4/25	Great Lakes Dragway, Union Grove, WI
4/27	Dallas Auto Show, Dallas, TX
5/1	Youngstown, OH
5/2	New York National, Long Island, NY
5/5	Morosos Speed Shop, York, PA
5/6	Pro Race Golf Tournament, York, PA
5/7–9	Super Stock Magazine Nationals, York, PA
5/11–12	Goodyear tire test, photo session
5/14–16	NHRA Division 7 WCS, Irwindale, CA
5/15–16	ETSA Safety Park, Syracuse, NY
5/20	Big Ed's Speed Shop, Alexandria, VA
5/21	Manassas Raceway Manassas, VA
5/22–23	NHRA Division 6 WCS, Bremerton, WA
5/23	Madison Township, NJ
5/27	Great Meadows Speed Shop, NJ
5/28	Santa Barbara, CA
5/29	Island Dragway, NJ
5/30	Lions, Long Beach, CA
5/30	Waynesboro, VA
6/3	Madison Township Speed Shop, NJ
6/4	Madison Township Raceway, NJ
6/5	Youngstown, OH
6/6	Niagara Raceway, NY
6/6	Long Beach CA
6/10–13	NHRA Springnationals, Columbus, OH
6/16	Atco Raceway, Atco, NJ
6/18–20	IHRA Bristol Nationals, TN
6/19–20	OCIR, Irvine, CA
6/24	Sharon, PA
6/25	New England Dragway, NH
6/26	Island Dragway, NJ
6/26–27	NHRA Division 7 WCS, Fremont, CA
6/27	Canadian Raceway
6/30	Capitol Raceway, Washington, D.C.
7/2–5	Great Lakes Dragway, Union Grove, WI
7/3–4	Irwindale Raceway, CA
7/7	Maple Grove Raceway, PA
7/8	Sharon, PA
7/10	Detroit Dragway, MI
7/11	Madison Township, NJ
7/10–11	Sacramento, CA
7/16–18	NHRA Summernationals, NJ
7/24	Island Dragway, NJ
7/25	Naperville, IL
7/25	Long Beach, CA
7/28	Rockford, IL
7/30	Union Grove, WI
7/31	Motor City Dragway, Detroit, MI
8/1	Continental Divide Raceway, CO
8/7–8	New England Dragway, NH
8/7–8	OCIR, Irvine, CA
8/12	Napierville, QC
8/13–14	Seattle, WA
8/15	Hartford, CT
8/19–22	AHRA, Salt Lake City, UT
8/26	Calahan Dodge (location unknown)
8/26–29	IHRA Nationals, Bristol, TN
8/27–28	NHRA Division 6 WCS, Seattle, WA
9/1–6	NHRA U.S. Nationals, Indianapolis, IN
10/22–24	NHRA Finals, Amarillo, TX
October	IHRA Finals, Rockingham, NC
11/20–21	NHRA Supernationals, Ontario, CA

Combined Events 1973–1974

*1973 Landy DLI Race and Display Dates**

1/25–28	AHRA Winter Nationals
1/30–31	Chrysler Testing, Irwindale, CA
2/1–4	NHRA Winternationals, Pomona, CA (rain)
2/10–11	NHRA Winternationals, Pomona, CA (rain)
2/17–18	NHRA Winternationals, Pomona, CA
2/24	Irwindale Raceway, CA
2/25	Orange County International Raceway, CA
3/2–4	March Meet, Bakersfield, CA
3/9–11	AHRA, Freemont, CA
3/24	All Pro Final, Orange County, CA
3/30	Swift Dodge, Sacramento, CA (display)
3/31–4/1	Sacramento Raceway, CA
4/6–8	AHRA, Tulsa, OK
4/14–15	Sacramento Raceway, CA
4/26	Freeway Dodge, Fort Worth, TX (display)
4/27–29	IHRA Longhorn, Dallas, TX
5/4–6	IHRA, Rockingham, NC
5/7	Chrysler test, Rockingham, NC
5/12	Thompson Raceway, Thompson, OH
5/13	Dragway 42, Cleveland, OH
5/15–17	Chrysler test, Milan, MI
5/18–20	Dragway 42, Cleveland, OH
5/24–25	Mattoon Mall JC Penney, Mattoon, IL (display)
5/26	Coles Co. Raceway, Charleston, IL
5/27	Union Grove, WI
6/1–3	AHRA, Denver, CO

6/6	USRT, Maple Grove, PA
6/8–10	NHRA, Columbus, OH
6/15–17	IHRA, Bristol, TN
6/19	Crown Auto Stores, Minneapolis/St. Paul, MN (display)
6/20	USRT, Minneapolis/St. Paul, MN
6/21	Sunset Raceway, Sharon, PA
6/22–23	Dragway 42, Cleveland, OH
6/27	Toronto, ON
6/29	Cincinnati, OH
6/30	Rockford, IL (display)
7/1	Rockford Center, Rockford, IL
7/3	Thompson, OH
7/4	USRT, Cayuga, ON
7/6	KC International, Kansas City, MO
7/7–8	AHRA, Kansas City, MO
7/12–15	NHRA Summer Nationals
7/17	JC Penney, Milwaukee, WI
7/18	USRT meet, Union Grove, WI
7/22	US 30 Dragway, Gary, IN
7/26	Gregory Speed Auto, Youngstown, OH (display)
7/27	Youngstown Raceway, Youngstown, OH
7/28	Thompson Raceway, Thompson, OH
7/31	Brunswick Mall, New Brunswick, NJ (display)
8/1	USRT meet, Englishtown, NJ
8/3	St. Louis International Raceway, St. Louis, MO
8/4–5	AHRA, St. Louis, MO
8/11–12	Charlotte Raceway, Charlotte, NC
8/14	Chess Mall, Boston, MA (display)
8/15	New England Dragway, NH
8/23–26	PRA race, Tulsa, OK
8/27	Monroe sales meeting, Los Angeles, CA (display)
8/29–9/1	NHRA Nationals, Indianapolis, IN
9/8	Sacramento Raceway, Sacramento, CA
9/14–16	AHRA, Orange County, CA
9/22–23	Sears Point, CA
9/29	All Pro, Irwindale, CA
10/5–7	AHRA Final Points, Fremont, CA (rain)
10/13–14	AHRA Final Points, Fremont, CA

* *only first three-quarters of year recorded*

*1974 Landy DLI Race and Display Dates**

1/21–22	Firestone, Phoenix, AZ (tire test)
1/24– 27	AHRA Winter Nationals, Phoenix, AZ
1/29– 30	Chrysler, Irwindale, CA (test)
1/31–2/3	NHRA Winternationals, Pomona, CA
3/1–3	Bakersfield, CA
3/6	Morningside High School, Los Angeles, CA (display)
3/14–17	NHRA Gatornationals, Gainesville, FL
3/18– 20	Chrysler Testing, Bradington, FL
3/28–29	Valley Dodge, San Jose, CA (display)
3/29– 31	AHRA Grandamerican, Fremont, CA
4/4–7	AHRA Orange County International Raceway
4/24–26	Chrysler School, Detroit, MI (display)
5/4–5	NHRA WCS, Pomona, CA
5/15–17	Prerace promotion and TV, Detroit, MI (display)
5/17–19	Detroit Dragway, Detroit, MI
6/1–2	Englishtown Raceway, NJ
6/5	Maple Grove Raceway, Maple Grove, PA
6/6–9	NHRA Springnationals, Columbus, OH
6/13	Sharon Raceway, Sharon, PA
6/15	Chess Mall, Boston, MA (display)
6/16	New England Dragway, Epping, NH
6/19	New England Dragway, Epping, NH
6/20	Capitol Dodge, Sacramento, CA (display)
6/21–22	WCS Sacramento, Raceway, Sacramento, CA
6/29	Island Dragway, Great Meadows, NJ
7/3	Puyallup Mall, Puyallup, WA (display)
7/4	Puyallup Raceway, Puyallup, WA
7/5	Jansen Beach, Portland, OR (display)
7/6	Portland International Raceway, Portland, OR
7/10	OCIR, Irvine, CA
7/11–14	NHRA Summernationals, Englishtown, NJ
7/16	Budds Creek Dragway, Budds Creek, MD
7/17	New England Dragway, Epping, NH
7/27	Youngstown, OH
8/3	Thompson, OH
8/8	Sharon Raceway, Sharon, PA
8/10–11	*Popular Hot Rodding* Magazine Championships, Martin, MI
8/17–18	NHRA WCS, Bonneville, UT
8/27– 31	Capital Dodge, Indianapolis, IN (display)
8/27–31	NHRA Nationals, Indianapolis, IN
9/6	Hackettstown Dodge, Hackettstown, NJ (display)
9/7	Englishtown Raceway, Englishtown, NJ
9/8	New England Dragway, Epping, NH
9/14	OCIR, Irvine, CA
9/20	Tucson, AZ (display)
9/21–22	Tuscan Dragway, Tucson, AZ
9/25–26	Promotion and TV, Boise, ID (display)
9/27–29	AHRA Grand American, Boise, ID

* *only first three-quarters of year recorded*

Dick Landy, impeccably dressed, at a 1969 clinic appearance.

INDEX

Additional books that may interest you...

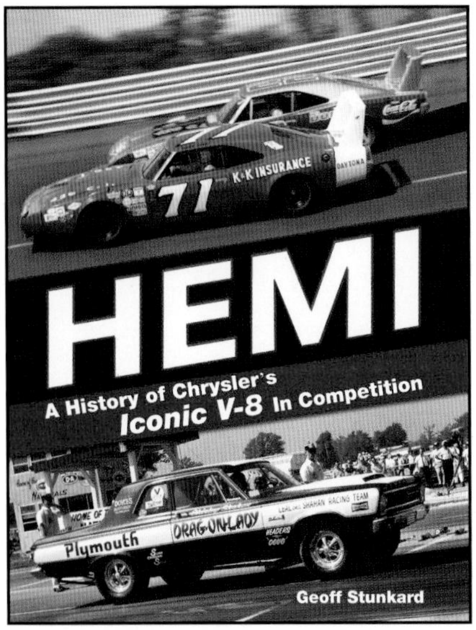

HEMI: A History of Chrysler's Iconic V-8 In Competition *by Geoff Stunkard* In the pages of this comprehensive Hemi history, the author goes behind the scenes and reveals how the engine was designed, built, tested, and eventually raced. He follows the engine as it rewrote racing history, became a highly sought-after engine in street cars, and redefined V-8 performance. Whether the Hemi was installed in a Charger, Super Bee, Baracuda, Superbird, or other car, it dominated in NHRA, NASCAR, and other forms of competition. The racing triumphs of Richard Petty, David Pearson, Dick Landy, Don Garlits, and countless others are brought back to life. Hardbound, 8.5 x 11 inches, 192 pages, 400 color photos. ***Item # CT537***

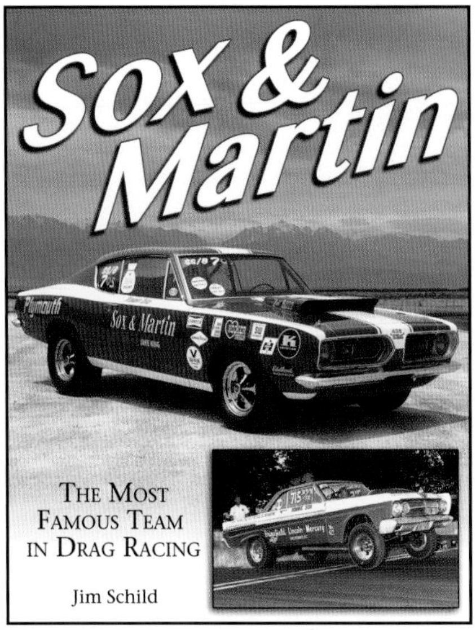

SOX & MARTIN: The Most Famous Team in Drag Racing *by Jim Schild* From their humble beginnings drag racing at local tracks in North Carolina to winning the prestigious US Nationals at Indianapolis, Ronnie Sox and Buddy Martin have seen it all. At their peak, Sox & Martin won 9 of 23 NHRA Pro Stock events, won 6 Championships in both AHRA and NHRA, and were invited to the White House. Never-before-seen photographs chronicle the team's Impalas, Comets, Colts, Omnis, Thunderbirds, Probes, etc. The author also includes a thorough examination of the record-breaking Belvederes, GTXs, Barracudas, Road Runners, and Dusters campaigned by the duo. Softbound, 8.5 x 11 inches, 176 pages, 350 color photos. ***Item # CT545***

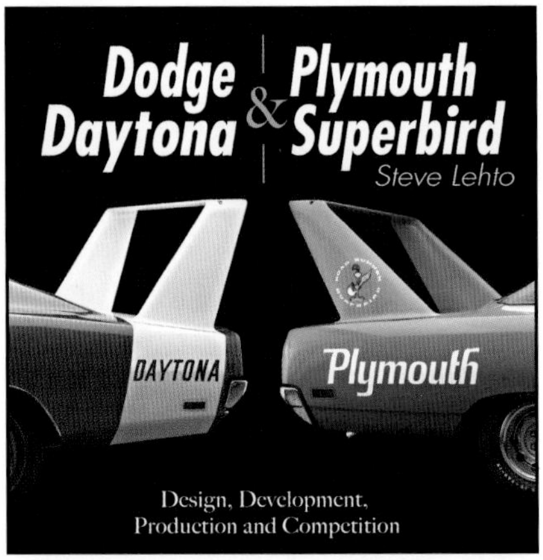

DODGE DAYTONA AND PLYMOUTH SUPERBIRD: Design, Development, Production and Competition *by Steve Lehto* In the fiercely competitive world of NASCAR, every manufacturer was looking for a competitive edge. Ford and Chrysler turned their attention to the aerodynamics of their race cars, resulting in a brief era affectionately called the Aero Wars. During the height of this competition, Chrysler and Ford produced, among other things, cars with radically altered grilles and tail sections. These exotic beasts became some of the most costly, creative, and collectible machines ever assembled in Detroit, whether in race trim or in stock street trim. Author Steve Lehto gives a thorough and detailed account of this battle that culminated with the final wars between the Ford Talladega/Mercury Cyclone and the Dodge Daytona/Plymouth Superbird. Hardbound, 10 x 10 inches, 204 pages, 360 photos. ***Item # CT543***

LOST MUSCLE CARS: 45 Stories of Hunting the Most Elusive and Valuable Muscle Cars *Wes Eisenschenk* In the world of the muscle cars, some of the greatest creations are still waiting to be discovered. This book is a collection of stories written by enthusiasts about their quest to find these extremely rare and valuable muscle cars. You find great stories that take you through the search for some of the most sought after muscle cars with names such as Shelby, Yenko, Hurst, and Hemi. Along the way, success stories including finding the first Z/28 Camaro, the 1971 Boss 302, and the 1971 Hemi 'Cuda convertible will make you wonder if you could uncover the next great muscle car find. Hardbound, 6 x 9 inches, 240 pages, 240 photos. ***Item # CT551***

Check out our website:

CarTechBooks.com

✓ **Find our newest books before anyone else**

✓ **Get weekly tech tips from our experts**

✓ **Get your ride or project featured on our homepage!**

Exclusive Promotions and Giveaways on Facebook
Like us to WIN! Facebook.com/CarTechBooks

www.cartechbooks.com or 1-800-551-4754